Historical Justice

The yearning for historical justice – that is, for the redress of past wrongs – has become one of the defining features of our age. Governments, international bodies and civil society organisations address historical injustices through truth commissions, tribunals, official apologies and other transitional justice measures. Historians produce knowledge of past human rights violations, and museums, memorials and commemorative ceremonies try to keep that knowledge alive and remember the victims of injustices.

In this book, researchers with a background in history, archaeology, cultural studies, literary studies and sociology explore the various attempts to recover and remember the past as a means of addressing historic wrongs. Case studies include sites of persecution in Germany, Argentina and Chile, the commemoration of individual victims of Nazi Germany, memories of life under South Africa's apartheid regime, and the politics of memory in Israel and in Northern Ireland. The authors critique memory, highlight silences and absences, explore how to engage with the ghosts of the past, and ask what drives individuals, including professional historians, to strive for historical justice.

This book was originally published as a special issue of *Rethinking History*.

Klaus Neumann is Professor of History at the Swinburne Institute for Social Research, Swinburne University of Technology, Melbourne, Australia. Recent books include *Across the Seas: Australia's Response to Refugees: A History* (Black Inc., 2015) and *Historical Justice and Memory*, co-edited with Janna Thompson (University of Wisconsin Press, 2015). He is currently researching issues of historical justice, the policy response to refugees, asylum seekers and other irregular migrants, and the politics of compassion.

Historical Justice

Edited by
Klaus Neumann

LONDON AND NEW YORK

First published 2016
by Routledge
2 Park Square, Milton Park, Abingdon, Oxon, OX14 4RN, UK

and by Routledge
711 Third Avenue, New York, NY 10017, USA

Routledge is an imprint of the Taylor & Francis Group, an informa business

© 2016 Taylor & Francis

All rights reserved. No part of this book may be reprinted or reproduced or utilised in any form or by any electronic, mechanical, or other means, now known or hereafter invented, including photocopying and recording, or in any information storage or retrieval system, without permission in writing from the publishers.

Trademark notice: Product or corporate names may be trademarks or registered trademarks, and are used only for identification and explanation without intent to infringe.

British Library Cataloguing in Publication Data
A catalogue record for this book is available from the British Library

ISBN 13: 978-1-138-93300-2

Typeset in Times New Roman
by RefineCatch Limited, Bungay, Suffolk

Publisher's Note
The publisher accepts responsibility for any inconsistencies that may have arisen during the conversion of this book from journal articles to book chapters, namely the possible inclusion of journal terminology.

Disclaimer
Every effort has been made to contact copyright holders for their permission to reprint material in this book. The publishers would be grateful to hear from any copyright holder who is not here acknowledged and will undertake to rectify any errors or omissions in future editions of this book.

Contents

Citation Information — vii
Notes on Contributors — ix
Dedication — xi

1. Introduction: Historians and the yearning for historical justice — 1
   Klaus Neumann

2. The disappearing museum — 21
   Marivic Wyndham and Peter Read

3. Stumbling blocks in Germany — 37
   Linde Apel

4. The ethics of nostalgia in post-apartheid South Africa — 51
   Judith Lütge Coullie

5. Excavating Tempelhof airfield: objects of memory and the politics of absence — 67
   Maria Theresia Starzmann

6. Jewish Haifa denies its Arab past — 86
   Gilad Margalit

7. Ghosts and *compañeros*: haunting stories and the quest for justice around Argentina's former terror sites — 100
   Estela Schindel

8. The desire for justice, psychic reparation and the politics of memory in 'post-conflict' Northern Ireland — 121
   Graham Dawson

Index — 145

Citation Information

The chapters in this book were originally published in the journal *Rethinking History*, volume 18, issue 2 (June 2014). When citing this material, please use the original page numbering for each article, as follows:

Chapter 1
Introductory Essay: Historians and the yearning for historical justice
Klaus Neumann
Rethinking History, volume 18, issue 2 (June 2014) pp. 145–164

Chapter 2
The disappearing museum
Marivic Wyndham and Peter Read
Rethinking History, volume 18, issue 2 (June 2014) pp. 165–180

Chapter 3
Stumbling blocks in Germany
Linde Apel
Rethinking History, volume 18, issue 2 (June 2014) pp. 181–194

Chapter 4
The ethics of nostalgia in post-apartheid South Africa
Judith Lütge Coullie
Rethinking History, volume 18, issue 2 (June 2014) pp. 195–210

Chapter 5
Excavating Tempelhof airfield: objects of memory and the politics of absence
Maria Theresia Starzmann
Rethinking History, volume 18, issue 2 (June 2014) pp. 211–229

CITATION INFORMATION

Chapter 6
Jewish Haifa denies its Arab past
Gilad Margalit
Rethinking History, volume 18, issue 2 (June 2014) pp. 230–243

Chapter 7
Ghosts and compañeros*: haunting stories and the quest for justice around Argentina's former terror sites*
Estela Schindel
Rethinking History, volume 18, issue 2 (June 2014) pp. 244–264

Chapter 8
The desire for justice, psychic reparation and the politics of memory in 'post-conflict' Northern Ireland
Graham Dawson
Rethinking History, volume 18, issue 2 (June 2014) pp. 265–288

For any permission-related enquiries please visit:
http://www.tandfonline.com/page/help/permissions

Notes on Contributors

Linde Apel is Director of the Werkstatt der Erinnerung at the Forschungsstelle für Zeitgeschichte in Hamburg, Germany. She is the author of *Jüdische Frauen im Konzentrationslager Ravensbrück 1939–1945* (Metropol, 2003) and of numerous papers on the politics of memory. Her research interests include the methodology of oral history and memories of the Holocaust.

Judith Lütge Coullie is Senior Research Associate at the University of KwaZulu-Natal, and Learning Advisor at the University of Canterbury, New Zealand. Publications include a collection of South African women's life writing, *The Closest of Strangers* (Wits University Press, 2004), a co-edited collection of essays on Breyten Breytenbach, *a.k.a. Breyten Breytenbach* (Rodopi, 2004), a CD on the poet Roy Campbell, *Campbell in Context* (UKZN, 2004) and interviews on southern African auto/biography, *Selves in Question* (University of Hawai`i Press, 2006). She has edited *Remembering Roy Campbell: The Memoirs of his Daughters, Anna and Tess* (2011). In 2014, *Antjie Krog: An Ethics of Body and Otherness* was published by the University of KwaZulu-Natal Press.

Graham Dawson is Professor of Historical Cultural Studies and Director of the Centre for Research in Memory, Narrative and Histories at the University of Brighton, UK. He is the author of *Soldier Heroes: British Adventure, Empire and the Imagining of Masculinities* (1994) and *Making Peace with the Past? Memory, Trauma and the Irish Troubles* (2007). He is also co-editor of *Trauma: Life Stories of Survivors* (2004), *Commemorating War: The Politics of Memory* (2004) and *Contested Spaces: Sites, Representations and Histories of Conflict* (2007). Alongside continuing work on the Irish peace process and legacies of the Troubles in Ireland and Britain, his current interests lie in the cultural dimensions of dealing with the past within conflict transformation processes, involving questions of memory, representation, imaginative geography, historical justice and human rights.

Gilad Margalit was Professor of General History at the University of Haifa, Israel. His research focused on German policies and attitudes towards Sinti and Roma, German memories of World War Two, and the identities of second and third generation Turkish Germans. His books include, among others, *Germany and its Gypsies: A Post-Auschwitz Ordeal* (University of Wisconsin Press, 2002) and *Guilt, Suffering, and Memory: Germany Remembers Its Dead in World War II* (Indiana University Press, 2010).

Klaus Neumann is Professor of History at the Swinburne Institute for Social Research, Swinburne University of Technology, Melbourne, Australia. He has written about postcolonial histories in Papua New Guinea, erupting volcanoes, German memories of the Nazi past, Australian refugee policies and World War Two civilian internment, among other topics. His latest books include *Across the Seas: Australia's Response to Refugees: A History* (Black Inc., 2015), and *Historical Justice and Memory*, co-edited with Janna Thompson (University of Wisconsin Press, 2015).

Peter Read is Adjunct Professor in the Australian National University's Centre for Aboriginal History. He works in Australian Aboriginal and Latin American history on issues of historical trauma and national reconciliation.

Estela Schindel studied Communications at the University of Buenos Aires and has a PhD in Sociology from the Free University Berlin, Germany. Her dissertation is a study about the social construction of the figure of Argentina's disappeared. She is a researcher at the Center of Excellence 'Cultural Foundations of Social Integration', the University of Konstanz, Germany. She is working on a project about the entanglements of violence, nature and technology in the EU border regime.

Maria Theresia Starzmann is an anthropologist whose work focuses on memory and materiality, institutions of confinement and carceral landscapes, colonialism and imperialism, as well as the history and cultural politics of archaeological practice. She is currently Assistant Professor of Anthropology at McGill University, Canada.

Marivic Wyndham is a Senior Lecturer in Latin American Studies, International Studies Program, Faculty of Arts and Social Sciences, University of Technology, Sydney, Australia. With Peter Read, she has published several articles on the theme of custodianship of place in contemporary Cuban society and, more recently, a series of studies of sites of conscience in Santiago, Chile, including Patio 29, the Víctor Jara Stadium, Loyola 6034, Villa Grimaldi and earlier studies of Londres 38.

In memoriam Gilad Margalit (1959–2014)

INTRODUCTION

Historians and the yearning for historical justice

Klaus Neumann

The Swinburne Institute for Social Research, Swinburne University of Technology, Melbourne, Australia

> The yearning for historical justice has become a defining feature of our age. The article discusses the extent and manifestations of this yearning for the redress of the wrongs of the past. It notes that, paradoxically, historians have not had a major influence on debates about historical justice. Referring to the seven other contributions to this themed issue of *Rethinking History*, the article suggests that historians have, however, made contributions in five crucial respects. They have provided critical analyses of processes of memorialising and historicising historic wrongs, highlighted silences and absences in representations of past injustices, drawn attention to pasts that have been largely forgotten, engaged with seemingly unbidden intrusions of the past into the present and identified and analysed the motives and desires of individual actors. Sketching promising future directions for relevant historical scholarship, the article proposes that historians problematise the idea that *all* historic wrongs need to be remembered comprehensively, and that historians reflect on the particular responsibilities and obligations of their discipline. Finally, this introduction suggests that practitioners of a critical history be cognisant of their emotional investment when writing about historic wrongs and historical justice.

As I am writing this, an international court has just upheld a 50-year prison sentence against Charles Taylor for war crimes, crimes against humanity and other violations of international humanitarian law (Sesay 2013; Simons and Cowell 2013; SCSL 2013). Taylor is a former president of Liberia (1997–2003). During his time in office, Liberia provided support to the Revolutionary United Front (RUF), an armed group fighting the government of neighbouring Sierra Leone. The RUF was responsible for the murder of tens of thousands of people, and the displacement of half of Sierra Leone's population. Its terror only came to an end in 2001 as the result of a United Nations-backed military intervention.

While Taylor, as president and, before then, as leader of the National Patriotic Front of Liberia (NPFL), was also responsible for serious human rights violations in Liberia, which between 1989 and 2003 experienced two brutal civil wars, he has so far only been tried for crimes that took place in Sierra Leone, and by an international court that drew both on international human rights law and Sierra Leonean domestic law and was set up jointly by the United Nations and the government of Sierra Leone. The injustices committed during Liberia's civil war were, however, investigated by a truth and reconciliation commission, which was inaugurated in 2006, collected almost 20,000 statements and delivered its final report in 2009 (Wiebelhaus-Brahm 2013; Hayner 2011, 66–68; see also James-Allen, Weah, and Goodfriend 2010). The commission made extensive recommendations, including, among others, to prosecute perpetrators, institute alternative arrangements for truth telling, bar perpetrators from public office, pay reparations to victims and build memorials (Republic of Liberia 2009).

The prosecution of Charles Taylor is unexceptional. In recent years, there have been numerous successful attempts to hold former high-ranking government officials accountable for crimes against humanity, war crimes and other human rights violations. The beginnings of what Sikkink (2011) has coined the 'justice cascade', the growing tendency to prosecute representatives of murderous regimes in domestic and international courts and tribunals, can be traced back to the Nuremberg and Tokyo trials in the immediate aftermath of the Second World War. While prosecutions such as those of Charles Taylor, Serbia's Slobodan Milošević, Argentina's Jorge Rafaél Videla or Cambodia's Ieng Sary aim for retributive justice, other means of redressing past wrongs, such as truth commissions, official apologies or the payment of compensation to victims, aim for reparative justice. Again, the Liberian truth and reconciliation commission is representative of a growing trend. Over the past 40 years, there have been truth commissions, or similar commissions of inquiry, in more than 30 countries to investigate extrajudicial killings, disappearances, arbitrary detention, torture, rape and other serious human rights violations, most of them perpetrated or condoned by representatives of the state (Hayner 2011).

The Liberian truth and reconciliation commission was also typical in that its commissioners explored a wide range of human rights violations: a plethora of crimes, perpetrated by a variety of actors over a long period of time. The commission investigated 23 different types of violations, including, among others, rape, arbitrary detention, forced displacement and torture (Republic of Liberia 2009, 262–263). While it attributed 39% of the crimes to the Charles Taylor-led NPFL, it identified some two dozen other organisations and groups that could be held responsible for violations, including the Liberian army and police, and various players in the Liberian civil wars (264). Although the commission was primarily formed to investigate and document incidents that occurred between 1979 and 2003 (the periods of the two civil wars, and the 10 years preceding them), it also tried to establish the 'root causes of our current conflict' (213), and in two chapters in its final report dealt with the pre-history of the violence that was the subject of its mandate (93–149).

Prosecutions such as Charles Taylor's and truth commissions reflect an intense yearning for historical justice, that is, for the redress of past wrongs. This yearning has become one of the defining features of the post-cold war era, from Argentina to Australia, from Canada to Cambodia and from Rwanda to Romania. The historic wrongs that are the subject of demands for redress extend beyond living memory; they include, for example, the Armenian genocide and transatlantic slavery. In Spain, scholars and activists are recovering the memory of the Moriscos, who were expelled from Spain in 1609, and have called for symbolic reparations (González García 2008). In 2001, Pope John Paul II justified his official apology for the sacking of Constantinople during the Fourth Crusade in 1204 by claiming that 'some events of the distant past have left deep wounds in the minds and hearts of people to this day' (John Paul II 2001). Even in cases in which the yearning for historical justice initially focuses on recent events, it is often felt necessary to go back further in time; the Liberian truth commission, for example, also delved into events in the nineteenth century. The demand for historical truth and justice has become seemingly boundless and, as Barkan (2005, 232) writes, 'almost insatiable'.

The idea that past injustices must be investigated, documented and redressed has become so widely accepted that it is difficult not to think of those who do not genuinely engage with past wrongs – for example, various Japanese governments, which refused to recognise and apologise for the suffering of Korean 'comfort women' – as being recalcitrant. But only 50 years ago, it would have made perfect sense for all participants in a prolonged civil war similar to the conflict in Liberia to make peace by deciding to let bygones be bygones. In fact, as recently as 20 years ago, at least one recommendation by the Liberian truth commission would have met with incredulity: that Ellen Johnson Sirleaf be barred from holding public office for 30 years because she provided financial support to Charles Taylor in the early stages of Liberia's first civil war (Republic of Liberia 2009, 361). Sirleaf has been Liberia's democratically elected president since 2006. In 2011, she was awarded the Nobel Peace Prize for her contribution to 'securing peace in Liberia' (Den Norske Nobelkomite 2011); arguably, the establishment of a truth and reconciliation commission in her first year in office was a crucial part of this contribution.[1]

Truth commissions and other transitional justice instruments are increasingly driven less by the urge to mete out punishments and more by the desire to do justice to the victims, and to tell the truth about human rights violations. 'The truth' often means: the victims' truth.[2] When reporting on the 1961 Eichmann trial, Arendt insisted that '[t]he purpose of a trial is to render justice, and nothing else; even the noblest of ulterior purposes [. . .] can only detract from the law's main business' (2006, 253). More than half a century later, it is taken for granted that national and international courts and tribunals ought to be aiming to do far more than 'the law's main business'. Although trials are ostensibly directed at holding perpetrators accountable, they have also become forums where those who had suffered injustices are given the opportunity to speak about them (see Karstedt 2010; Brants 2013). In such trials, the role of victims of historical injustices exceeds both that assigned to witnesses in an ordinary criminal trial, and that of informants who could furnish oral histories. In 2006, the Outreach Programme of the International Criminal Tribunal for the Former Yugoslavia (ICTY) described the Tribunal's accomplishments in the following terms:

> [M]any victims play a crucial role in the proceedings at the Tribunal as witnesses. By displaying exceptional courage in testifying at the Tribunal, they contribute to the process of establishing the truth. In turn, the Tribunal's proceedings provide these victims and witnesses the opportunity to be heard and to speak about their suffering. [...] the ICTY guarantees that the suffering of victims across the former Yugoslavia is acknowledged and not ignored. (Outreach Programme of the ICTY 2006)

While victims of human rights violations are not yet *entitled* to testify and to be heard,[3] international law now recognises the right of victims to receive reparations and to learn the truth; in December 2005, the United Nations General Assembly adopted 'Basic Principles and Guidelines', which Mahmoud Cherif Bassiouni, one of its architects, has justifiably hailed as 'a monumental milestone in the history of human rights as well as international criminal justice' (2006, 278). They include the following:

> Remedies for gross violations of international human rights law and serious violations of international humanitarian law include the victim's right to the following as provided for under international law:
> (a) Equal and effective access to justice;
> (b) Adequate, effective and prompt reparation for harm suffered;
> (c) Access to relevant information concerning violations and reparation mechanisms. (United Nations 2006, principle 11)

The Basic Principles further state that 'victims and their representatives should be entitled to seek and obtain information on the causes leading to their victimization [...] and to learn the truth in regard to these violations' (principle 24). According to Bassiouni (2006, 275),

> Understanding and public disclosure of the truth is important to victims because the truth (1) alleviates the suffering of the surviving victims; (2) vindicates the memory or status of the direct victim of the violation; (3) encourages the State to confront its dark past; and (4) through it, seek reform.

The proliferation of initiatives designed to attain historical justice by confronting 'dark pasts' ought to be seen in the context of a broader shift in focus, at least in the global north:[4] collectively, we now look backwards and inwards, more so than forwards. Fifty years ago, the future loomed large. It held great promises – of material advancement and technological progress – but it also encompassed the threat of a war that would extinguish humankind. The past was seen as something to be left behind – it did not appear to generate substantive dividends, and whatever evil could be associated with it was, or at least could be, seemingly safely contained. In 1963, a nuclear war was a distinct possibility, but it seemed by no means inevitable. In 2013, doom awaits us not as the result of a rash decision made by individuals in Washington or Moscow, but as the outcome of practices embraced in the past, over many decades and by many actors, particularly in Europe and North America, and also as the consequence of a prevailing global inertia that hampers attempts to abandon and undo the consequences of these practices. Yet in 2013 it is the past, at least as much as the future, that looms menacingly large. And much as people in 1963 were ambivalent about the future, 50 years later they are ambivalent about the past: it is the object of a nostalgic yearning for long-lost good times, but at least as often it is also seen as a liability. In 1963, the past seemed to have been over and done with, notwithstanding the fact that for some the memories of the horrors they experienced were fresh; in 2013, 'dark pasts' keep encroaching upon our present, regardless of whether or not we experienced them ourselves – and intriguingly also regardless of how often we try to 'lock up the past' with the help of an array of transitional justice instruments (Hazan 2010, 157).

Would that not be reason enough for us to try averting our eyes? After all, is that not exactly what many of us *are* doing with respect to the future – as if the melting of the glaciers could be halted if only we stopped fretting about it? It seems paradoxical: the more the past appears to intrude into the present, the more we want to know about it – as if the present had no legitimacy unless we kept attending to the past. The more we know, however, the more we want to be reminded of what we know. It seems ever more important to hold on to what we take to be the truth, to make that knowledge appear safe. Much more so than in 1963, in 2013 the past appears to be ephemeral and elusive.

Given this preoccupation with the past in general, and with producing knowledge about the perpetration of heinous crimes, in particular, professional historians ought to be in high demand. One could expect them to take centre stage as mediators of and guides for our engagement with 'dark pasts' because of their skills in uncovering the past, interpreting it, analysing it and rendering it as history. Admittedly, historians do play a part in this effort to know, but they occupy centre stage only on rare occasions. More often than not, they find themselves in auxiliary roles: as consultants or expert witnesses. The discourse about the past is shaped by politicians and poets, artists and advocates, journalists and judges – not because they possess specific talents or qualifications, but because seemingly these are not required. Anybody is entitled to retell and interpret the past. No Ph.D. in history is needed to contribute to debates about, say, heritage – or about historic wrongs, for that matter. In fact, such debates are not about history: at stake is not so much how to historicise the past, but how to remember it and to seemingly keep it alive. The traditional authority of scholarship – of texts that have been penned by qualified experts and whose claims are supported by copious notes – is greatly diminished; the general public is unlikely to privilege them over Wikipedia entries or television documentaries. The latter's truth claims are often credible not so much because they employ historians as talking heads, but because they draw on the accounts of witnesses who recount personal experiences. Historians' traditional claim that they are able to better understand the past because they can contemplate it from a safe distance is upstaged by the allure of experience, which collapses the distance from the past (cf. Chakrabarty 2007, 81). The expert witness who reports on her research about an event in the past is no match for the eyewitness who was involved in that event. Presumed authenticity now trumps professional authority.

The role of critical history

Historians and others with specialist knowledge about the past, such as archaeologists or historical anthropologists, have failed to shape recent public debates about historical justice, but they have played a crucial role in providing detailed knowledge about past wrongs, and thus have contributed to satisfying the urge to know about past human rights violations. Truth commissions have relied on their expertise. They have provided briefings to governments pondering whether or not to issue an official apology. Historians have identified the exact extent to which institutions and businesses have perpetrated wrongs or benefited from them. They have given evidence to parliamentary inquiries and have testified in court rooms; in fact, international criminal trials would now be unthinkable without some contextualisation provided by historians (see Wilson 2011, 20–23).

Historians have also helped to defuse historic tensions, by serving on historical commissions designed to expose partisan myths and to identify narratives that all parties in a conflict can agree on (see Karn 2005). They have lent their authority as arbiters of competing versions of the past to bodies that try to effect a reconciliation between perpetrators (and their descendants) and victims and survivors (and their descendants) (see Barkan 2005, 2009). Apart from being involved in the process of securing historical justice, historians – and scholars from other relevant disciplines, such as anthropology, cultural studies, sociology or archaeology – have also *critically* accompanied the process. The other seven papers assembled here are representative of this latter contribution, which has manifested itself in numerous critiques of public memory-making, in particular (see the contributions by Read and Wyndham, Apel, and Coullie). Historians and practitioners of related disciplines have engaged with the process of historical justice also in other fruitful ways: by highlighting absences and silences (as does Starzmann in this issue); by drawing attention to pasts that have been condemned to oblivion (see Margalit's contribution); by engaging with the phenomenon of the 'ghostly' reappearance of 'dark pasts' (as in Schindel's article) and by trying to understand the specificity of a yearning for justice (see Dawson's paper in this issue).

Critiquing memory

Scholars in the humanities and social sciences have provided critical accounts of the historicisation and memorialisation of past injustices. They have identified the beneficiaries of particular renderings of historic wrongs, and analysed the politics of history and politics of memory that have shaped historical redress. They have shown how particular memories emerge in the course of contests over the interpretation of the past, and have insisted on the distinction between official memory and 'vernacular memory' (Gluck 2007). The process of publicly working through historic wrongs has become a prominent subject of historical research – one that is often no less attractive to scholars than a study of the wrong itself. Much of the scholarship on historical redress has been informed by attempts to understand the phenomenon of *Vergangenheitsbewältigung*, German attempts to come to terms with and pay symbolic and material reparations for the historic wrongs perpetrated in the name of Nazi Germany. The German case alone has been the subject of dozens of book-length analyses. Elsewhere, too, historians have critically analysed the process by which 'dark pasts' have been unearthed, debated or addressed; it could be argued that the scholarship on issues of historical justice in countries such as Argentina, France or South Africa is sufficiently substantive to constitute discrete fields of research.[5]

In the tradition of James Young's pioneering scholarship (for example, Young 1989), Marivic Wyndham and Peter Read provide a critical 'biography' of a memorial: they chronicle the disputes over the use of Londres 38, a building in the centre of Santiago de Chile, where opponents of the Pinochet regime were tortured and detained. They are critical of the appropriation of the site by the Chilean state, and the concomitant sidelining of victims' organisations. While they write about the commemoration of historic wrongs in Chile as outsiders, Linde Apel is personally and professionally involved in the issues she explores in her paper. She writes about the *Stolpersteine* memorials, plaques embedded in the footpath that commemorate individual victims of Nazi Germany. She is suspicious of the motivations of those sponsoring a *Stolperstein* or using them to make public claims about the supposed righteousness of post-Holocaust generations. Implicitly, both Wyndham and Read, and Apel argue for alternative ways of commemorating the victims of the Chilean dictatorship, and the Nazi regime, respectively.

A critique of history and/or memory can focus our attention on silences and absences. The processes of remembering and forgetting are related: memories are never comprehensive, and remembering one aspect of the past often comes at the expense of others (Vivian 2010, 8–12). In her contribution to this issue, Judith Coullie rises to the defence of a much-criticised memoir by the South African writer Jacob Dlamini, who fondly remembers aspects of life under apartheid. She argues that the focus on the historic wrong that apartheid undoubtedly was not only hides integral aspects of the past from view, but also diverts attention from the darker sides of post-apartheid, democratic South Africa. In other words, Coullie suggests that a focus on injustices in the past obscures injustices in the present.

Highlighting silences and absences

In many cases, the vast majority of sources about a past injustice were generated by those responsible for it. Often, the voices of victims only survive in the accounts of their tormentors. In fact, the more horrific an injustice was, the greater is the chance that the kind of truth the draftees of the 2005 Basic Principles had in mind needs to be winnowed from the testimonies of perpetrators – who tend to be interested in obfuscation rather than revelation. In the absence of survivors, the telling of truth becomes doubly problematic: because those speaking on behalf of victims lack the authorisation of surviving witnesses and because they need to conjure voices that make themselves heard. Rather than bemoaning the one-sidedness of their sources, scholars have successfully accepted the challenge of according agency to people whose voices were silenced. In this issue, Maria Theresia Starzmann reflects on the results of an archaeological excavation at the site of a forced labour camp in Berlin, and engages supposedly mute objects, conjuring both the presence of those who had used them, and their absence.

Rescuing from oblivion

In 2005, two historians, Caroline Elkins and David Anderson, published books about injustices that had been largely forgotten: the human rights violations perpetrated by the British colonial administration during the Mau Mau emergency in Kenya. Elkins' *Imperial Reckoning*, in particular, soon prompted calls by Kenyan government ministers for an apology from the British government (Human Rights House 2005; BBC News 2005). In 2013, British Secretary of State William Hague not only issued a statement of regret in the House of Commons; he also announced that his government had agreed to make an out-of court payment totalling £19.9 million to 5228 Kenyans who had suffered as a result of British policies during the emergency, and to contribute funding for a memorial to be built in Nairobi to the victims of abuse during the colonial era (House of Commons (United Kingdom) 2013, 1692–1693). Much like Elkins and Anderson, historians have played a crucial role in bringing past injustices to the attention of a wider public. Often, this attention has spawned campaigns by victims or their descendants for recognition and compensation. In other instances, historians have responded to campaigns by survivors and documented human rights violations, thereby providing survivors or the relatives of victims with the hard evidence required to launch successful claims for compensation or memorialisation. In both cases, the initiative to explore injustices in the past has come from historians.[6]

The *Nakba*, the expulsion of Palestinians from the territory of the newly formed state of Israel in 1948, is not an injustice that needs to be rediscovered and thereby rescued from oblivion. Neither is the fact that in 1948 – and in later years – many Palestinian homes were bulldozed to make room for Jewish settlements or simply to prevent the return of their former residents. Gilad Margalit, whose paper discusses aspects of the *Nakba* in Haifa, is thus not breaking new ground in the way Elkins and Anderson were when writing about the Mau Mau emergency, but he is as proactive in his engagement with past wrongs as they were. For him, historical justice means recognising Haifa's Arab past in general, and, in particular, the founding of modern Haifa in 1761 by Daher el-Omar, the Arab ruler of the Galilee. He argues that such recognition, including the celebration of modern Haifa's 250th birthday in 2011, has been avoided by the city's local government because a narrative that included the city's founding father would also have had to mention the demolition of Haifa's historic centre by the Israeli army in 1948.

Engaging with the ghosts of the past

In Florian Cossen's film *The Day I Was Not Born* (originally released as *Das Lied in mir*; Cossen 2010), the swimmer Maria Falkenmeyer has a stop-over in Buenos Aires. Although she does not speak any Spanish, a Spanish lullaby she hears while waiting for her connecting flight literally throws her off course and makes her abandon her travel plans and check into a local hotel. She then learns that as a baby she was taken from her parents, who were disappeared under the military dictatorship, adopted by a German couple and taken to Germany. Maria's journey of discovery in Buenos Aires is prompted by a strong emotional response to something she cannot grasp cognitively. The provenance of the memories that torment Fausta, the main character in Claudia Llosa's film *The Milk of Sorrow* (originally released as *La teta asustada*; Llosa 2009), similarly defies rational explanation. Her mother had been raped during the violence that gripped Peru between 1980 and 2000, and transmitted her suffering to Fausta with her breast milk, as if the traumatic experience of rape were an infectious disease.[7] In both films, a 'dark past' makes an unbidden appearance. Maria and Fausta have no choice but to accept its presence.

Inspired by Avery Gordon's, Jacques Derrida's and, albeit to a much lesser extent, Nicholas Abraham and Maria Torok's work on haunting (Gordon 2008; Derrida 2006; Abraham and Torok 1986), scholars have tried to come to terms with the fact that in the aftermath of historic wrongs, 'the time is out of joint', to use the words of Shakespeare's Hamlet, and the dead reappear as ghosts. They have done so both in the sense that people experience the presence of something or somebody that, strictly speaking, cannot be there, and in the sense that writers and film makers have summoned ghosts to draw out a past that could not be spoken about. The latter has been a prominent phenomenon in Spain, where the dictatorship ended 'naturally', when the dictator died of old age, and the transition to democracy was premised on the agreement to a so-called *pacto de olvido* (pact of forgetting). While this pact remained intact for about 25 years, the past of the Spanish civil war and of the subsequent Francoist repression nevertheless *made itself felt* (see Labanyi 2000).

The spectral presences that feature in Estela Schindel's contribution to this issue are not conjured by novelists and film makers, but appear unbidden to security guards, construction workers and janitors who work at sites of trauma in

Argentina. As in the cases explored by Jo Labanyi in Spain, however, these ghosts are the symptom of silences about the dictatorship. While in Spain – until about 2000 – the persecution of Franco's opponents and the summary execution of Republicans during the civil war were not to be publicly talked about, in Argentina the talking about the disappearances orchestrated by the military junta is often formulaic and beholden to the ideology and celebratory rhetoric of the political left of the 1970s, thus leaving a remainder that cannot be spoken. In both countries, ghosts 'are reminders of a need for justice' (Wilke 2010, 77), to cite Christiane Wilke's observation on yet another country, Germany, with a 'dark past' that is prone to make unbidden appearances.

Focusing on specific actors

Much of the scholarship on memories of historic wrongs is heavily indebted to Maurice Halbwachs' writings about the social dimensions of processes of remembering. While the experience of suffering is regularly individualised, the yearning for historical justice tends to be ascribed to collectives. The instruments addressing this yearning may not offer remedies that are meaningful for all, or even most, individual victims; for example, the Special Court for Sierra Leone, which tried Charles Taylor, does not necessarily respond to the needs and expectations of ordinary Sierra Leoneans – not because they do not yearn for justice, but because they are faced with enduring injustices that did not come to an end simply because Charles Taylor was tried in The Hague (Mieth 2013; see also Shaw 2010).

Sometimes the same collectives – for example, nations or ethnically defined groups – that were invoked to justify the perpetration of wrongs feature as actors in accounts of the subsequent response to such wrongs. Critical historical scholarship has exposed abstract accounts of group identities, memories and sentiments as fiction by focusing on the drivers of *specific* thought processes and emotions. In this issue, Dawson (2007) follows up on his previous research into the Irish peace process by exploring the stance of the members of West Tyrone Voice, an organisation representing the victims of sectarian violence. Dawson draws on object relations theory to identify and analyse their *specific* desire for justice. His work strongly suggests that we ought to identify actors and their particular predispositions, motivations, affects and choices when exploring the response to violence: not only is it unhelpful to attribute acts of violence to ill-defined collectives or institutions (such as 'the Hutu' or 'the Chilean military'), it is equally unproductive to talk about 'national' or 'ethnic' memories of such acts.

For future reference

I suggest that historians could productively respond to the yearning for historical justice by focusing on two further issues which have not yet received the attention they deserve. Following on from their critiques of individual acts of memorialisation, they could revisit a discussion triggered by two controversial public lectures delivered by Arno Mayer and Charles Maier, respectively, in

1992. Both wondered aloud whether there was a surfeit of memory in relation to historic wrongs in general, and the Holocaust in particular (see Neumann, 2014). At the time, their interventions caused a stir, and an article by Bartov (1993) accusing them of being the bedfellows of Holocaust deniers was rushed into print before Mayer's (1993) and Maier's (1993) own papers had been published.

Contrary to what could be assumed if one read only Bartov's critique, Mayer and Maier drew attention to important epistemological quandaries. They asked whether all historical knowledge is intrinsically valuable. They tried to understand how the shift in focus that I described earlier – away from the future and onto the past – affected their work as historians. They did not dispute claims of Jewish suffering. Maier did not deny that the injustices highlighted by minority groups in the USA occurred; he merely objected to the level of attention paid to them, claiming that the focus on past suffering has been accompanied by a 'retreat from transformative politics' (1993, 150). Both Maier and Mayer suggest that memories privilege the suffering of some and disregard the suffering of others – in other words, that a surfeit of memory regarding some aspects of the past is responsible for a silencing of others.

The public's often slightly hysterical response to any suggestion that forgetting could be productive and remembering debilitating has made it difficult to extend the line of argument developed by Maier and Mayer. This is despite the fact that the scholarship on public remembering has provided ample evidence for the contention that processes of remembering and forgetting are dynamically intertwined, and notwithstanding convincing arguments for a reappraisal of a public forgetting (see Huyssen 2005; Vivian 2010; Rieff 2011). In his contribution to this issue, Gilad Margalit argues that school textbooks portray Haifa's development from a sleepy fishing village to a vibrant city as the work of Zionist settlers. That narrative omits mentioning the fact that modern Haifa was founded in 1761 by Daher el-Omar. A history that focused on his role as a founder, however, could as easily silence the fact that modern Haifa supplanted an older town, Haifa El-Atika, which was a few kilometres from the site of the new city, and which Daher el-Omar ordered to be demolished. In Germany, to give another example, the focus on the suffering of the victims of Nazi Germany overshadows, if not thwarts, attempts to remember perpetrators, accomplices, beneficiaries and bystanders. The *Stolpersteine* memorials, which are the subject of Linde Apel's critical reflection in this issue, are often sponsored by non-Jewish Germans who have no personal connection to the victims of Nazi Germany whose lives they wish to commemorate. Those who strive to remember somebody who once lived in their street before she was deported to Auschwitz comfortably forget how their own parents or grandparents may have been compromised – and that their and their friends' household effects may include the odd item that had once belonged to a deportee and could be cheaply acquired when the opportunity presented itself. Arguably, the focus on the fate of individual victims diverts attention from the way many Germans who had no connection to the murderers in the SS or in the *Einsatzgruppen* were nevertheless implicated in the Holocaust.[8]

The second issue that in my view warrants further attention is related to the first. In recent years, moral and political philosophers have put forward powerful arguments in favour of remembering historic wrongs and satisfying the urge to know about past injustices (see, in particular, Margalit 2002; Thompson 2002; Booth 2006; Blustein 2008; Walker 2010). Historians have tended to shy away from tackling these or similar issues, which would require an engagement with the ethics of writing history. Do historians have a particular obligation to write the histories of genocides? Do they have a responsibility towards the victims of human rights violations? Are they beholden to survivors and the descendants of victims to provide 'information on the causes leading to their victimization' and to assist them in 'learn[ing] the truth in regard to these violations', to cite once more the words of the 2005 Basic Principles?[9]

Possibly because he had earlier been accused of anti-Semitism, in his controversial lecture Arno Mayer was anxious to clarify his professional commitment, and in doing so invoked his biographical background as a European Jew. He claimed to 'follow Marc Bloch's injunction to maintain a continuing dialogue with the dead' (Mayer 1993, 5), and suggested that his work was informed by the desire to be faithful to the victims. Earlier, in *The Unmasterable Past*, his account of the German *Historikerstreit* about the historicisation of the Holocaust, Maier (1988, 97–98) had responded to the suggestion that historians, rather than agonising over 'nonhistorical questions', 'need only tell it as it was': 'The problem is that "as it was" implies a moral stance; historians just cannot avoid having judgments implicated in the marrow of existential and causal statements'. He objected to Holocaust revisionism because it 'denies respect' (Maier 1993, 146). With these statements, Maier and Mayer went further than most historians in the academy, then and now, would be willing to go, perhaps owing to a fear that a moral stance could be seen to interfere with a commitment to their discipline's famed rigour. There are few scholars who would freely admit, as the Australian historian Dening did, that they have opted to focus their efforts on writing the history of those 'on whom the forces of the world press most hardly' (2004, 12), and that they are guided by the *moral* impetus 'to give a voice to the dead' (Dening cited in Dymond 2001, 2).

Before the late nineteenth-century birth of history as a discipline, historians were less likely to have such scruples. In 1781, Gibbon remarked in the third volume of his *Decline and Fall of the Roman Empire* that violent historical actors are 'less detestable than the cool unfeeling historian' (2013 [1781], 267n.84). In 1872, Jules Michelet suggested in the second volume of his *Histoire du XIXe siècle* that the historian was duty-bound to concern himself with all those *miserabiles personae* who had no friends to care for their memory:

> I have given many of the too-forgotten dead the assistance which I myself shall require. I have exhumed them for a second life. Some were not born at a moment suitable to them. Others were born on the eve of new and striking circumstances which have come to erase them, so to speak, stifling their memory [...] History greets and renews these disinherited glories; it gives life to these dead men,

resuscitates them. Its justice [...] offers reparation to some who appeared so briefly only to vanish. (cited in Barthes 1987, 101–102)

Michelet's sentiment – which finds a perhaps unexpected echo in Benjamin's 'Theses on the Philosophy of History' (1968) – could remind us that history began as a moral discipline and that historians, however detached they pretend to be, can hardly avoid making moral claims. A foregrounding of that understanding would allow historians to play a greater role in debates about the past, rather than be seen as 'technical' experts who provide the material that allows others (tribunals, truth commissions or governments) to proclaim truths. Such a division of labour also gives the misleading impression that at the end of the day, we can all agree on one truth and one history, devoid of uncertainty. In other words, rather than waving their freshly laundered white gloves, proclaiming their innocence (Southgate 2006, 53) and at the same time accepting their impotence, historians may as well get their hands dirty and take a moral stance.[10]

'Disciplined historians' (see Dening 1988, 23) are prone to reject the idea once put forward by Michelet that they could resuscitate the dead or offer reparation to them. Meanwhile, many of them bemoan the privileging of memory over history in contemporary societies (for example, Nora 2002, 2011). The appeal and power of memory are fed by the realisation that the past *can* be brought to life and that thereby justice *can* be done. In their role as critics of memory, historians ought to lay bare the hubris of memorial projects. But they may also want to be less sceptical about the efficacy of their own work. The past, at least to the extent that it intrudes in the present, is not beyond their reach.

Historians are neither prosecutors nor judges, but they cannot pretend that what Michelet calls 'history's justice' has nothing to do with them. They are involved in the production of truth (albeit not 'objective' or 'scientific' truth), and if such production takes place in the context of attempts to redress historic wrongs, then there is no clear-cut distinction between history's truth and history's justice.

The seven papers that follow strongly suggest that the pursuit of the question, How do historians respond to past injustice?, ought to be more than an exercise in the philosophy of history and take into account the historian's personal – if not to say emotional – entanglement. Most of the authors put forward their arguments with palpable passion, and are informed by a sense of compassion towards the victims of the past, be they forced labourers in Nazi Germany, left-wing activists in Pinochet's Chile or Arab residents of Haifa who were driven from their homes in 1948. Graham Dawson's text is marked by an empathetic engagement with the people he interviewed in the borderlands of Northern Ireland, which goes well beyond the empathy of historicists. Marivic Wyndham and Peter Read write a partisan biography of Londres 38, the former torture and detention centre; they side with the survivors and are critical of moves by the government to dictate the agenda of the memorial museum. Linde Apel is affronted by some of the memorial practices she describes in her paper. Maria Theresia Starzmann's reflections on her professional practice cannot be divorced from her emotional response: towards the men and women whose living quarters she unearthed, and towards the companies that profited from forced labour. Estela Schindel listens attentively to stories about ghosts because she finds the official rhetoric about the dictatorship in Argentina unsatisfactory; she is longing for other voices and other registers. Gilad Margalit, finally, begins his paper by embracing his dual position as a professional historian and as a Jewish resident of Haifa who is hoping that his granddaughter will live to see a different history emerge.

Historians cannot 'make whole what has been smashed' (Benjamin 1968, 257). Yet, how many of us studying murderous regimes, genocides or colonial atrocities secretly wish we could? And how many others despair because they know that they cannot? Elsewhere I observed that historians writing about historic wrongs and the search for historical justice are 'almost willing [their] protagonists [...] to right the wrong' (Neumann 2012, 128). It seems to me that the initial problem here is not so much the arousal of emotions such as anger or compassion, but an unwillingness to admit to the possibility of such arousal.

In recent years, historians have increasingly explored the role of emotions in shaping the past (Matt 2011). They have tried to elicit affective responses from their readers by conveying their own empathetic engagement with historical actors (see Phillips 2008). They have reflected on the affective appeal of their practice (Robinson 2010). The questions of how particular affective dispositions are aroused by particular subject matters and how historians could harness such dispositions have received less attention. Could it be that while historians no longer deny the role of emotions – and, for that matter, of moral judgements – they still harbour suspicions about them?

To varying degrees, the seven papers in this themed issue suggest that the historian's 'dialogue with the dead', to which Arno Mayer refers, may become charged in particular ways if the dead were the victims of an injustice. In a recent article on the East Asia Collaborative Workshop, whose members research the history of Korean labour conscripts in Japan, Morris-Suzuki (2013, 100) writes: 'Of course, from a standard academic point of view it is irrational to speak to the dead. The dead cannot hear us'. However, she also acknowledges that the Workshop members' ability to address – and, to some extent, *redress* – historic wrongs is due not least to their 'willingness to speak to the dead', and in doing so to let themselves be touched by the dead. That begs two questions: Are historians writing about issues of historical justice prone to disregard 'standard academic points'? And could it be that their subject matter warrants such disregard?

At the end of her book, *The Era of the Witness*, Wieviorka (2006, 144) asks: 'How can the historian incite reflection, thought, and rigor when feelings and emotions invade the public sphere?' Perhaps the answer is: if she is not pretending that her work has been successfully quarantined from emotions and moral concerns. As somebody trained in critically analysing sources, including the testimonies of survivors, and as somebody who ought to be able to reflect on her emotional response to human rights violations in the past, she could provide the kind of truth sought by Sierra Leoneans, Liberians and others grappling with the presence of 'dark pasts'.

Acknowledgements

I thank *Rethinking History*'s editor Alun Munslow, the contributors, the referees of all papers considered for this special issue, and Xan Karn and Audrey Mallet for helpful suggestions and advice. I am indebted to the generous and incisive comments an anonymous reader, Katharine McGregor, Peter Read, Maria Theresia Starzmann and Marivic Wyndham made on the introduction. The idea to put together this issue germinated at the Historical Justice and Memory conference which I convened in February 2012 in Melbourne; four of the contributions (by Wyndham and Read, Dawson, Margalit and Coullie) grew out of papers presented there. I am grateful to those attending the conference for exceptionally engaging discussions about issues of historical justice. Finally, I would like to extend a special 'thanks' to Nira Pancer for helping to facilitate the publication of Gilad Margalit's essay.

Funding

The Melbourne conference and my research on historical justice have been supported by Swinburne University of Technology and the Australian Research Council (through a Discovery grant).

Notes

1. Sirleaf has been open about her initial support for Taylor. Following the release of the truth and reconciliation commission's report, she said, referring to the period of conflict in Liberia:

    Sometimes, the circumstances were opaque, the distinctions between evil and good were not so clear – this is the nature of conflict and war. Like thousands of other Liberians at home and abroad who did, I have always admitted my early support for Charles Taylor to challenge the brutality of a dictatorship. It was equally clear that when the true nature of Mr. Taylor's intentions became known, there was no more impassioned critic or strong opponent to him in a democratic process. (Sirleaf 2009)

2. This rarely means: '*all* victims' truth'. Truth commissions and tribunals may privilege some victims over others, be it on account of their gender, their ethnicity or their ability to be articulate.
3. However, the International Criminal Court has come close to recognising such a right in its Rome Statute by allowing victims 'to participate in trials even if they are not called as witnesses' (Groome 2011, 189; see also Pena and Carayon 2013).
4. In the global south, trials and truth commissions may not necessarily be a symptom of an obsession with the past (see, for example, Bevernage 2011, 76–80); it should be noted, however, that at least some transitional justice mechanisms in the global south have been instigated at the behest of actors in the global north.
5. To get a sense of the dynamics of the scholarship on historical justice, see, for example, the journals *History & Memory* and *International Journal of Transitional Justice*, and the website of the international research network Dialogues on Historical Justice and Memory, which lists more than 700 researchers, many of them historians, who have published at least one substantial article on issues of historical justice and memory http://historicaldialogues.org/affiliates/database-of-researchers/.
6. In many other instances, the initiative has come from institutions or groups that have commissioned historians, often in an attempt to define an appropriate response to past wrongs.

7. The film's plot was inspired by a testimony retold by Kimberly Theidon (2013, 43–44), an anthropologist who has done extensive research in Quechua-speaking communities who bore the brunt of the violence in Peru's 20-year internal conflict.
8. Recently, there have been some tentative moves to question Germany's *Erinnerungskultur*, its official and public memories of the Holocaust (for very different perspectives, see Meier 2010; Jureit and Schneider 2010; Giesecke and Welzer 2012; for a critique of the latter two, see Assmann 2013).
9. The main exception to the claim that historians have avoided such issues is De Baets' (2009) work. For engagements with broader, but related questions, see Wennberg (1998) and Gorman (2004); incidentally, both authors are philosophers rather than practising historians.
10. For a more conventional approach to the 'moral turn', see Cotkin (2008), which I read as a rather unconvincing attempt to take a moral stance without dirtying one's gloves.

References

Abraham, Nicolas, and Maria Torok. 1986. *The Wolf Man's Magic Wand: A Cryptonymy*. Translated by Nicholas Rand. Minneapolis, MN: University of Minnesota Press.

Anderson, David. 2005. *Histories of the Hanged: The Dirty War in Kenya and the End of Empire*. London: Weidenfeld and Nicholson.

Assmann, Aleida. 2013. *Das neue Unbehagen an der Erinnerungskultur: Eine Intervention*. München: Beck.

Barkan, Elazar. 2005. "Engaging History: Managing Conflict and Reconciliation." *History Workshop Journal* 59: 229–236.

Barkan, Elazar. 2009. "Introduction: Historians and Historical Reconciliation." *American Historical Review* 114 (4): 899–913.

Barthes, Roland. 1987. *Michelet*. Translated by Richard Howard. New York: Hill and Wang.

Bartov, Omer. 1993. "Intellectuals on Auschwitz: Memory, History and Truth." *History & Memory* 5 (1): 87–129.

Bassiouni, M. Cherif. 2006. "International Recognition of Victims' Rights." *Human Rights Law Review* 6 (2): 203–279.

BBC News. 2005. "Kenya Wants UK 'Atrocity' Apology." 4 March. http://news.bbc.co.uk/2/hi/africa/4318277.stm

Benjamin, Walter. 1968. "Theses on the Philosophy of History." In *Illuminations: Essays and Reflections*, edited by Hannah Arendt and translated by Harry Zohn, 253–264. New York: Schocken Books.

Bevernage, Berber. 2011. *History, Memory and State-Sponsored Violence: Time and Justice*. New York: Routledge.

Blustein, Jeffrey. 2008. *The Moral Demands of Memory*. Cambridge: Cambridge University Press.

Booth, W. James. 2006. *Communities of Memory: On Witness, Identity, and Justice*. Ithaca, NY: Cornell University Press.

Brants, Chrisje. 2013. "Transitional Justice: History-Telling, Collective Memory, and the Victim-Witness." *International Journal of Conflict and Violence* 7 (1): 36–49.

Chakrabarty, Dipesh. 2007. "History and the Politics of Recognition." In *Manifestos for History*, edited by Keith Jenkins, Sue Morgan, and Alun Munslow, 77–87. New York: Routledge.

Cossen, Florian, dir. 2010. *Das Lied in mir*. TeamWorx.

Cotkin, George. 2008. "History's Moral Turn." *Journal of the History of Ideas* 69 (2): 293–315.

Dawson, Graham. 2007. *Making Peace with the Past? Memory, Trauma and the Irish Troubles*. Manchester: Manchester University Press.

De Baets, Antoon. 2009. *Responsible History*. New York: Berghahn.

Dening, Greg. 1988. *History's Anthropology: The Death of William Gooch*. Lanham, MD: University Press of America.

Dening, Greg. 2004. *Beach Crossings: Voyaging Across Times, Cultures, and Self*. Philadelphia, PA: University of Pennsylvania Press.

Den Norske Nobelkomite. 2011. "The Nobel Peace Prize for 2011." Press release, 7 October. http://www.nobelprize.org/nobel_prizes/peace/laureates/2011/press.html

Derrida, Jacques. 2006. *Specters of Marx: The State of the Debt, the Work of Mourning and the New International*. Translated by Peggy Kamuf. New York: Routledge.

Dymond, Tim. 2001. "A Library Sailor: An Interview with Greg Dening." *Limina* 7: 1–9. http://www.archive.limina.arts.uwa.edu.au/__data/page/186570/dening_new.pdf

Elkins, Caroline. 2005. *Imperial Reckoning: The Untold Story of Britain's Gulag in Kenya*. New York: Henry Holt and Company.

Gibbon, Edward. 2013 [1781]. *The History of the Decline and Fall of the Roman Empire*, edited by J. B. Bury. Vol. 3. Cambridge: Cambridge University Press.

Giesecke, Dana, and Harald Welzer. 2012. *Das Menschenmögliche: Zur Renovierung der deutschen Erinnerungskultur*. Hamburg: Edition Körber-Stiftung.

Gluck, Carol. 2007. "Operation of Memory: 'Comfort Women' and the World." In *Ruptured Histories: War, Memory, and the Post-Cold War in Asia*, edited by Sheila Miyoshi Jager, and Rana Mitter, 47–77. Cambridge, MA: Harvard University Press.

González García, José M. 2008. "Cultural Memories of the Expulsion of the Moriscos." *European Review* 16 (1): 91–100.

Gordon, Avery. 2008. *Ghostly Matters: Haunting and the Sociological Imagination*. 2nd ed. Minneapolis, MN: University of Minnesota Press.

Gorman, Jonathan. 2004. "Historians and Their Duties." *History and Theory* 43: 103–117.

Groome, Dermot. 2011. "The Right to Truth in the Fight Against Impunity." *Berkeley Journal of International Law* 29 (1): 175–199.

Hayner, Priscilla. 2011. *Unspeakable Truths: Transitional Justice and the Challenge of Truth Commissions*. 2nd ed. New York: Routledge.

Hazan, 2010. *Judging War, Judging History: Behind Truth and Reconciliation*. Translated by Sarah Meyer de Stadelhofen. Stanford, CA: Stanford University Press.

House of Commons (United Kingdom). 2013. "Mau May Claims (Settlement)." Hansard, 6 June, 1692–1699, http://www.publications.parliament.uk/pa/cm201314/cmhansrd/chan13.pdf

Human Rights House. 2005. "Vice President Demands British Apology over Mau Mau." 3 March. http://humanrightshouse.org/Articles/6424.html

Huyssen, Andreas. 2005. "Resistance to Memory: The Uses and Abuses of Public Forgetting." In *Globalizing Critical Theory*, edited by Max Pensky, 165–184. Lanham, MD: Rowman and Littlefield.

James-Allen, Paul, Aaron Weah, and Lizzie Goodfriend. 2010. "Beyond the Truth and Reconciliation Commission: Transitional Justice Options in Liberia." May. New York: International Center for Transitional Justice. http://ictj.org/sites/default/files/ICTJ-Liberia-Beyond-TRC-2010-English.pdf

John Paul II. 2001. "Apology for the Sack of Constantinople (2001)." 4 May. Facts on File, http://www.fofweb.com/History/MainPrintPage.asp?iPin=SIWH0189&DataType=WorldHistory&WinType=Free

Jureit, Ulrike, and Christian Schneider. 2010. *Gefühlte Opfer: Illusionen der Vergangenheitsbewältigung*. Stuttgart: Klett-Cotta.

Karn, Alexander. 2006. "Depolarizing the Past: The Role of Historical Commissions in Conflict Mediation and Reconciliation." *Journal of International Affairs* 60 (1): 31–50.

Karstedt, Susanne. 2010. "From Absence to Presence, from Silence to Voice: Victims in International and Transitional Justice Since the Nuremberg Trials." *International Review of Victimology* 17 (1): 9–30.

Labanyi, Jo. 2000. "History and Hauntology; or, What Does One Do with the Ghosts of the Past? Reflections on Spanish Film and Fiction of the Post-Franco Period." In *Disremembering the Dictatorship: The Politics of Memory in the Spanish Transition to Democracy*, edited by Joan Ramon Resina, 65–82. Amsterdam: Rodopi.

Llosa, Claudia. 2009. *La teta asustada*. Generalitat de Catalunya.

Maier, Charles S. 1988. *The Unmasterable Past: History, Holocaust, and German National Identity*. Cambridge, MA: Harvard University Press.

Maier, Charles S. 1993. "A Surfeit of Memory? Reflections on History, Melancholy and Denial." *History & Memory* 5 (2): 136–152.

Margalit, Avishai. 2002. *The Ethics of Memory*. Cambridge, MA: Harvard University Press.

Matt, Susan J. 2011. "Current Emotion Research in History: Or, Doing History from the Inside Out." *Emotion Review* 3 (1): 117–124.

Mayer, Arno J. 1993. "Memory and History: On the Poverty of Remembering and Forgetting the Judeocide." *Radical History Review* 56 (5): 5–20.

Meier, Christian. 2010. *Das Gebot zu vergessen und die Unabweisbarkeit des Erinnerns: Vom öffentlichen Umgang mit schlimmer Vergangenheit*. München: Siedler.

Mieth, Friederike. 2013. "Bringing Justice and Enforcing peace? An Ethnographic Perspective on the Impact of the Special Court for Sierra Leone." *International Journal of Conflict and Violence* 7 (1): 10–22.

Morris-Suzuki, Tessa. 2013. "Letters to the Dead: Grassroots Historical Dialogue in East Asia's Borderlands." In *East Asia Beyond the History Wars: Confronting the Ghosts of Violence*, edited by Tessa Morris Suzuki, Morris Low, Leonid Petrov, and Timothy Y. Tsu, 87–104. London: Routledge.

Neumann, Klaus. 2012. "Icebergs and Other Hazards: An Epilogue." *Time & Society* 21 (1): 121–131.

Neumann, Klaus. 2014. "History, Memory, Justice." In *A Companion to Global Historical Thought*, edited by Prasenjit Duara, Viren Murthy, and Andrew Sartori, 466–481. Chichester: Wiley-Blackwell.

Nora, Pierre. 2002. "Reasons for the Current Upsurge in Memory." *Eurozine*, 19 April. http://www.eurozine.com/pdf/2002-04-19-nora-en.pdf

Nora, Pierre. 2011. "Recent History and the Dangers of Politicization." Translated by Mike Routledge. *Eurozine*, 24 November. http://www.eurozine.com/pdf/2011-11-24-nora-en.pdf

Outreach Programme of the International Criminal Tribunal for the Former Yugoslavia (ICTY). 2006. "The Tribunal's Accomplishments in Justice and Law." *Justice in Transition* 3, http://www.icty.org/x/file/Outreach/view_from_hague/jit_accomplishments_en.pdf

Pena, Mariana, and Gaelle Carayon. 2013. "Is the ICC Making the Most of Victim Participation?" *International Journal of Transitional Justice* 7: 518–535. [Advance online publication].

Phillips, Mark Salber. 2008. "On the Advantage and Disadvantage of Sentimental History for Life." *History Workshop Journal* 65: 49–64.

Republic of Liberia, Truth and Reconciliation Commission. 2009. "Consolidated Final Report, Vol. 2." 30 June. Monrovia: Truth & Reconciliation Commission of Liberia. http://trcofliberia.org/resources/reports/final/volume-two_layout-1.pdf

Rieff, David. 2011. *Against Remembrance*. Carlton: Melbourne University Press.

Robinson, Emily. 2010. "Touching the Void: Affective History and the Impossible." *Rethinking History* 14 (4): 503–520.

Sesay, Alpha. 2013. "Charles Taylor's Conviction and Sentence Upheld: What Next for Him?" Open Society Justice Initiative, *The Trial of Charles Taylor*, 26 September. http://www.charlestaylortrial.org/2013/09/26/charles-taylors-conviction-and-sentence-upheld-what-next-for-him/

Shaw, Rosalind. 2010. "Linking Justice with Reintegration? Ex-Combatants and the Sierra Leone Experiment." In *Localizing Transitional Justice: Interventions and Priorities after Mass Violence*, edited by Rosalind Shaw, and Lars Waldorf, with Pierre Hazan, 111–132. Stanford, CA: Stanford University Press.

Sikkink, Kathryn. 2011. *The Justice Cascade: How Human Rights Prosecutions Are Changing World Politics*. New York: W.W. Norton.

Simons, Marlise, and Alan Cowell. 2013. "50-Year Sentence Upheld for Ex-President of Liberia." *New York Times*, 26 September. http://www.nytimes.com/2013/09/27/world/africa/charles-taylor-sierra-leone-war-crimes-case.html

Sirleaf, Ellen Johnson. 2009. "Special Message by Her Excellency Mrs. Ellen Johnson Sirleaf, President of the Republic of Liberia, on the Occasion of the 162nd Independence Anniversary of the Republic of Liberia." 27 July. http://www.emansion.gov.lr/doc/7_26_09_President26Remarks.pdf

Special Court for Sierra Leone (SCSL). 2013. "Judgement – Prosecutor Against Charles Chankay Taylor.", SCSL-03-01-A (10766-11114). 26 September. http://www.sc-sl.org/LinkClick.aspx?fileticket=t14fjFP4jJ8%3d&tabid=53

Southgate, Beverley. 2006. "'A Pair of White Gloves': Historians and Ethics." *Rethinking History* 10 (1): 49–61.

Theidon, Kimberly. 2013. *Intimate Enemies: Violence and Reconciliation in Peru*. Philadelphia, PA: University of Pennsylvania Press.

Thompson, Janna. 2002. *Taking Responsibility for the Past: Reparation and Historical Justice*. Oxford: Polity Press.

United Nations. 2006. "Resolution Adopted by the General Assembly on 16 December 2005: Basic Principles and Guidelines on the Right to a Remedy and Reparation for Victims of Gross Violations of International Human Rights Law and Serious Violations of International Humanitarian Law." United Nations Document A/RES/60/147, 21 March. http://www.un.org/ga/search/view_doc.asp?symbol=A/RES/60/147

Vivian, Bradford. 2010. *Public Forgetting: The Rhetoric and Politics of Beginning Again*. University Park, PA: Pennsylvania State University Press.

Walker, Margaret Urban. 2010. "Truth Telling as Reparations." *Metaphilosophy* 41 (4): 526–545.

Wennberg, Robert. 1998. "The Moral Standing of the Dead and the Writing of History." *Fides et Historia* 30 (2): 51–63.

Wiebelhaus-Brahm, Eric. 2013. "Liberia." In *Encyclopedia of Transitional Justice*, edited by Lavinia Stan, and Nadya Nedelsky. Vol. 2, 280–286. Cambridge: Cambridge University Press.

Wieviorka, Annette. 2006. *The Era of the Witness*. Translated by Jared Stark. Ithaca, NY: Cornell University Press.

Wilke, Christiane. 2010. "Enter Ghost: Haunted Courts and Haunting Judgments in Transitional Justice." *Law Critique* 21 (1): 73–92.

Wilson, Robert Ashby. 2011. *Writing History in International Criminal Trials*. Cambridge: Cambridge University Press.

Young, James E. 1989. "The Biography of a Memorial Icon: Nathan Rapoport's Warsaw Ghetto Monument." *Representations* 26: 69–106.

The disappearing museum

Marivic Wyndham[a] and Peter Read[b]

[a]Faculty of Arts and Social Sciences, University of Technology Sydney, Sydney, Australia;
[b]Department of History, University of Sydney, Sydney, Australia

> Since its official opening to the public in 2007, the curators of the site of conscience Londres 38 have presented a variety of histories of its past. Gradually, the state has wrested the site's interpretation from the victims and their families, at the cost of particularity in time, place and precise historical detail. We trace the struggles between the civil society *colectivos* ('collectives') and a variety of state agencies for the dominant narrative, and argue that today the state controls the interior of the building; the *colectivos* control only the street – not unlike the situation as it was before the building opened six years ago.

This paper examines the conflicting agendas between the state and the supporters of a Santiago site of conscience,[1] as to how the building should be historically interpreted. The building is Londres 38, one of the most infamous of the many hundreds of torture, extermination and disappearance centres notorious during the Pinochet regime. The protagonists, on one side, are the survivors, families and other victims of the *Pinochetistas*. They formed themselves into three *colectivos* ('collectives'), working sometimes discordantly after the dictatorship ended in 1990 to have the building released into their hands from a quasi-military organisation. In 2005, Colectivo 119 focused on the 119 political prisoners, members of the radical Left party MIR (Movimento de Izquierda Revolucionaria [Revolutionary Movement of the Left]), who were connected with Londres 38 as survivors or family members. A second group, Amigos y Familiares de los 119, comprised individuals with less personal interest in the site and more current political concerns. In 2005, some members of Colectivo 119 formed a third collective, Colectivo Londres 38, which sympathises broadly with the Socialist Party. The issue of exactly which leftist grouping each politically executed/

disappeared prisoner belonged to has remained a much more significant issue than at other such sites.

On the other side are a variety of government agencies and local administrative interests, including the Ministry of the Interior, the Metropolitan Regional Administration, the Council for National Monuments and the Ministry of Public Works, each of which seeks to utilise the historical interpretation for their own purposes. At Londres 38, some of these agencies were in conflict with each other; however, all of them have shared the cautious reluctance shown by successive Concertacíon governments to investigate and prosecute individual perpetrators and to memorialise sites of terror for fear of a return to military rule, which makes possible to subsume these disparate agencies under the label of 'the state'.

Londres 38, at length acquired by Michelle Bachelet's Concertación government in 2005, was opened to the public in 2007, the first time in more than 30 years. Family members immediately began to place mementoes of their loved ones in corners of the building, and the *colectivos* began to plan how the terrible past was to be interpreted if not expiated. But the government's own disparate agencies, irritated by the lack of agreement among the *colectivos* and anxious to prosecute their own agendas, have little by little edged out the voices of precise locality and exact event. Tracing the process by which the particular has become generalised in place and time in the interpretation of state violence within the building is the focus of our paper.

Among several roles, our analysis as historians here rests on a complete photographic record of the changes in presentation which we have maintained. What follows here is a continuous narration, from the first curatorial statement to the unfinished present, of events that exemplify the profound interpretative struggle between a focus narrow or wide, graphic or poetic, brutal or meditative. In this way, we build upon the personal testimonies which currently comprise 90% of the histories about Chilean sites of conscience. Historians tell stories, but we must do more than merely record and recount. Our account, which draws on many discussions we held when attending vigils outside Londres 38 over several years, would be spineless without a conviction that what occurred at this, or at any, site of conscience, was of sharp significance. The events that occurred at Londres 38, and their evolving interpretation, clearly matter profoundly to the survivors and the families of the politically executed and the disappeared. Their interactions with others relate to the history of Chile, to the history of the cold war, to the history of twentieth-century state violence and to the evolution of international human rights. As authors, through our training and interests, we follow, collect, record, relate and reflect upon their journey; as outsiders, we try to bring to the story both impartiality and compassion.

The increasing sophistication of the management of trauma sites is exemplified in the study of the continuing academic exchanges over what should become of the sites of conscience.[2] In Chile, however, historical discussion is still mostly limited to online or published testimonies of the experiences of survivors. Impassioned curatorial discussion takes place at board of management meetings and within communities. Every former torture and extermination centre in Santiago, each infamous in its own way, has its own band of devotees composed of victims, their families, survivors and others, who are united, divided or perplexed, as to its future (Read and Wyndham 2008). For instance, in 2008 the supporters of the internationally best-known Villa Grimaldi reconstructed one of its torture chambers, established a Memory Room and built an open-air theatre amidst rolling lawns and serene gardens (Corporación Parque de la Paz Villa Grimaldi 2005, 36). These developments were not without controversy. D'Orival Briceño, a critic of the reconstructed centre, exclaimed in a conversation with us in 2009: 'They fill it with plaques and objects rather than tell the story of what happened there. Now they're having a rock concert there!'

The debate about what to do with the changing rooms and passageways of the National Stadium, where 14,000 people were temporarily held, tortured or executed in the early months after the coup, began at about the same time; but it was only in 2006 that plans were finally drawn up by heritage professionals as to how the rusting, decrepit and in some cases bullet-holed facilities might be conserved. The process of actually conserving them, however, is unlikely to begin in the near future (Ministerio de Educación, Republica de Chile 2007). It was not until 2007 that local residents and others were able to enter the airforce maintenance camp and secret police establishment in Loyola/Neptuno Street, Quinta Normal, to celebrate its opening to the public; but a memorial stone to the victims was later destroyed by a section of the local community (Read and Wyndham 2012). A memorial at a fourth centre, at 1367 José Domingo Cañas, was inaugurated in April 2010, 10 years after the site was declared a historic monument (Corporación José Domingo Cañas 1367 2003, 19), and two years after the José Domingo Cañas 1367 Corporation obtained a government grant to erect a memorial, offices and a library. In the late 1990s, victim families drawn mainly from the MIR and the Socialist and Communist Parties formed a *colectivo*, and in a gesture of solidarity, invited *poblaciones*, people from the poorest suburbs – who had been particularly victimised by the *Pinochetistas* – to paint powerful slogans and murals. But interventions by *poblaciones* have by no means been invited nor welcomed at all sites of conscience.

Thus sites of recent but very great trauma in Chile, as in Argentina (see Estela Schindel's contribution in this issue), are variously open to the public, privatised, destroyed, levelled, forgotten or unknown. Each may carry no interpretation, minimal interpretation or detailed and multifaceted interpretation. A few are in the process of being preserved, conserved, reconstructed and memorialised (Andreani and Cerda 2000). Each may be made brutal, or serene or both; but each holds the potential for deep conflict. Sites of wickedness remain not only concrete and material but also 'visible and invisible, past and present, [where] physical and metaphysical came to exist and share a common space' (Tumarkin 2005, 233). In daily life, the polarities of these dilemmas are very wide: Should the remaining centres of torture, disappearance and execution be allowed to be destroyed for a larger contemporary public purpose like a housing estate? Should a former torture and extermination centre privilege the experiences of one particular group of victims, such as women? From the perspective of the Left, the critical question is: should older people who suffered during, and young people who have only heard about, the terrible Pinochet years throw their best efforts into current problems of housing, education and unemployment, or into the researching, revealing, memorialising and demanding compensation for the iniquities done several decades ago?

Londres 38

Londres 38 is an elegant nineteenth-century three-storey mansion in one of the most graceful areas of Santiago's central business district (CBD). During the Allende years of the early 1970s, it was the headquarters of the Chilean Socialist Party. Possibly out of a sense of irony, more probably because it was a building that could be seized quickly to house and interrogate prisoners, the building was occupied by the Dirección de Inteligencia Nacional (DINA), Pinochet's secret police, two months after the coup.

While the two Santiago stadiums – the National Stadium and the Chile Stadium – were first used as holding centres, Londres 38 was the destination to which the best known and, to Pinochet's forces, the most dangerous militants of the Left were taken by summary arrest (Read and Wyndham 2008). In particular, they included members of the elite MIR. Probably by the beginning of November 1973, the security services were setting up Londres 38 as the first of its interrogation, torture, detention and execution centres. The building functioned for 10 months as one of hundreds of secret sites of torture, execution and disappearance operated by the Pinochet government. A total of 98 people are known to have died within the building during this period. Others of the more than 3500 Chileans who were disappeared during the Pinochet years may have been killed there too.

Londres 38 remained distinct. Thanks again to its high status, physical elegance and prime location half a kilometre from the seat of government, the centre was not levelled by the dictatorship. Rather, in 1978, the building was gifted by Pinochet to the O'Higgins Institute, a politically reactionary and quasi-military organisation. The Institute's membership contained a significant number of former Army officers who could still summon deference in each of the centre-left governments elected since Pinochet's departure. The members objected strongly to any reference to the brief but terrifying role of their headquarters as the first of Pinochet's torture centres. They denied knowledge to any enquiry and changed the number of the building from 38 to 40. For a decade the centre-left Concertación governments, implicitly acknowledging the potential of the O'Higgins Institute to encourage a further military coup, resisted any attempt at an official recognition of the building's past (Stern 2010, 270–271).

HISTORICAL JUSTICE

Within a few months, the techniques of the DINA would grow more sophisticated: rather than carrying out an arrest at home, which involved witnesses and disturbance, wanted suspects walking in the streets were identified secretly by spies and collaborators in a passing car, bundled into another car and 'disappeared' (Castillo 2007). Prisoners thereafter were kept separate from each other, the torture centres secret. But in these very early days of the coup, the DINA had not yet established its procedures. Although the government continued to deny its existence until 1979, Londres 38 was always known for what it was. Held near the well-known church of St Francisco, blindfolded prisoners could hear the pealing of the bells; others recognised, by peering below their blindfolds, the distinctive black and white marble tiling of the entrance hall, and whispered to each other their location. Several times a day came a roll-call, therefore every prisoner knew who had arrived, or Left or died. In this way, partly because of its central position in one of the most elegant areas of the CBD, partly because its location was an open secret, Londres 38 began its infamous career as a notorious, internationally known icon of Chilean state terrorism. Patricio Rivas, a leading MIR official held in Londres 38 for 72 hours in late December 1973, recalls his arrival at the torture centre:

> A kind of infernal choir tilled the place. I heard screams of different tones, from different mouths, which blended with the summons of the agents. They were screams of horror that bit the air and which, even when they ended, still vibrated in space. They weren't screams of fear, they were of loneliness in the face of the incomprehensible. The voices of those young people remained there forever. (Rivas 2007, 115)

Many Chilean survivors of torture have described their experiences in dozens of centres. We cite here the testimony of Raimundo Belarmino Elgueta Pinto relating to Londres 38, in the conviction that one cannot usefully analyse curatorial changes without, at least, catching a glimpse of the emotions which survivors or families of the detained/disappeared bring to the site of suffering:

> In London 38, I was tortured daily, with the exception of Sundays which in those times were still deemed for compulsory rest, punched and kicked and applied electrical currents while sitting on a chair, lying on the 'grill' or hanging from a metal bar. The principal method consisted of applying an electrical current on the 'grill', for which I was made to take all my clothes, they would tie me by the hands and feet to the electric bed, and connect cables to the fingers of my hands and feet and also to the penis and/or testicles and left a 'floating' cable which they applied to the different parts of the body. The 'sessions' were of variable duration, some very prolonged and others very brief, and were generally conducted by Reyes Zapata and Romo Mena, although I remember that on one occasion I was interrogated and tortured directly by Moren Brito and on another occasion I was interrogated, without torture, directly by Krassnoff Martchenko. (Belarmino Elgueta Pinto, n.d.)

Interpreting the site

2004

While the Institute remained *in situ*, public commemoration of the building's past was severely restrained. Unlike at José Domingo Cañas, there could be no question of allowing permanent graphic artwork even on the facade. But now, as news spread that the building was soon to be released from hostile control, it was probably no coincidence that those advocating a memorialisation of Londres 38 began to fracture. At least two collectives demanded a distinct voice. The members of Colectivo 119, drawn together to resolve issues connected with the 119 murdered political prisoners, were personally connected with Londres 38 as survivors, families or descendants. They demanded, first of all, recognition of the 119. Amigos y Familiares de los 119, headed by Ximena Muñoz, occupied a lower socio-economic place and believed themselves to be the ideological inheritors of working-class struggles. It was they who began to convoke the solemn weekly vigils to the dead staged after business hours for several years on the pavement, away from silent witnessing towards political slogans and noisy critiques of the Concertación (Read and Wyndham 2012). Colectivo 119 and Colectivo Amigos y Familiares de los 119 split over whether to accept the government as partner in memorialising the building, and how and what should be remembered. The inexperienced, and somewhat anarchic Amigos y Familiares, unused to negotiating with the state at any level, held that no one associated with the building should deal with a government that had prevaricated and compromised with the military. The rival collective, better educated and confident in negotiation, thought this attitude counterproductive.

The discussions about the building's future became more urgent: Should the interior present a minimalist exhibition of images and texts in key places or become a public space for the larger contemporary issues of education and workers' employment? The footpath activities became more discordant. Songs and recitals at the evening vigils included fewer personal testimonies, more theatrical roll-calls for oppressed minorities like Indigenous people, more displays and puppet shows, and more denunciations – not of Pinochet's regime, but of Bachelet's!

2005

It was in the context of the 2004 Valech Report's multiple testimonies of torture at Londres 38 and elsewhere, and in the expectation that the O'Higgins Institute might be prepared to move to new quarters, that Michelle Bachelet's centre-left government declared the building a historic monument (Valech et al. 2004). A bronze tablet sunk into the pavement outside the building, rectangular, somewhat obscure and bureaucratic in design, gave away few details of what atrocities might have occurred inside:

Londres 38
   Secret Centre of detention, torture, disappearance and execution 11 September 1973–September 1974
   It is estimated that more than 2,000 people were detained in Londres 38, 96 of whom were executed, are currently disappeared or died later as a consequence of the tortures; 83 were men and 13 women, two of whom were pregnant.
   Declared a Historic Monument in 2005

The position of the plaque on the pavement rather than on the wall of the building indicated that the third player, the Department of Historic Monuments, in joining the site's interpretation, was still anxious not to offend the powerful and dangerous. Meanwhile the Bachelet government continued to negotiate with the Institute by offering several attractive sites elsewhere in the city to exchange for Londres 38.

The state's recognition of the site as a historic monument acted to release those local frictions which had been in larger tension for many years between the Chilean intellectual Left and the working-class Left. Some members of Colectivo 119 split to form a new but not unfriendly group, Colectivo Londres 38, composed of survivors and families of the Socialist Party, to make plans for the future of the building. Survivors and family members who once belonged to the ultra-left MIR remained behind in Colectivo 119. The fractures widened. The Amigos y Familiares de los 119 criticised the other two collectives for entering into direct negotiation with the government. Only peaceful protest and patient negotiations would convince the government that the Institute should be persuaded to leave. Trying to smash in the front door of Londres 38, as some were demanding, would be highly counterproductive. They would finish up with nothing. The demand by the Amigos y Familiares that free education and health benefits should be granted not only to the children of victims of repression, but to all working-class children was wrong-headed. If there was to be a central archive of historical research, what would be its purpose? Who would control it? In the last resort – should the leftist groups work with the government towards reconciliation – or against it?

2006

Unexpectedly, in February 2006 the Institute put the building up for sale. The collectives claimed victory, but the government trumped the discussion by announcing that it, not the collectives, had become the owner of Londres 38 and that it planned to install on the site a yet-to-be-established Institute for Human Rights (*La Nación*, 12 October 2006).

2007

At last here was something that could unite the collectives. Almost everyone, it seemed, opposed the government's plan. In March 2007, Colectivo 119 invited all interested parties to a meeting to decide the preferred purpose. The Colectivo Londres 38 demanded that the building should become a public space dedicated to the history of the Pinochet repression and the memories of those who had suffered within its walls. A participatory process should define its uses, after which the state should have no role beyond ensuring that its management was public, democratic and participatory.

Still unable to enter the building, the collectives planned their own exterior memorialisation, which they wanted to be more informative than the state's minimalist plaque. In the pavement of the public street, 300 black and white granite tiles would imitate the floor inside the building which victims could glimpse through the bottom of their blindfolds. A further 98 iron placards would list the names and ages of the 85 men and 13 women who died in the building. Almost as significant as the name would be a statement of political affiliation. One read, for example:

> Abundio Alejandro Conteras Gonzales
> 28 years old
> MIR

No sooner had the divisions closed in opposition to the government's plans, than they reopened on the alternative conservation and memorialisation of the building. Now that the plaques and memorials were in place outside, what should be interpreted inside, and how, and when? One end of the collectives' spectrum was an empty, silent building, bare and darkened rooms for quiet contemplation. Concerned with a wider agenda beyond the interests of the local and particular, it was this vision that the state's agencies would progressively challenge.

The official opening and re-occupation of the building was scheduled for 10 December 2007, marking the point at which the divisions between the state and victims, a national future opposed to a precise and local past, became tangible. Colectivo 119 wanted a solemn and respectful ingress: only they should first be admitted to exorcise their memories and conduct their rituals. Tensions rose as the Ministry of National Assets announced that, contrary to the wishes of seemingly everyone else, it would take charge of the formal opening as a major media event. The collectives debated whether to boycott the event; most decided that it was in their interests to attend. But during the morning, rumours had spread that the minister, hearing of a planned counter-demonstration by the Amigos y Familiares de los 119, had postponed the formal opening until further notice. By three o'clock in the afternoon, few in the crowd gathering outside knew what was to happen, or when. By four, a crowd of a hundred people stood outside awaiting developments, chatting, listening to speeches and performers. The building's windows and door on the bottom floor were wide open, but representatives of the Amigos y Familiares de los 119 stood outside barring entry to all but, it seemed, their own members. By half past four, the numbers of people being allowed to walk in and out of the main entrance were increasing. Suddenly a spokesperson for the Colectivo Amigos y Familiares announced defiantly that since the minister had forbidden entry, those present should 'force' their way in: 'We must repudiate the Ministry, *compañeros*, for [all] government still represents the long repression of the workers. The entry of we urban unionists will be like a vigil, but something more. Treat it with the utmost respect, but move in'. A hundred people surged forward.

Different intentions at once emerged. While mourners on the upper floors pored over walls and floors in search of evidence like painted-over messages, down in the marble-tiled entrance hall a noisy discussion began as to the future of the building. The drama of the afternoon was precipitating a climax of tensions months or years in the making: to express individual grief, to give voice to national workers' movements, to bind the site to international human rights and to further the cause of national reconciliation. Boiling over here were not only the emotions of the terror but also of the years of frustration at the Institute, at the government, at the other collectives and at each other in a divided political Left with nowhere to go. In the broadest terms, the question was: Who in the end holds the emotional and moral rights to this building? Were they intellectuals or workers, sufferers or supporters, professionals or amateurs? Would the opening of the building be a victory for *local* activism and the current struggles of Santiago urban workers – the present; or a victory for *local* memory, truth and justice set in a context of international human rights – the past; or the state's *national* agenda of investigation of victims (not perpetrators) and reconciliation – that is to say, the future?

2008

The first interpretations of the terror were personal, precise and agonising: the ornaments and drawings appeared unobtrusively probably within hours of the opening, presumably done by those with the most painful connections. In a cramped and windowless cell (probably originally a storage pantry) were depicted four blindfolded handcuffed individuals jammed together on the floor. In another, the infamous torturers Krasnoff and Moren Brito, flanked by a guard, stood in threatening poses. A blindfolded naked man hung upside down suspended by the knees and hands from a pole. A naked man was plunged by two guards into a barrel, probably of sewage. Some of the reproductions hung on three corners, or were crooked or slightly torn. Their positioning was unmistakably urgent, in no sense decorative, answering a private motive rather than one of public information. Since each was only some 8 × 12 centimetres, it was easy for visitors to the building – which could not yet be called a museum – not to notice them. Each depicted an event in the relevant room: for example, the drawing of the figure in the barrel hung in the upstairs bathroom nearest to the torture chamber. There is no reason to doubt that each of these torture sites had become a private altar for perhaps a solitary mourner. While some of the punishments were not specific to Londres 38, the drawings memorialised several exact and unspeakable events that had occurred there.

2009

Probably early in the year, still within the first outpouring of deepest grief, an unknown mourner placed six identical photocopied cards depicting, on a dirty floor still stained with marks of a yellow paintpot, five members of probably a single family, Alberto Gallardo, Roberto Gallardo, Catalina Gallardo, Rolando Rodriguez and Monica Pacheco, arranged against the wall of the first room that one entered. Beside each card was propped a paper rose. Below each photograph was typed:

> Executed by the DINA
> 9th of November 1975.

On the ground floor, in another bathroom, someone had glued an image of a young man's face on an inlet valve that served poignantly to frame it. Throughout the building, the mood of the impromptu signage was one of barely restrained horror and grief at what had happened here, not there, and to this person, not that.

To this point, neither the Department of National Assets nor the collectives had agreed on the direction of a Londres 38 display. It was a full year before the first indications of the shift from the minutely particular to a general statement about the building itself took form. Sometime in 2009, a rather bureaucratic notice appeared propped against the chimney wall on the marble mantelpiece, directly above the memorial cards to the Gallardo family. The wording of this first interpretative signage inside the building was significant, illustrating the compromises between the three collectives. Note the prioritising of the achievements of the different protagonists:

> Had it not been for the actions of the ex-detained [Colectivo 119], the families of the victims [Colectivo Londres 38] and the social organisations [Colectivo Amigos y Familiares de los 119], this site would still remain ignored. Virtually 'erased' from the city.

And yet, no doubt intended as a countermeasure against this intrusion, someone had taken the cards memorialising the Gallarado family from the floor and arranged them on the mantelpiece to lean against the sign itself, partly obscuring it.

2010

Visitors to the building might well have noticed a subtle but sure direction away from precise location to generality. The reception room, the largest space on the ground floor, where the detainees were held handcuffed and blindfolded, was the only room whose purpose was identified. Here, Patricio Rivas had absorbed the 'infernal choir, those screams of horror that bit the air' and which, 'even when they ended, still vibrated in space, screams not of fear, but of loneliness in the face of the incomprehensible'. The signage, however, was far more prosaic:

> DETENTION ROOM. Common room in which during the day the male and female detainees remained seated and blindfolded. During the night the chairs were removed and they slept on the floor.

The rest of the 2010 signage appeared to have been directed by another, more poetic hand, but one which still eschewed both precision and location. Nor was it clear who had written them, nor for whom. This caption in another room seemed to reflect the horror that Rivas could not forget:

> The problem was not, nor is, only to speak or tell of what was experienced, rather to find ears that want to listen.

This caption appeared on a door on the first floor:

> The ear allowed them to see without eyes, identify the house and its surroundings, recognise days and nights and hold in their memory the voices of friends and comrades.

And prominently inscribed on the walls of another room:

> How does one fill this void so full of entrapped memories?
> This is a past that continues to be part of our present.

Finally, visitors reflected upon this message, scribbled on a cigarette packet by a woman prisoner, Muriel Dockendorff Navarrete, to her friend Sandra Machuca, a fellow detainee in the Santiago torture centre Cuatro Alamos. Muriel died, Sandra survived:

> I remember when I met you in the house of terror [...] In those moments in which a light was a dream. Or a miracle, however, you were light in those darknesses. We were one in one misfortune. Today thousands of misfortunes. Later I see you as before, as I know you will be today, in some other place, always looking to windward.
> We will meet through the mists that we will dispel.
> Do not forget me.

Heart-stopping as Muriel Dockendorff's farewell message was to her friend, the explanation below the major caption for the first time introduced a new element into the display. Though it is not necessary to read this explanation as anything but an attempt to convey the horrors of interrogation, torture and disappearance or execution, it indicated for the first time that the history of Londres 38 might not only set aside the minutiae of every room, but also the particularity of the building itself:

> Letter written by Muriel Dockendorff Navarrete – today a detained disappeared, to her friend Sandra Machuca, 10 October 1974, while both were detained in the camp [now site of conscience] Cuatro Alamos.

2011

The purposes and intentions that the government had indicated in 2010 were now to weigh much more heavily on the interpretation. Dominating the display, and marking the starting point of the guided tours established during the year, was a historical timeline that began with the story of the 119 disappeared – while noting that such psychological warfare was practised by other dictatorships of the time. In each annual summary of events, Londres 38 did not always figure. The text for the year 1983, for instance, noted only the first of the widespread nationwide strikes against the government. The caption for 2005 noted the year in which Londres was handed over to the collectives. For 2010, the year in which the state assumed a more direct control over interpretation, the signage traced its own role precisely. A laboriously worded sign explained that, 'meeting the will of the current government', a Working Group had been formed of the three collectives, along with representatives of the Presidential Assessors Commission of Human Rights, the Programme of Human Rights of the Ministry of Interior, the Metropolitan Regional Administration, the Executive of Architecture of the Ministry of Public Works and the Council for National Monuments, among others.

Equally significantly, the drawings of the detainees cramped in a tiny cell, the six photocopies of the Gallardo family members, the individual tortures, the tiny photograph of the young man in the lower bathroom, all were gone. When we asked the building's solitary guide, Leopoldo Montenegro, he replied that did not know that they ever had been there. To the question as to why, for example, there was no physical evidence of torture instruments such as the *parrilla* displayed at José Domingo Cañas or the National Museum of Human Rights, he replied that such an object would be 'contrary to the aesthetic of the display'.

2012

The display assumed a new irony. The most dominant voice when the building was still in the hands of the O'Higgins Institute, that of the Colectivo 119, remained absent inside, relegated to that familiar pavement of vigil and posters, apparently the only area where it was allowed to mount its own display. This took the form of a nine-panel temporary exhibition, packed away each night, presenting a photograph and biographical information on each of the disappeared 119 (Wadi 2012). Inside, the most significant innovation was an electronic display of as many of the executed and disappeared – from the whole country – of whom photographs could be obtained. The display marked a new humanising direction: fewer of the serious traditional head and shoulders photos, more of people playing with their children or a dog, or relaxing at a party.

The years of struggles to rescue Londres 38 as a specific site of conscience appear to have come a full circle. The same spatial tensions of the time prior to that day in 2007 when Londres 38 first opened its doors, between the public and private, the outside and the inside of the site, hold today. The years of vigils and pasted photographs of victims of Londres 38 outside, when the building was occupied by the O'Higgins Institute, now seem almost futile. Once again, the physical and metaphorical spheres of interior and exterior impose themselves: the state in control over the politics of the interior of the building, and the collectives in charge of the various public exhibitions staged outside. The extent to which some members of the collectives have resigned themselves to these divisions of space and power is reflected in a recent anonymous justification of the status quo that argues in phrases as cumbersomely opaque in English as they are in Spanish:

> [W]e aim to go beyond the traditional concepts of museum or commemorative space, privileging the relationship with the community, in pursuing a collective and participatory conception. This means that the memories related to the site involve other groups and sectors of society, whose participation is necessary in order to

generate processes of elaboration of those memories and the construction of collective knowledge a constant and always inconclusive dynamic. Therefore, the realisation of the project necessarily meets in the convocation of other social sectors, creating new links and networks which facilitate the process of the recuperation and elaboration of memories. (Cited in Perez and Glavic 2011, 2)

Londres 38 has been bedevilled by internal divisions between its many claimants. Situated in the city centre, only metres from the lobby of a prominent hotel, it is controlled by the state, after its grieving families have been outmanoeuvred. By contrast, the Frei government passed over the site of the former torture and extermination centre Villa Grimaldi to its dominant collective with few strings attached (Read, December 2013). Barely a year after the transition to democracy, Villa Grimaldi survivors and supporters had agreed to present and proclaim the centre as an International Site of Conscience. At the suburban José Domingo Cañas, local groups united behind the leadership of a dominant spokesperson. Although purchased through a government grant, it is removed from casual tourism and has maintained a fiercely independent stance as to how its past should be interpreted.

At this point in the ongoing negotiations between state and victim stakeholders of Londres 38, it is clear who holds the balance of power. The history and politics of memorialisation of Londres 38, reflected so eloquently in the constantly changing signage, reflect the local tensions and the way in which the state has been able to turn these divisions in its favour. A generous interpretation of the state's role in robbing Londres 38 of its particularity as a site of conscience is that it was done in pursuit of a wider agenda of reconciliation. There are good reasons why the state should choose such an iconic and centrally placed site as the principal vehicle to carry information on all such centres of state violence. But equally, the several government departments involved in the planning and maintenance of the building have clearly taken advantage of the lack of unity between the collectives, the victims, their families and supporters. And in the end, the state holds the trump card: it owns the building and like all such state-controlled museums, in the last resort it can do as it pleases. The newcomer may well find the current display informative, general and moving. It is only through what is *not* displayed that one glimpses the torment still felt by the excluded.

Equally, the interpretation of Londres 38 reflects the wider Chilean tensions that exist beyond the human rights movement. The Chilean polarities still working themselves out are those between memory and suppression, human rights and national interest, reparations and contemporary economic ills, amnesty and forgiveness, restorative justice and expedience, and reconciliation and political stability. These are the antagonisms felt and expressed today and for past decades, even among those who thought they were on the same side. Struggles for control over sites of torture and disappearance resonate both with the unresolved party political tensions of the Allende years and with the frustrations of the Left that has few real political spaces in which to articulate its many grievances.

HISTORICAL JUSTICE

Yet attempts by the state to undermine the integrity and character of Londres 38 over such a long history cannot be altogether ascribed to the ideological divide of Left and Right. As we have suggested, both the centre-left Concertación governments between 1990 and 2010 and the current centre-Right government of Sebastian Piñera have sought to rob this site of conscience of its potent particularity as witness to the violations of human rights committed during state terrorism. The localised and specific past remains a threatening force to the policy of 'reconciliation' (meaning national governability), consistently pursued by successive post-Pinochet governments that privilege censorship and impunity over truth and justice (Fernándo 2008, 140).

In the end every generation finds new uses for every site, however sinister. In April 2012, besides the street display about the 119 disappeared prisoners, stood a blackboard inviting visitors to write messages. Some chalked the expected, though perfectly justified *Nunca Más* (Never Again); but others wrote slogans which would have surprised and disappointed the members of the revolutionary Left of 40 years ago:

The worst dictatorship is the one that masks as a democracy.

And even:

The seizure of power as a revolutionary strategy does not work.

In the last resort, it may be said that it is not people but a time that occupies a historic site. For in September 2011, the streets around Londres were again thronged with police, tear gas, water cannon and thousands of students demonstrating for free education. Inside Londres 38, where a school group was being instructed by Leopoldo Montenegro, the rumble of running feet and the stink of tear gas penetrated every room. As another throng of fleeing young people swept past, the security guard shouted at the students to seek shelter. In they tumbled, most probably unaware of where they were. The police made no attempt to follow. Marivic Wyndham invited them, relieved, nervous and excited as they were, to be photographed. Down they sat, not with political slogans, no shouting down of the dictatorship, but with chatter; they sat on the same stairs where, on the momentous day of opening, 10 December 2007, the survivors and their families had entered, trembling with emotion, overwhelmed with their memories. These young people too now were demonstrators but in a different time and what seemed almost to be a different building. They held hands for the photo, they grinned, they made signs. One in the front made Mickey Mouse ears behind his companion.

Notes

1. Sites of conscience is a generic term for sites of what we may broadly call 'infamy', which may involve murder, torture, disappearance, execution, imprisonment or slavery. Very often such deeds are an instrument of state repression. While there are thousands of such sites, the International Coalition of Sites of Conscience recognises

only a small number (www.sitesofconscience.org/). In Chile, Villa Grimaldi, Estadio Nacional and Casa Memoria José Domingo Cañas are members of the International Coalition, while Londres 38 is not.
2. These academic debates, sometimes led by survivors of torture, extend over several disciplines and areas of research, including individual and collective memory; heritage management; dark tourism; and the politics of memory, among others. Key texts include Tunbridge and Ashworth (1996); Savage (2009); Goodall, Keene, and Read (2010); Ashworth and Hartman (2005); Edkins (2003); Foote (2003); Pennebaker, Paez, and Rimé (1997) and Lennon and Foley (2000).

References

Andreani, M., and Marianne Cerda. 2000. *El si-no de le reconciliación representaciones Sociales de la Reconciliación en los jóvenes*. Santiago: Fundación Documentación y Archivo de la Vicaría de e Solidaridad.

Ashworth, Gregory, and Rudi Hartman, eds. 2005. *Horror and Human Tragedy Revisited: The Management of Sites of Atrocity for Tourism*. New York: Cognizant.

Belarmino Elgueta Pinto, Raimundo. n.d. "Testimonio di Raimundo Belarmino Elgueta Pinto." www.memoriaviva.com/testimonios/testimonio_de_raimundo_belarmino_elgueta_pinto.htm

Castillo, Carmen, dir. 2007. *Calle Santa Fe*. Paris: Agnes B. Productions.

Corporación José Domingo Cañas 1367. 2003. *Una experiencia para no olvidar*. Santiago: Corporación José Domingo Cañas 1367.

Corporación Parque de la Paz Villa Grimaldi. 2005. *A Museum in Villa Grimaldi for Memory and Education in Human Rights*. Santiago: Corporación Parque de la Paz Villa Grimaldi.

Edkins, Jenny. 2003. *Trauma and the Memory of Politics*. Cambridge: Cambridge University Press.

Fernándo, Roberto. 2008. "Memoria y conmemoració delo qq de septiembre de 1973: entre el recuerdo y el silencio." In *Memorias en Busca de Historia*, 139–154. Universitario Bolivariana. Santiago: LOM Ediciones.

Foote, Kenneth. 2003. *Shadowed Ground: American Landscapes of Violence and Tragedy*. Austin: University of Texas Press.

Goodall, Heather, Judith Keene, and Peter Read, eds. 2010. *Where Are the Bodies? A Transnational Examination of State Violence and Its Consequences. The Public Historian*. Vol. 32, No. 1.

Lennon, John, and Malcolm Foley. 2000. *Dark Tourism: The Attraction of Death and Disaster*. London: Continuum.

Ministerio de Educación, Republica de Chile. 2007. *Consejo de monumentos nacionales*. Santiago: Ministerio de Educación.

Pennebaker, James, Dario Paez, and Bernard Rimé, eds. 1997. *Collective Memory of Political Events: Social Psychology Perspectives*. Mahwah, NJ: Lawrence Erlbaum.

Perez, José M., and Karen Glavic. 2011. "La experiencia de la visita y la visita como experiencia: memorias criticas y constructivas." Photocopy held in library, Londres 38.

Read, Peter. December 2013. "You Have to Let Out the Scream." *History Australia*, 10 (3): 215–235.

Read, Peter, and Marivic Wyndham. 2008. "Putting Site Back into Trauma Studies: A Study of Five Detention Centres in Santiago, Chile." *Life Writing* 5 (1): 79–96.

Read, Peter, and Marivic Wyndham. 2012. "Those Who Have No Memorial: Contested Memories of a Pinochet Site of Conscience." *Encounters* 5: 169–182.

Rivas, Patricio. 2007. *Un largo septiembre*. Santiago: LOM Ediciones.

Savage, Kirk. 2009. *Monument Wars*. Berkeley: University of California Press.

Stern, Steve J. 2010. *Reckoning with Pinochet: The Memory Question in Democratic Chile*. Durham, NC: Duke University Press.

Tumarkin, Maria. 2005. *Traumascapes*. Carlton: Melbourne University Press.

Tunbridge, J. E., and G. J. Ashworth. 1996. *Dissonant Heritage: The Management of the Past as a Resource in Conflict*. Chichester: Wiley.

Valech, Sergio, María Luisa Sepúlveda, Miguel Luís Amunátegui, Luciano Fuillioux, José Antonio Gómez, Lucas Sierra, Álvero Varela, and Elizabeth Lira. 2004. "Informe de la Comisión Nacional sobre Prisión Política y Tortura." Gobierno de Chile, November 28. www.latinamericanstudies.org/chile/informe.htm

Wadi, Ramona. 2012. "The Right to Memory in Chile: An Interview with Erika Hennings, President of Londres 38." *Upside Down World*, May 4. www.upsidedownworld.org/main/chile-archives-34/3618-the-right-to-memory-in-chile-an-interview-with-erika-hennings-president-of-londres-38

Stumbling blocks in Germany

Linde Apel

Forschungsstelle für Zeitgeschichte in Hamburg, Hamburg, Germany

In the early 1990s, German artist Gunter Demnig initiated the commemoration of individual victims of Nazi Germany by means of cobble stone-sized memorials, so-called *Stolpersteine* ('stumbling blocks'), that are inserted in the footpath. While initially *Stolpersteine* were hotly debated, today they are no longer considered controversial. The fact that dedicating a *Stolperstein* means to have to research the fate of an individual victim distinguishes this commemorative form from others. In this article, I explore a variety of approaches to and motives for sponsoring *Stolpersteine*, and responses to them. I argue that the success of the *Stolpersteine* is due to the fact that they make complex and burdensome historical relationships manageable, and that they offer emotional relief because they are a public sign of expressing empathy with victims.

Recently I had a visit from Leo Arbel and his wife Lea. They live in Israel, where we had met and become friends in 2010. At the time, I had been doing interviews with Yekkes, Jews with German roots and living in Israel, and Leo Arbel had been one of my interviewees. He was born in 1931 in Hamburg. In the late 1930s, Leo's mother arranged for her husband, and later also for Leo and his sister, to emigrate to Uruguay. She stayed behind, was later deported and did not survive.

Leo had put the past behind him, or so he had thought. It was not until I peppered him with questions about the life histories of his parents that he realised how little he knew. When I published a biographical sketch about him (Apel 2011a), he was delighted, had it translated for his children into Hebrew and undertook some research himself. However, when I told him that somebody in Hamburg had sponsored a *Stolperstein* (literally: stumbling block) for his mother, he responded with irritation.

The *Stolpersteine* memorial project is the brainchild of Gunter Demnig, a West German artist born in 1947, whose father was a member of the Condor Legion, the German military unit responsible for the bombing of Guernica during the Spanish civil war (Debus 2007). In the early 1990s, Demnig became involved in attempts to commemorate the 50th anniversary of the deportation of Sinti and Roma from Cologne. He created memorials the size of cobble stones by engraving the names and dates of birth and death of individual victims on small brass plaques, 10 × 10 cm, which he attached to concrete cubes. In 1995 he began to implant these memorials in the sidewalks in front of the last known residences of victims of Nazi Germany, initially in Cologne but soon also elsewhere in Germany, and in the beginning without permission from the local authorities. Demnig's *Stolpersteine* are level with the pavement, presumably to prevent pedestrians from literally stumbling over them (Photo 1).

Today, there are more than 40,000 *Stolpersteine* in Germany alone. In recent years, *Stolpersteine* have also been installed to commemorate the lives of survivors, and in other European countries, such as Hungary, Italy and Ukraine.[1] In a speech in the Hamburg city hall on 28 August 2007, the then mayor, Ole von Beust, who had sponsored *Stolpersteine* for the four siblings of his Jewish grandfather, rightly called Demnig's project the 'largest citizens' initiative in the world'. While Demnig manufactures all *Stolpersteine* in his Berlin workshop – and sells them for €120 each – and then personally installs them, anybody can sponsor such a memorial cube.

In the early years of the project, when Demnig had sometimes put up his memorials against the express wishes of residents and local councils, the *Stolpersteine* were often widely and hotly debated. Objectors claimed, for instance, that *Stolpersteine* were a potential hazard and that they would disrupt the flow of pedestrian traffic, or that they attracted the attention of neo-Nazis (for example, Vorrath 2009). Today, such arguments are no longer made publicly, and

Photo 1.   One of the first *Stolpersteine* installed in Cologne. Courtesy: Karin Richert.

the installation of new *Stolpersteine* is usually reported favourably in the media and received with public approval. Mayors and other local dignitaries gratefully acknowledge the work of *Stolpersteine* groups and individual sponsors, and regularly invoke the memorials as a cure-all for historical forgetfulness. Only the city of Munich still opposes the laying of *Stolpersteine*, thereby adhering to a position taken by Charlotte Knobloch, the former president of the Central Council of Jews in Germany, who finds it unacceptable that people step on the names of the dead (Goebel 2010). In East Germany, dedication ceremonies are sometimes still protected by the police, and in some cases, memorials have been vandalised or stolen,[2] but overall, the *Stolpersteine* project is no longer controversial.

Taking responsibility for laying a *Stolperstein* usually involves researching the biography of a known victim. Sometimes prospective sponsors first do research about the former residents of their own house or apartment building because many of them are particularly interested in commemorating the life of somebody with whom they can claim to have a personal connection. In my capacity as director of the Werkstatt der Erinnerung, the oral history archive of the Forschungsstelle für Zeitgeschichte in Hamburg, I am often approached by individuals and groups who are interested in sponsoring a *Stolperstein* and seek my help in sourcing information about a particular victim. I have been intrigued

Photo 2. Flyer (detail) for the dedication ceremony in Berlin Kreuzberg, 2011. Courtesy: KIgA e.V.

by the sponsors' urge to gather as much biographical information as possible, and by the level of detail in some of the narratives resulting from their research.

The research of *Stolpersteine* activists is made available in booklets, on leaflets and on the Internet. In Hamburg, biographical information is available on the website of the organisation Stolpersteine, www.hamburg.de/stolpersteine, through an application for smartphones, and in several brochures about *Stolpersteine* in particular neighbourhoods.[3] Similar (but individually designed) websites and publications, which provide biographical information and the locations of *Stolpersteine*, exist for many other German cities.[4]

While occasionally sponsors are related to those they wish to memorialise, the overwhelming majority of sponsors have no such family connections. Individual sponsors and members of *Stolpersteine* groups range from secondary school students to old age pensioners. Nearly all of them are German by birth, but occasionally they also include immigrants; in Berlin-Kreuzberg, for example, a group of teenagers from a range of ethnic and religious backgrounds sponsored *Stolpersteine* for Bernhard, Günther and Horst Lewin, three brothers who had been murdered in concentration camps after violating anti-Semitic laws (Coppi 2011) (Photo 2).

Stolpersteine prompt non-historians to do microhistory and to produce biographical knowledge about individual victims of Nazi Germany. On account of its decentralised and self-directed character, the *Stolpersteine* movement is reminiscent of West German initiatives of the 1970s and 1980s which instigated the writing of local history 'from below' under the catch cry *Grabe wo du stehst* (literally: 'dig where you stand'). Then, there had been a boom of local historical research, both by amateurs and by trained historians outside the academy (Lindqvist 1989). Many of these researchers were organised in history workshops; some of those with professional training used the workshops to develop credible alternatives to the histories produced and taught in universities (Heer and Ullrich 1985). The *Grabe wo du stehst* movement was particularly interested in *Alltagsgeschichte* (the history of everyday life) and often focused on the Nazi period.

The preoccupation with local social history was a response to the crisis of the academic discipline of history, but was also symptomatic of crises of identity experienced by many practitioners of *Alltagsgeschichte*: left-wing political activists who had become disillusioned with the organised labour movement and its history (Siegfried 2008). They turned to the past to look for role models. They were hoping to unearth the stories of the Nazis' victims and, even more importantly, those of ordinary Germans who had opposed the Nazi regime. Their research often revealed that opportunism and acquiescence had played a far greater role in the lives of their protagonists than resistance. Because many in the *Grabe wo du stehst* movement came to strongly identify with those they were writing about, the *Grabe wo du stehst* movement also generated narratives that were hardly less apologetic than the historical interpretations its practitioners railed against, namely histories that paid little attention to how sections of the West German elites had been complicit in the crimes perpetrated between 1933 and 1945.

Alltagsgeschichte has become respectable and is no longer a radical alternative to conventional history. Its epistemological and methodological foundations have been accommodated within the discipline's canon. At least in the German context, its innovative potential has largely been exhausted. Many of those who criticised the West German historical discipline from the outside in the 1970s and 1980s have since become part of the academic establishment (Lüdtke 1989). Unlike many of the historians who were practicing *Alltagsgeschichte* in the history workshops of the 1980s, the amateur historians involved in the *Stolpersteine* movement do not set out to challenge historiographical orthodoxy. Unlike the *Geschichtswerkstätten* of the 1980s, however, today's *Stolpersteine* groups are not prone to produce apologetic histories, as they focus exclusively on the lives of victims. This focus has become a central feature of the public memory of the Nazi past, particularly in Germany. Admittedly West Germans have embraced the biographies of select victims at least since the phenomenal success of the Anne Frank diary in the 1950s; until the 1990s, however, the vast majority of victims could only be thought of as part of a face- and nameless mass of people who were represented by 'the Holocaust', 'six million Jews' or 'Auschwitz' rather than by Anne Frank, the Weiss family of the television mini-series *Holocaust*, Janusz Korczak or the Children of Bullenhuser Damm (see Neumann 2000, 136–156, 241–258).

The *Stolpersteine* project has successfully emphasised individual aspects of persecution. It has resulted in the generation of thousands of – often detailed – biographies of victims who had previously remained anonymous. But individual sponsors and *Stolpersteine* groups have often been prompted to do detailed historical research not so much for its own sake, that is, to add to our knowledge of the complexity of the Nazi past, but because they empathise and identify with those they are commemorating. Many non-Jewish Germans of the post-war generations readily embrace the victims of Nazi Germany and distance themselves from perpetrators and bystanders. As discussed by Jureit (2010), this identification is closely related to a perceived need for reconciliation and a yearning for release from a perceived collective guilt.

Many of the sponsors say that they are prompted to act out of *Betroffenheit*, a sense of dismay paired with compassion (see Neumann 2000, 10, 261). *Stolpersteine* offer relief because they make it possible to confront emotionally burdensome and barely comprehensible crimes by reducing complex instances of persecution to simple relationships and by expressing empathy with individual innocent victims. Emotions could easily thwart our understanding of the past by obscuring historical points of reference. Sponsors who focus on individual biographies because of their emotional investment in the lives of victims easily lose sight of the context within which these lives were destroyed. The fact that the majority of Germans did not object to Nazism is a crucial part of that context. In order to understand how the persecution of Jews, Sinti and Roma, and other minorities was possible, and in order to be able to explain why Germans supported, accepted, condoned, put up with or actively opposed the Nazi regime, affective responses must be complemented with an awareness of relevant historical contexts and a critical examination of historical evidence. The apparent ability of the *Stolpersteine* to make complex relationships manageable accounts for the success of these unimposing memorials.

The interest in the *Stolpersteine* as an individual and a social practice is growing at a time when the contemporary witnesses to the Holocaust are dying out. At the very time when the last perpetrators, bystanders and victims are passing away, public interest in the fate of the victims is increasing. For the overwhelming majority of Germans, the years from 1933 to 1945 are no longer part of a past they experienced personally. Knowledge about the Nazi regime is now largely transmitted in the public sphere, rather than in families. The rapid shrinking of the generation of witnesses to history has prompted renewed efforts to put the last remaining known perpetrators, like John Demjanjuk (see Wefing 2011), on trial. At the same time, attention is focusing, more so than ever before, on the last remaining survivors, who are sought out to provide testimony. Often they are required to lend credibility and gravitas to official commemoration ceremonies, particularly in Germany, where their first-hand accounts are also considered to make audiences immune against racist sentiments.

Some of the *Stolpersteine* sponsors develop a sense of ownership towards the person whose biography they have been researching; in conversation they tend to refer to 'my victim' or 'our victim'. The surviving relatives of those to be commemorated are understandably often wary of attempts by the descendants of perpetrators and bystanders to appropriate the lives of victims. At the Stolpersteine – zwischen Gedenken und Bedenken event on 29 September 2010 in Berlin, Ulrike Schrader, the director of a memorial museum in the West German city of Essen, recounted how a woman who objected to the installation of a *Stolperstein* commemorating the death of her parents in the Holocaust pointed out that they were special only to her and not to anybody else. She also doubted the sincerity of the *Stolpersteine* activists and the efficacy of the memorials: Would Germans really think about Holocaust victims every time they saw a *Stolperstein*? Leo Arbel voiced different, albeit related reservations. He was uncomfortable with the idea that there were people in Hamburg who were complete strangers to him but knew more about his mother than he did, and wished he had been consulted before the *Stolperstein* for his mother was created.

Other descendants of victims have welcomed the work of *Stolpersteine* initiatives. Jackie Kohnstamm lives in London and is a third-generation Holocaust survivor. She inherited a cardboard box that contained a few surviving mementoes, documents and photos of her grandparents, which her parents had kept hidden. Over time, she collected more items from other relatives. One day, she searched the names of her grandparents in Google, and landed on the Berlin *Stolpersteine* website to discover that only four days earlier *Stolpersteine* had been laid for them. Kohnstamm was touched by this gesture and the fact that the Berlin memorial activists devoted their energies to commemorating the lives of people who had been complete strangers to them. She described meeting the sponsors of her grandparents' *Stolpersteine* and the conveners of the *Stolpersteine* group:

> I was not the only one to have grown up during decades of silence – so had they. How much of the horrors had our parents and grandparents known about at the time? That had been a no-go area for all of us. We each had a piece missing from our jigsaw of the past, and I realised in that schoolroom that I represented their missing piece. It was a disconcerting moment. (Kohnstamm 2007)

Although the starting point for the *Stolpersteine* project was the commemoration of the persecution of Sinti and Roma, for a long time the focus was almost exclusively on Jewish victims of the Holocaust. In recent years, members of the political resistance, gays, Sinti and Roma, and some of the so-called 'forgotten victims' (see Projektgruppe 1986) have also been on the agenda of *Stolpersteine* activists. In the following I briefly discuss two cases involving the memorialisation of individual German Sinti in 2010 to give a sense of the range of approaches adopted by *Stolpersteine* groups.

When in 1995 Demnig wanted to commemorate the deportations of Sinti and Roma in Cologne via *Stolpersteine* as we know them today, Sinti living in Cologne objected to his plans because they did not want the names of Sinti victims made public out of fear of discrimination, and they did not want people to step on the names of the dead. Therefore, the first 100 or so *Stolpersteine* ever installed do not carry a name, but instead bear the inscription 'Romm', 'Rommni', 'Sinto' or 'Sintezza'.[5] Since then, hundreds of *Stolpersteine* have been installed for individually named Roma and Sinti victims all over Germany, including five in Cologne. But the reservations encountered by Demnig in 1995 are still shared by some Sinti and Roma. In 2009, Rudko Kawczynski, founding member of the Hamburg Rom and Cinti Union, gave a speech at the opening of an exhibition about the deportation of Jews, Sinti and Roma from Hamburg, in which he took issue with the enthusiasm of memorial activists:

> The well-meaning *Stolpersteine* project installed nine memorial stones with the names of Sinti victims in the sidewalks of Hamburg, even though it had been pointed out many times that their relatives consider it to be an insult to the dead, when passers-by step on the names of their fathers and mothers, and dogs defecate on their people's memorials ... None of the survivors were listened to. The victims had to be 'commemorated' at all costs. End of discussion. (Kawczynski 2009)

Following Kawczynski's comments, the local umbrella organisation of *Stolpersteine* groups, Stolpersteine Hamburg, which has overseen the installation of more than 4000 memorials since 2002, removed all previously installed *Stolpersteine* for Sinti victims and returned them to their sponsors.[6] But the *Stolpersteine* movement is heterogenous, and groups not associated with Stolpersteine Hamburg have continued to lay *Stolpersteine* for Sinti victims. In 2010, I was contacted by a group in Elmshorn, a small town about 30 km north of Hamburg. They were adamant that Kawczynski's objections were irrelevant, and on 20 April 2010 – of all days – unveiled a *Stolperstein* for Benno Winterstein, a Sinto who had been murdered in Auschwitz.[7]

By contrast, the memorialisation of the life of another German Sinto, Johann 'Rukeli' Trollmann, involved individuals and groups outside of the circle of Hamburg *Stolpersteine* activists, such as Trollmann's family and a Hamburg sports club. Trollmann was a well-known boxer, who had been controversially deprived of the German light-heavyweight title in 1933. In 1942, he was imprisoned in the Neuengamme concentration camp, and two years later killed in its satellite camp Wittenberge.[8] In 2010, a *Stolperstein* was installed in front of Hamburg's Rote Flora, a squat currently occupied by radical left-wing groups, which used to serve as a dance hall and hosted boxing matches. The dedication ceremony was unusually well attended, with around 120 participants, including members of the Trollmann family and people associated with Rote Flora. The building was decorated with posters with comprehensive biographical information about Trollmann. Inside the building, a boxing ring with an image depicting Trollmann functioned as an ephemeral memorial. That evening, a nearby bookstore hosted a reading from a book about his life. Trollmann's life and boxing career were very present during the ceremony, although in her speech, one of the organisers of the event seemed to be more concerned with her own political activism, the multiculturalism of her sports club and her personal discovery of Johann Trollmann, than with his life. *Stolpersteine* have also been laid for Trollmann in Berlin and Hannover. In 2010, the first Rukeli-Trollmann Cup, a tournament for young boxers, was held, and a year later a gymnasium in Berlin was named after him (Photo 3).

The successful installation of a *Stolperstein* tends to reflect back on the sponsor, which helps explain why there have been very few attempts to install *Stolpersteine* for convicted criminals who had been imprisoned in concentration camps as so-called *Berufsverbrecher* ('professional criminals') and died there. There have been heated debates in Hamburg's *Stolpersteine* groups about the

Photo 3. Stumbling block dedicated to Johann Trollmann, Hamburg 2009. Courtesy: Manuel Trollmann.

merits of memorialising people who were not innocent but whose crimes did not warrant their murder in concentration camps. What kind of inscription could be engraved on the *Stolperstein* for a pimp, or that for a murderer who was killed as a result of a power struggle involving fellow prisoners? Until recently, there were also no *Stolpersteine* for those deemed *asozial* (anti-social) and *arbeitsscheu* ('work shy') by the Nazis and imprisoned in concentration camps.[9]

Demnig, *Stolpersteine* groups and the sponsor make a joint decision about which victim is worth remembering (Schulz 2008, 37). The artist, however, has the final say about whether a *Stolperstein* should be installed or not. Thus, a man who had survived the Nazi regime and later lived and died in the German Democratic Republic was denied a *Stolperstein* because Demnig discovered that he had worked for the East German secret police, the Stasi.[10] For Demnig, the life of a victim must be exemplary to warrant its memorialisation. But such distinctions between 'deserving' and 'undeserving' victims oversimplify the past and pay no attention to the power structures of the Nazi regime. *Stolpersteine* often hide more than they reveal: despite the extensive biographical research that often precedes them, they do not shed light on the complexity of Nazi society, which cannot be adequately depicted by applying the concepts of perpetrators, victims, accessories and bystanders.

Stolpersteine commemorate a particular aspect of somebody's biography. Trollmann, for example, has been made into a resistance fighter, although his biography does not seem to warrant such an emphasis (Herold and Robel 2012). A memorial for a convicted rapist who was murdered in a concentration camp would focus on his status as a victim rather than on the fact that he was also a perpetrator. While selective remembrance is unavoidable, *Stolpersteine* groups often exclude aspects of a biography that might be considered controversial. A few years ago I witnessed a *Stolpersteine* dedication ceremony in Ahrenshoop, a village by the Baltic Sea that was once popular with artists and the Weimar Republic's boheme. Speeches provided biographical details for two Jewish women: Edla Charlotte Rosenthal, an artist who was eventually murdered at Treblinka, and Elza Kohlmann, a bacteriologist who died in Berlin's Jewish Hospital in 1943. The fact that they had been a couple and had lived together for more than 20 years was not mentioned. Apparently the speakers at the ceremony – and the authors of texts documenting the women's lives on a *Stolpersteine* Internet site (Beier and Kuhlbarsch 2010a, 2010b) – avoided mentioning that the two women were in a relationship perhaps because they could not be sure that Rosenthal and Kohlmann would have wanted others to know about it. But it is also not known whether the two women identified as Jewish, and whether they would have approved of the label 'Jewish victim'.

Leo Arbel was born in Hamburg's Isestrasse, one of the most prestigious addresses in a status-conscious city. Owing to the fact that in the 1930s many of the street's inhabitants were Jewish, there are comparatively many *Stolpersteine* in Isestrasse: at the last count, 245 (out of a total of 4511 in Hamburg). In 2008, Hamburg-based journalist Hans Michael Kloth (2008) discovered that one of the main perpetrators of the Holocaust, Robert Mulka, had also lived in Isestrasse. Mulka had been deputy to the Auschwitz concentration camp commandant Rudolf Höss; in 1965, he was convicted to 14 years imprisonment in the first Frankfurt Auschwitz trial, was released in 1968 and died one year later in Hamburg. The journalist realised that very few of the residents, who were otherwise well versed in the history of their neighbourhood and readily empathised with the Holocaust's 'poor victims', knew about Mulka – despite the infamy he had acquired during his trial.

It would be highly inappropriate to install anything resembling a *Stolperstein* for Mulka. But a marker for a perpetrator, whatever form it might take, could be a useful provocation that would make many people stop in their tracks.[11] It could act as a reminder of the fact that perpetrators like Mulka were often able to continue seamlessly in their careers and businesses after 1945. By focusing on the lives of 'poor victims', *Stolpersteine* could in fact divert attention away from those who were responsible for, condoned or benefited from Nazi persecution. *Stolpersteine* bear no reminders of the non-Jewish neighbours who looked on as Jewish residents were picked up or had to go to assembly points (see the remarkable images in Nachama and Hesse 2011). Nor do they make reference to those who attended the auctions, which occasionally took place in people's homes after their deportation, in the hope of finding a bargain (Apel 2010).

Representatives of the City of Hamburg often boast of the fact that Hamburg has more *Stolpersteine* than any other city. Ruth Klüger, who as a child survived deportation from Vienna, has critically observed that remembering and memorialising also serve as a 'mirror of the self, taking pleasure in savouring its own sensitivity' (1996, 32). The sense of pride about Hamburg's achievements vis-à-vis those of other German cities – or, for that matter, about the plethora of German attempts to come to terms with its past, as compared with the reluctance

Photo 4. Stephan Kramer, general secretary of the Central Council of Jews in Germany with a group of young Muslim activists, Berlin 2011. Courtesy: Alina Braml.

of other nations to address historic wrongs – suggests that memorials are understood as means by which guilt and responsibility can be erased. The large number of *Stolpersteine* is not so much seen as a reflection of Hamburg's implication in the Holocaust (after all, there would be fewer *Stolpersteine* in Hamburg, if fewer of its residents had been murdered), but rather as evidence of its exculpation. As Schrader (2006) has observed, the sponsorship of *Stolpersteine* amounts to an 'absolution of guilt through the buying of indulgences'.

After being erected and unveiled, memorials tend to fade quickly from public and private consciousness. This is especially true of the small, inconspicuous *Stolpersteine*. Therefore, local authorities, church groups, political parties and other organisations often run public awareness campaigns by calling on residents to clean the *Stolpersteine* in their neighbourhoods (Photo 4). Sometimes celebrities are enlisted to lend weight to such campaigns and to motivate local residents. Often the initiators of such campaigns provide prospective volunteers with precise instructions about the kinds of detergents and brushes they ought to use, and publish images that depict people, who always seem eager and proud, scrubbing the footpath.[12] Does the pride reflected on those photos amount to what in German is referred to as *Sündenstolz* (the pride in having been a sinner)? What exactly is being scrubbed and polished when *Stolpersteine* are cleaned: the brass nameplates, or perhaps also the German conscience? Do the *Stolpersteine*, when they gleam brightly, represent the righteousness of today's Germans, who are always ready to recall past crimes? Admittedly, not too long ago I went to work with rubber gloves, sponge and detergent to restore the shine on the *Stolperstein* that informs passers-by that Hasia Arolowitsch, Leo Arbel's mother, was deported to Riga in December 1941 and murdered soon afterwards. Leo was moved and deeply grateful for the attempt to care for the *Stolperstein* that he viewed as a symbol for her gravestone.

The *Stolpersteine* highlight the commemorative commitment of those sponsoring them and researching the biographies of individual victims – and of those publicly polishing them later on. When sponsors and researchers organise themselves in *Stolpersteine* groups and when residents have working bees to clean memorials in their neighbourhood, they are able to reassure one another of their righteousness (compare Dohnke 2009) and be collectively appalled by less enlightened fellow citizens, such as those belonging to the perpetrator generation who still claim that their Jewish neighbours suddenly disappeared or simply went away (see Apel 2011b, 1026). It could thus be argued that the *Stolpersteine* have little to do with historical justice; they do not redress historic wrongs, but rather allow the descendants of perpetrators and bystanders to be less troubled by their history.

There are, however, at least two good reasons to continue the *Stolpersteine* project. One is provided by Kohnstamm, who, as a descendant of Holocaust victims, appreciates the respectful work done by *Stolpersteine* activists to remember her grandparents. I was reminded of the other reason when the Arbels and I wandered around the affluent district of Eppendorf to trace the footsteps of Leo's family. We made very slow progress because we frequently stopped to decipher the inscriptions of *Stolpersteine* that were embedded in the pavement in front many of the buildings we passed. As the footpaths in Eppendorf are comparatively wide, our little group did not constitute an obstacle. Besides, Eppendorf residents have become accustomed to the sight of passers-by who stop to examine *Stolpersteine*. I was therefore taken aback when an elderly woman, who was wearing an elegant dress and straw hat, refused to give way and jostled me with surprising force as she passed. In Hamburg – and particularly in affluent neighbourhoods – people do not jostle, but keep their distance and mind their manners. It seems that *Stolpersteine* are useful as long as there are some people who are still unsettled by them.

Stolpersteine provide knowledge in fragments. In themselves, they are not particularly informative, but at a time when Germans' interest in the history of Nazi Germany is declining (Heitmeyer 2009, 141, 148), they create a symbolic link between the present and the past. Researchers and passers-by acquire a connection to the living environment of a victim: where she grew up, went to school, raised a family or established a business, and was ostracised by her neighbours, which made it possible to deport her to be murdered out of sight. They share a space with particular victims and thereby may be able to convey a sense of the ordinariness of Nazi Germany.

Notes

1. See Demnig's website www.stolpersteine.com for more information about the *Stolpersteine* project. Similar forms of commemoration exist in Chile for the victims of the military dictatorship; see Peter Read and Marivic Wyndham's article in this issue of *Rethinking History*. In Argentina, the victims of state terrorism are commemorated with *baldosas de la memoria*, large and colourful 'tiles of memory' that also are installed in the pavements.
2. A couple of recent examples: In the East German town of Greifswald, 11 *Stolpersteine* disappeared in the night of 9 November 2012 (the anniversary of the 1938 *Reichskristallnacht* pogrom); see www.ndr.de/regional/mecklenburg-vorpommern/stolpersteine127.html. In December 2012, five *Stolpersteine* were stolen in the East German town of Sassnitz; see www.aktuell.meinestadt.de/sassnitz/2012/12/05/stolpersteine-in-sassnitz-gestohlen-und-beschaedigt/
3. See www.stolpersteine-hamburg.de/index.php?RECORD_ID=98 and www.stolpersteine-hamburg.de/index.php?MAIN_ID=8
4. See, for example, for Berlin: www.stolpersteine-berlin.de/; for Leipzig: www.stolpersteine-leipzig.de/; for Bremen: www.stolpersteine-bremen.de/; for Frankfurt: www.stolpersteine-frankfurt.de/
5. See the database about the *Stolpersteine* in Cologne, http://www.museenkoeln.de/ns-dokumentationszentrum/default.aspx?s=1204&vgr=Sinti%20und%20Roma. Natascha Winter, who later became the head of the Cologne-based Sinti-Allianz, convinced Demnig to change the inscriptions and helped him decide whether a particular victim was a Sinti or a Roma. I thank Karola Fings for this information.
6. Email communication, Johann-Hinrich Möller to the author, 17 February 2009.

7. www.antifaelmshorn.blogsport.de/2010/04/15/20-04-2010-stolpersteine-elmshorn/. Many Germans would be aware that Adolf Hitler was born on 20 April. In Nazi Germany, Hitler's birthday was an occasion for large-scale celebrations. Even 60 years after Hitler's death, the designated premier of the state of Baden-Württemberg considered the date sufficiently problematic to ask that his swearing-in be deferred for a day.
8. The story of Trollmann's persecution is told on a website created by his great-nephew Manuel Trollmann: www.johann-trollmann.de
9. For an example of a campaign to install a *Stolperstein* for a man who was arrested for vagrancy and later murdered in a concentration camp, see www.stolpersteine-fuer-norddeich.blogspot.de/
10. Oral communication, Gunter Demnig, Haifa, 17 November 2010.
11. The suggestion to 'memorialise' perpetrators was made by Neumann (2005, 2006) in the context of public discussions about the commemoration of the Celle '*Hasenjagd*'.
12. See, for example, the instructions provided by Stolpersteine Hamburg: www.stolpersteine-hamburg.de/?MAIN_ID=21

References

Apel, Linde. 2010. "'Hier war doch alles nicht so schlimm.' Die Hamburger Deportationen aus Sicht der Opfer, Täter und 'by-stander'." In *Stolpersteine in der Hamburger Isestraße. Eine biografische Spurensuche*, edited by Christa Fladhammer and Maike Grünwaldt, 251–258. Hamburg: Landeszentrale für Politische Bildung.

Apel, Linde. 2011a. "'Ich mache alles alleine.' Leo Arbel, Hamburger, Latino, Israeli." In *Aus Hamburg in alle Welt. Lebensgeschichten jüdischer Verfolgter in der Werkstatt der Erinnerung*, edited by Linde Apel, Klaus David, and Stefanie Schüler-Springorum, 18–31. Hamburg: Dölling und Galitz.

Apel, Linde. 2011b. "Voices from the Rubble Society: 'Operation Gomorrah' and its Aftermath." *Journal of Social History* 44 (4): 1019–1032.

Beier, Astrid, and Daniel Kuhlbarsch. 2010a. "Elza Kohlmann. Stolpersteine in Mecklenburg-Vorpommern." www.stolpersteine-mv.de/stolperstein/elza-kohlmann

Beier, Astrid, and Daniel Kuhlbarsch. 2010b. "Edla Charlotte Rosenthal. Stolpersteine in Mecklenburg-Vorpommern." www.stolpersteine-mv.de/stolperstein/edla-charlotte-rosenthal

Coppi, Hans. 2011. "Stolpersteine für die Brüder Lewin, Sizi 'Stolperstein' dösenmesine davet ediyoruz." *Antifa, Magazin der VVN für antifaschistische Politik und Kultur*, November/December: 11.

Debus, Lutz. 2007. "Steine des Anstosses." *Jüdische Zeitung*, October. www.j-zeit.de/archiv/artikel.754.html

Dohnke, Kay. 2009. "Steine und Gefühle. Überlegungen zum Gedenken an die Opfer des Nationalsozialismus." *Informationen zur Schleswig-Holsteinischen Landesgeschichte* 51: 69–81.

Goebel, Anne. 2010. "Neue Diskussion über die 'Stolpersteine'." *Süddeutsche Zeitung*, May 17. www.sueddeutsche.de/muenchen/opfer-des-ns-terrors-neue-diskussion-ueber-die-stolpersteine-1.677117

Heer, Hannes, and Volker Ullrich. 1985. *Geschichte entdecken. Erfahrungen und Projekte der neuen Geschichtsbewegung*. Reinbek: Rowohlt.
Heitmeyer, Wilhelm. 2009. *Deutsche Zustände, Folge 7*. Frankfurt: Suhrkamp.
Herold, Kathrin, and Yvonne Robel. 2012. "Zwischen Boxring und Stolperstein. Johann Trollmann in der gegenwärtigen Erinnerung." In *Die Verfolgung der Sinti und Roma im Nationalsozialismus: Beiträge zur Geschichte der nationalsozialistischen Verfolgung in Norddeutschland*, edited by KZ-Gedenkstätte Neuengamme, 144–155. Bremen: Edition Temmen.
Jureit, Ulrike. 2010. "Opferidentifikation und Erlösungshoffnung. Beobachtungen im erinnerungspolitischen Rampenlicht." In *Gefühlte Opfer. Illusionen der Vergangenheitsbewältigung*, edited by Ulrike Jureit and Christian Schneider, 17–103. Stuttgart: Klett-Cotta.
Kawczynski, Rudko. 2009. "Rede von Rudko Kawczynski, zur Eröffnung der Ausstellung 'In den Tod geschickt. Die Deportationen von Juden, Roma und Sinti aus Hamburg 1940 bis 1945'." February 16. www.hannoverscher-bahnhof.hamburg.de/eroeffnungsveranstaltung/
Kloth, Hans Martin. 2008. "Mein Nachbar, der KZ-Kommandant." *Spiegel Online*, January 21. www.einestages.spiegel.de/static/authoralbumbackground/1258/mein_nachbar_der_kz_kommandant.html
Klüger, Ruth. 1996. *Von hoher und niedriger Literatur*. Göttingen: Wallstein.
Kohnstamm, Jackie. 2007. "A Heavy, Lonely Legacy." *AJR Journal*, April. www.ajr.org.uk/journal/issue.Apr07/article.796
Lindqvist, Sven. 1989. *Grabe, wo du stehst. Handbuch zur Erforschung der eigenen Geschichte*. Bonn: Dietz.
Lüdtke, Alf. 1989. "Einleitung. Was ist und wer treibt Alltagsgeschichte." In *Alltagsgeschichte. Zur Rekonstruktion historischer Erfahrungen und Lebenswelten*, edited by Alf Lüdtke, 9–49. New York: Campus.
Nachama, Andreas, and Klaus Hesse. 2011. *Vor aller Augen. Die Deportation der Juden und die Versteigerung ihres Eigentums. Fotografien aus Lörrach, 1940*. Berlin: Hentrich & Hentrich.
Neumann, Klaus. 2000. *Shifting Memories: The Nazi Past in the New Germany*. Ann Arbor: University of Michigan Press.
Neumann, Klaus. 2005. "Ketzerische Nachsätze." *Celler Hefte* 1–2: 63–69.
Neumann, Klaus. 2006. "Täter, Opfer, Mitläufer: Überlegungen zur Erinnerungskultur in Deutschland." *Celler Hefte* 3–4: 76–82.
Projektgruppe für die 'vergessenen' Opfer des NS-Regimes in Hamburg, ed. 1986. *Verachtet, verfolgt, vernichtet. Zu den 'vergessenen' Opfern des NS-Regimes*. Hamburg: VSA.
Schrader, Ulrike. 2006. "Die 'Stolpersteine' oder Von der Leichtigkeit des Gedenkens. Einige kritische Anmerkungen." *Geschichte im Westen* 21: 173–181.
Schulz, Sandra. 2008. "Verortung der Vergangenheit. 'Stolpersteine' des Künstlers Gunter Demnig." *Informationen. Wissenschaftliche Zeitschrift des Studienkreises Deutscher Widerstand* 67: 33–37.
Siegfried, Detlef. 2008. "Die Rückkehr des Subjekts. Gesellschaftlicher Wandel und neue Geschichtsbewegung um 1980." In *Geschichte und Geschichtsvermittlung*, edited by Olaf Hartung and Katja Köhr, 125–146. Bielefeld: Verlag für Regionalgeschichte.
Vorrath, Jonathan. 2009. "Stolpersteine ängstigen Anwohner." *Frankfurter Rundschau*, October 13. www.fr-online.de/bad-homburg/schmitten-stolpersteine-aengstigen-anwohner,1472864,3001840.html
Wefing, Heinrich. 2011. *Der Fall Demjanjuk. Der letzte große NS-Prozess*. München: Beck.

The ethics of nostalgia in post-apartheid South Africa

Judith Lütge Coullie

School of Arts, University of KwaZulu-Natal, Durban, South Africa

The ethics of memory, for Avishai Margalit and Paul Ricoeur, means, respectively, remembering the past so as to foster more caring relationships and seeking the truth of the past and building a better future. In post-apartheid South Africa, a variety of memory practices bring to public attention reminders of apartheid, a past that must be remembered so that it will strengthen relationships amongst once-divided citizens and so that iniquities will not be repeated. In general, these diverse efforts – official, publicly funded initiatives and individual endeavours to preserve personal memory – seek to shape collective memory in ways that invoke the horrors of the past. *Native Nostalgia* (2009), by Jacob Dlamini, both conforms to this trend and challenges it. It follows convention by contending that apartheid was without virtue; it defies the norm by insisting that the life that Dlamini lived in Katlehong is worth remembering with nostalgia – reflective nostalgia – because it was an ordered world in which ethically laudable principles governed social interactions, principles and practices, all of which are rare in post-apartheid South Africa.

> I see memory as a gift but also as a duty. We ought to cultivate our memories, we should not let them go to ruin. (Primo Levi, *The Voice of Memory*)

It would seem to be self-evident that it cannot be ethically defensible to remember life during apartheid nostalgically, as does Dlamini in *Native Nostalgia* (2009). Yet how can ethics – concepts of right and wrong behaviour – apply to memory which is, for most of us, much of the time, beyond our control? Margalit asks if there can be obligations to remember, or, the converse, to forget (2002, ix). He points out that we can only say that something *ought* to be done if it *can* be done (55). Clearly, we cannot entirely bring memory traces under conscious control. But are there ever circumstances in which we are able to do so? In *Memory, History, and Forgetting*, Ricoeur discusses the dual characteristics of memory: it is not only the 'welcoming' of stored impressions, but also the active search for images of the past (2004, 56). It is in the now of intentional remembering that ethics is pertinent: 'use implies the possibility of abuse' (2004, 57).

In this essay, I examine Dlamini's act of exploring and representing the past, his use or abuse of individual memories of life during apartheid. *Native Nostalgia* is a personal response to past and present South Africa, to hegemonic versions of the past and to contemporary state-sponsored endeavours to shape communal memory. My concern, in line with Dlamini's, is with the ethics of both individual memory and communal memory in post-apartheid South Africa. In this analysis the line between the politics of memory and the ethics of memory is thin. I ask: what are the 'ethico-political' (Ricoeur 2004, 57) implications of state-endorsed uses of memory which Dlamini condemns and how does Dlamini represent his own remembered experience?

Memory work: post-apartheid South Africa

In post-apartheid South Africa, in accordance with the Constitution adopted in 1996, a variety of memory practices bring to the public reminders of a past of institutionalised oppression that must be remembered so that it will not be repeated and so that redress can be effected. The preamble to the Constitution is clear:

> We, the people of South Africa,
> Recognise the injustices of our past;
> Honour those who suffered for justice and freedom in our land;
> Respect those who have worked to build and develop our country; and
> Believe that South Africa belongs to all who live in it, united in our diversity.
> We therefore, through our freely elected representatives, adopt this Constitution as the supreme law of the Republic so as to
>
> - heal the divisions of the past and establish a society based on democratic values, social justice and fundamental human rights;
> - lay the foundations for a democratic and open society in which government is based on the will of the people and every citizen is equally protected by law;
> - improve the quality of life of all citizens and free the potential of each person; and
> - build a united and democratic South Africa able to take its rightful place as a sovereign state in the family of nations. (Republic of South Africa 1996)

Memory practices include new history curricula in schools, the massive archive of public testimony generated by the Truth and Reconciliation Commission, new museums, memorial gardens, public statuary and commemorative public holidays. There has also been an outpouring of life writing. Typically, memory work attempts to contribute to the shaping of collective memory by staking a claim in the interpretation of the past. Statues, commemorative public holidays, published biographies and memoirs – each represents a public declaration of what the institution or individual deems important about the past: *this*, they assert, should be more widely known and remembered. Almost all commemorative undertakings – including by former leading proponents of the apartheid regime, such as ex-president F.W. de Klerk – invoke shared condemnation of the apartheid past, but some have nevertheless provoked controversy: for instance, the Women's Day public holiday, commemorating the 1956 protest march of around 20,000 women,[1] a recent biography of Nelson Mandela by David James Smith (2010) (described as 'malicious' by one reviewer and 'valuable' by another) and Dlamini's *Native Nostalgia*.

Ethics, memory and post-apartheid South Africa: Dlamini's *Native Nostalgia*

Dlamini's evocation of 'the tapestry of township life' through fragments of memory is, one reviewer declares, 'a magnificent achievement' (McKaiser 2009); another influential commentator refuses to even read it (Miyeni 2011). Why is *Native Nostalgia* controversial? As is the norm in post-apartheid personal and public histories, the narrator reviles apartheid as that 'deformed world' in which 'order and authority became confused with state violence and depravity' (Dlamini 2009, 13, citing Jonny Steinberg). He reminds us that disenfranchised black South Africans endured daily humiliations, poverty, landlessness, random pass raids, police brutality, government death squads and state graft (15). There was 'crime' and 'moral degradation' (19). 'Apartheid was', Dlamini proclaims, 'without virtue' (13). In this, then, *Native Nostalgia* corresponds with diverse commemorative endeavours which remember apartheid so as to condemn it. Where it differs from many is that the text's primary emphasis is not on the malevolence of apartheid but rather on Dlamini's own cherished experiences during those oppressive and increasingly bloody decades.

Born in 1973 to a working-class mother in a single-parent family, in his formative years in a typical overcrowded township, Dlamini would have experienced some of the most horrifying repression, civil unrest and violence. In the aftermath of the student uprisings beginning in the late 1970s, one state of emergency followed another and the increasingly militarised state needed more conscripted white males to contain 'the black peril' (Dlamini 2009, 130). Dlamini's high school was, he recalls,

> under military occupation. There was barbed wire all around the school [...]. You had to present your ID to the soldiers to be let into the schoolyard. After 8am [...] the gate was shut, and the soldiers [...] would then patrol the grounds. (87)

Police and soldiers would fire tear gas at 'interchangeable black bodies' (122) as state paranoia grew to fever pitch. Dlamini recalls that his mother was once at a night vigil when a passing military patrol heard the congregation singing *Nkosi Sikelel' iAfrika* (a hymn adopted by the African National Congress (ANC) as its anthem and thus banned); they 'fired teargas into the tent and told the old women [...] to disperse' (123). In Katlehong and elsewhere, blood was spilled in conflict not only between state and activist but also in what was known as 'black-on-black' violence (in many – perhaps most – cases, fomented by the state). Dlamini notes that in the early 1990s, when tense negotiations between apartheid government and liberation movements were underway, 'Katlehong was the eye of the violent storm that claimed more than two thousand lives [...] and left thousands injured and hundreds displaced' (133). Dlamini stresses that he does not yearn for this horrific past. The controversy of *Native Nostalgia* arises from the fond recollection of the life he lived then, provocatively announced in the title.

The label 'native' has some powerfully negative connotations: in the early decades of apartheid, 'native' was the nomenclature used for those who, in contradistinction to 'Europeans', were not entitled to an education above that which would fit them for manual labour and were denied citizenship and freedom of movement. Moreover, 'native' also carries the Fanonian sense (articulated in *The Wretched of the Earth*) of the self-abasing colonised: 'The status of "native" is a nervous condition introduced and maintained by the settler among colonized people *with their consent*' (Sartre 1963, 20). Initially, Dlamini's title might seem to sanction the deprivations endured by such natives. Then, to add insult to injury, Dlamini pairs this with nostalgia!

What could be affectionately recollected of apartheid? Dlamini's memories are largely positive because the 'great jumble of objects' (Steinberg 2010, 16) remembered were imbued with conviviality and warmth: the radio dramas, the sense of community, the love which transformed township matchbox houses into homes, the social order manifested in class distinctions and rituals of politeness, and even the residents' use of Afrikaans.[2]

Nostalgia

As the blending of memoir with scholarly analysis in *Native Nostalgia* implies and Dlamini's resume (Dlamini, n.d.) confirms, he is an educated man. Although his account of past experience is imbued with nostalgia's 'warm glow from the past' (Davis 1979, 16), he is no naïve reactionary or amnesiac. In acknowledging past difficulties, Dlamini sets himself apart from the common or garden nostalgic. Nostalgia, originally coined to refer to the yearning to return home, now connotes longing for the 'personally experienced' (Davis 1979, 8) past.[3] Although typically a bitter-sweet emotional complex, nostalgia is usually experienced as more positive than negative (see Barrett et al. 2010, 401). In popular parlance, and amongst some key theorists in the field, nostalgia ordinarily elicits censure for romanticising the past. Margalit says nostalgia is 'not as innocent a trait as one might think [for it harbours a] tendency to *kitsch* representations of the past' (2002, 62). The problem, morally, with nostalgic kitsch is its sentimentality. 'Nostalgia distorts the past by idealizing it. People, events, and objects from the past are presented as endowed with pure innocence' (Margalit 2002, 62). However, for Dlamini, nostalgia works in two ways: as yearning, embedded in critical reflection, for a lost home, and also as longing for a 'specific' and 'problematic' 'time and place in South African history' (2009, 152).

Dlamini (2009) concedes that nostalgia is 'something of a bad word [... worse] if it is uttered in the same breath as the term apartheid' (16). For surely, there can be nothing ethical about yearning for what Dlamini agrees is 'a dark chapter in South Africa's history' (22)? Thus, Miyeni (2011) writes in the *Sowetan* that he finds the premise of *Native Nostalgia* 'that growing up in apartheid-designed townships was fun [...] so sickening [that] I decided never to read it'. Miyeni likens apartheid to the Holocaust and argues that 'The only purpose [*Native Nostalgia*] serves is to reduce white South Africa's guilt'. This book creates 'barriers to black success. [It weakens] our struggle for black economic freedom'.[4]

Nevertheless, there is, Dlamini (2009) avers, a way out 'for nostalgics such as me' (17). He adopts Boym's (2001) distinction between two kinds of nostalgia, restorative and reflective[5]: whereas the former 'takes itself dead seriously' (18) and 'proposes to build the lost home' (17), the latter 'can be ironic and humorous' (18) and unite longing and critical thinking. Restorative nostalgia undermines the ethical search for truths about the past; reflective nostalgia, on the other hand, scrutinises personal memory, analysing it in an endeavour to represent the past truthfully and fully. As the blurb on the book's back cover puts it, *Native Nostalgia* is 'part-history, part-memoir, part-meditation and part-ethnography about Katlehong'; for Dlamini (2009), the conjunction of affect and analysis 'makes reflective nostalgia an attractive narrative frame for the kind of idiosyncratic engagement with the past essayed here' (18).

Ethics and memory: Avishai Margalit and Paul Ricoeur

But the 'narrative frame' for represented memory can only be deemed 'attractive' if it does not offend commonly held ethical standards. What are these, in relation to memory? I referred earlier to Ricoeur's distinction (*pace* Aristotle) of 'simple memory in the manner of an affection' and 'recollection [which] consists in an active search' (2004, 17). The ethical implications of memory relate to remembering as act, the purposeful adoption by individuals and communities of strategies to preserve specific memories of events and people and the conscious decision *not* to rehearse particular past occurrences, *not* to commemorate certain people. So the obligations we attach to memory apply to what we deliberately select for such recall or neglect, and how our decisions influence our actions.

For Margalit (2002, 37), ethics has to do with thick relations, that is personal relations with those who are near and dear such as family members, friends and lovers, and those we might never meet but with whom we nevertheless feel an affinity, such as fellow-countrymen. Thus, ethics pertains not only to face-to-face relations but also to what Benedict Anderson referred to as an imagined community.

At the centre of ethical relations, Margalit argues, is caring: 'At its best caring enhances a sense of belonging. It gives the other a feeling of being secure in having our attention and concern, irrespective of their achievements. Caring [...] is a selfless attitude' (2002, 34–35). Caring, Margalit explains, involves the expectation that we share a common past and memories; 'memory is the cement that holds thick relations together, and communities of memory are the obvious habitat for thick relations and thus ethics' (8). An ethics of memory means remembering people we care about; remembering is *part of* the caring and there is therefore an ethical duty to remember those we care about and, I would add, to remember also what is significant to the relationship. Thus, the emphasis, in *Native Nostalgia*, on positive aspects of relationships amongst members of the community and Dlamini's love for his mother (to whom the book is dedicated) is an ethical use of memory for it denotes – and promotes – caring and strengthens bonds of mutual consideration in the representation of memory.

Ricoeur reminds us that our belief that we can contest the accuracy of a memory implies that memory has a truth claim. 'To memory is tied an ambition, [...] that of being faithful to the past' (Ricoeur 2004, 21). The ethics of memory obliges us to verify and authenticate, to the best of our ability, our recollection and representation of the past. Memory stands in contrast to imagination which is not 'constrained by the reality of the past' (Margalit 2002, 140) because imagination 'has as its paradigm the unreal, the fictional, the possible' (Ricoeur 2004, 21). There is, Margalit notes, 'very good moral reason to seek the truth' (2002, 6), no matter how uncomfortable or tentative or provisional that may be. Dlamini's disconcerting challenge to orthodox interpretations of life for apartheid's oppressed lies in his claim that *despite* the evils of apartheid, the oppressed of Katlehong were resilient, resourceful, principled, dignified and mutually respectful; this personal truth must, he insists, be configured in a reckoning of the larger historical truth.

Memory's truth claim marks its relevance to ethics, as does the way that we allow memory to inform our present and future actions. Memory can be used and abused. Citing key essays by Freud, Ricoeur contrasts 'the work of remembering' (2004, 71) – by means of which we mourn lost objects of love and are ultimately reconciled with the loss, retaining self-esteem – with the abuse of memory, that is, the melancholic response to loss which remains obsessively trapped in repetition of what is remembered, unresponsive to the call of reality.

In 'Memory and Forgetting', Ricoeur (1999a) applies this model to both individual and collective uses and abuses of memory. The ethical use of memory avoids ritualised commemoration, in which excesses of memorialisation employ myth so as to fix memories in a kind of reverential relationship to the past; there are also dangers attendant upon remembering wrongdoing: as Margalit notes, memory breathes revenge as often as it breathes reconciliation (2002, 5). For Ricoeur, the ethico-political level of the problem of memory has to do with the shaping of the future: 'the duty to remember consists not only in having a deep concern for the past, but in transmitting the meaning of past events to the next generation' (1999a, 9). The collective is ethically bound to remember and teach: 'a basic reason for cherishing the duty to remember is to keep alive the memory of suffering over against the general tendency of history to celebrate the victors' (1999a, 10). But there is also a duty to forget, to be reconciled with the past, so as to be liberated from past anger and hatred. Thus, for Ricoeur, the ethics of memory means remembering the past, as accurately as is possible, so as to learn from it and build a better future (1999a, 10).

Post-apartheid South Africa

In the eyes of the world, South Africa is now living its better future. The new South Africa has risen phoenix-like from the humiliations and bloodshed of apartheid to embrace a constitution which respects all citizens' rights. Yet Dlamini's insistence that there is much to be valued in past experience emerges, as is typical of nostalgia, out of the awareness that the present context is wanting. Living in an economically thriving democratic state – albeit one with its share of woes including unemployment and a disparity in incomes (Mapenzauswa 2012), with one of the most liberal constitutions in the world – what possible contemporary malaise might occasion Dlamini's nostalgia? Might his simply be an ahistorical response to extreme and rapid social change? After all, as Chase and Shaw (1989, 8) observe: '[If] our consciousness [now] is fragmented, there must have been a time when it was integrated; if society is now bureaucratised and impersonal, it must previously have been personal and particular'.

Certainly, regret at loss of community and mutual care experienced during apartheid features prominently in *Native Nostalgia*. Katlehong, laid out by apartheid town planners in grid formation so as to maximise state surveillance, was made meaningful by residents who 'did not so much undermine the grid as neutralise it with practices such as cutting double laps, shortcuts, through neighbours' properties, and erecting stop-nonsense fences' (Dlamini 2009, 45). Undermining Verwoerd's goal of strict tribal segregation, the population of Katlehong comprised an ethnic and linguistic mix. The neighbourhood, although not immune to endemic violence, was part of a world in which there was 'a quiet dignity and respect for the dead in the midst of daily humiliations' (55); it was a world with its own 'moral logic' (101), held together by rituals of politeness, sharing and mutual kindness; a world peopled by larger-than-life characters and children at play; a world in which scholastic achievement was rewarded and adults like Dlamini's 'proud working class' (92) mother 'reigned supreme' (91).

Although Dlamini does not use the term, he describes a community which operated largely in terms of *ubuntu* or African humanism (see Murove 2009). Dlamini (2009) notes that 'Families in our neighbourhood participated' in a 'moral economy' in which people refused 'to treat each other as means' and believed that 'old-fashioned courtesies still had their place'; 'they sought in their imperfect ways to see humans in their fullness' (102–103).

Dlamini's (2009) mourning for belonging and connectedness occurs in the context of the present-day profit economy which has 'corrupted humans, instrumentalised social relations and turned individuals into means and ends', thus stunting human qualities and severing 'everything tender' (102). In contrast, *ubuntu* values human interrelatedness and mutual respect, and deems each person's very being dependent on such connections. *Ubuntu* is a disposition towards good which makes one perceive, feel and act in a humane way towards others. It [...] is best realised [...] in harmonious relations within society. [...] It signifies recognition of another person's humanity. [...] People are recognised *and regarded as equals* by virtue of their humanity. (Munyaka and Motlhabi 2009, 65–66, emphasis added)

For black South Africans now, there is, Dlamini contends, an absence of mutual regard, social order, neighbourliness, solidarity. Dlamini longs for these and for a time when, contrary to the struggle slogan which declared 'liberation before education', people like his mother insisted that 'education *was* liberation' (2009, 93, emphasis added). His regret at what people have lost is informed by a keen sense that such qualities characterised life in black townships during apartheid and that they are not acknowledged in hegemonic post-apartheid versions of that past. This failure to appreciate the complexity and richness of both past and present township life persists. Dlamini condemns Miyeni's equation of townships to sewers as 'warped' (163) for it fails to acknowledge that townships continue to be vital and indestructible parts of contemporary South Africa.

As one of those who refuse to see the past 'as one vast desert of doom and gloom' (12), is Dlamini (2009) a 'sell-out' or a 'self-hating' black (13)? His nostalgic recollection of his apartheid youth might seem to be contrary to the ethical quest for truth about past cruelties. In emphasising the remembered good, rather than past suffering, Dlamini perhaps does not exploit fully the ethical potential inherent in the latter: the recollection of affliction, Margalit (2002, 82) argues, is a first step on the road to repentance for wrongdoers (necessary so that they can distance themselves from past transgressions) and accords victims respect and acknowledgement of the wrongs suffered. There is, notwithstanding, an ethical merit to Dlamini's focus on how township residents rose above their oppression. By showing how he values residents' self-esteem, decency, kindness and commitment – recounting how they triumphed over their oppressive circumstances – Dlamini is *using* memory, in the positive Freudian sense, rather than *abusing* memory in ritualised repetitions of a version of the past, indifferent to present realities. *Native Nostalgia* works through what is recalled, thus, reinforcing self-worth – his own and that of other township residents. It is ethical, also, because by remembering these shared experiences, Dlamini endorses ethical values such as respect and love; remembering this way enacts the ethical link between caring and memory that Margalit contends cements thick relations.

Furthermore, Dlamini's nostalgia is ethical, too, in its search for the truth through a nuanced, carefully articulated assessment of both past and present. So while Dlamini (2009) acknowledges the validity of Boym's claim that 'a sentiment of loss and displacement [...] is an incurable condition of modernity', his is not wholly ascribable to a non-specific, generalised and globalised 'longing for continuity in a fragmented world' (16). For it is precisely the assault on historical specificity and accuracy – the sweeping generalisations, the inaccuracies taken as fact, the reverential rehearsals of ritualised memory – which he finds offensive in the new 'master narrative' (19). *Native Nostalgia* challenges 'facile accounts of black life under apartheid that paint the forty-six years [...] as one vast moral desert [...] as if blacks produced no art, no literature or music, bore no morally upstanding children' (19). This 'corruption of black history' is not merely skewed; it is a 'fiction' (21). The politically expedient distortions continue: for example, the year after *Native Nostalgia* was published, Julius Malema (then President of the ANC Youth League) claimed falsely that the Pan Africanist Congress (PAC) had 'hijacked' the memory of the Sharpeville massacre from the ANC and that young people should learn to 'correct' South Africa's history (du Plessis 2010).

Dlamini's appreciation for aspects of past experience does not arise out of a false certainty of either the coherence or the simple knowability of the past – indeed, he stresses his desire to reinsert ambiguity and depth into contemporary historical and political discourse. Dlamini (2009) objects to the crudely homogenised account of events, places and people in the apartheid past. In current 'jargon', black South Africans are generally characterised as 'faceless' victims who 'experienced apartheid the same way, suffered the same way and fought the same way' (18). This failure or refusal to admit 'gender, class, ethnic, age and regional differences (to name only the most obvious distinctions)' (18) leads to a fraudulent narrative which erases the richness and 'complexity of life amongst black South Africans, that not even colonialism and apartheid [...] could destroy' (19). It is both inaccurate and demeaning. Dlamini denounces the ruling party's persistent harking back to apartheid.[6] The insistence that memory be used as a weapon[7] against past, present and future human rights abuses is, Dlamini argues, obfuscatory, since it fails to take cognisance of the fact that 'not everything people did was a response to apartheid' (14). In this respect, Dlamini's use of the term 'native' undermines the negative connotations embedded in its use by apartheid's officialdom; for Dlamini, 'native' refers to indigeneity and to its politically charged sense of 'person of African descent' (152). Ultimately, he appropriates the negative term and uses it to affirm self-esteem.

Distortions of history: the ethical implications

Misrepresentations of the past have serious implications at both micro- and macro-levels of society. Individuals whose memories are scorned in dominant discourses could feel alienated from the nation and lose self-respect. This is because, as Ricoeur (1999a, 7–8) and others have argued, one's memories are linked to identity. We value our memories, no matter how trivial they may be, because they are special, irreplaceable. The present self is composed of, relies on and values what is remembered; thus, when hegemonic discourse is contemptuous of individuals' memories it undermines individuality. In effect, the state and its organs are saying to black South Africans: you are all the same because your experiences are all the same; your past is not special, particular or worthy of fond recollection, therefore your present self can make little claim to such qualities. This denial of the 'validity of experience' (Orwell 1990, 83) is the antithesis of ethical remembering for it denies the individual's right to value what she/he remembers and thus undermines the unique self.

Dlamini (2009) argues that the only importance assigned to black South Africans in officially sanctioned homogenising discourse lies in their belonging to the statistically important majority, as apartheid's oppressed natives (whose freedom, as politicians from the ruling ANC have it, came 'courtesy of [the] liberation movement' (13)[8]) and who can now be paraded as the passive beneficiaries of state beneficence. The current refutation of complexity and difference is unethical, furthermore, in that it seeks to suppress the complexity, incompleteness, of the truth. Ironically, it relies on and reinforces apartheid's obsession with racial classification (there is hardly a form to be filled in South Africa today which does not require declaration of racial classification) while its aim, paradoxically, is to 'erase the legacies of apartheid' (20).

At the macro-level of social relations, Dlamini (2009) maintains that the 'corruption of black history' (21) is a key element of the ANC government's 'anti-politics machine' (20). In terms of this, ordinary black South Africans are racial stereotypes, 'nothing more than objects of state policies or, worse, passive recipients of state-led service delivery' (20). This not only further disempowers the black electorate – 'now turned into abstract entities called PDIs (previously disadvantaged individuals)' (153) – but also '[breeds] political entrepreneurs and racial nativists' (20) who 'play the race card' so as to '[allow] a few black faces to get rich at the expense of millions of blacks' (21).[9] In the romantic narrative of mouthpieces of the governing party, 'the men and women who led the struggle' are transformed into 'the heroes and heroines of legend' (14). Challenges to this mythical version are labelled as reactionary or even racist.

Victors write the history. In the politics of remembering, even when the victors were engaged in a just struggle, their account of that past is no less presentist than any other and will be in the service of their own current needs and future desires. The kind of commemorative practice increasingly employed by the South African state is objectionable because, as Todorov notes, memory of the past can only help to prevent the repetition of past evil if it refrains from attributing to a select group 'the appealing, respected role of hero and victim and confining others to the less glorious role of villain, criminal and executioner, or the passive recipient of our heroic deeds' (2010, 9–10).[10] Instead of the current rhetoric,[11] memories of the past need to include the acknowledgement that apartheid collaborators and resisters were sometimes one and the same person (Dlamini 2009, 8).

It must be remembered that the apartheid state's manipulation of remembrance and history in the service of racist exploitation represents an extreme which the post-apartheid state has not come close to approximating. The latter is, nevertheless, failing to treat memory and history ethically by skewing memory, by attempting to stifle debate, by obsessively rehearsing and ritualising selected past events so as to deflect attention from contemporary abuses of power.

The self-serving recasting of history is a key element in the exploitation of the powerless by the powerful; it permits corruption to flourish as long as it is committed by one of the favoured. So what might seem to be a minor, or even trivial, instance of what is surely common amongst nation-states, namely the imposition of a romanticised version of the past on the populace, in Dlamini's (2009) analysis can be seen to be part of a larger, more profoundly unethical skewed deployment of public resources. The post-apartheid state fails to uphold law and order (156); it provides schooling which seems 'determined to rob young people of their futures' (93); it views diverse black townships as undifferentiated 'sites of struggle' (154) when they are actually 'a constitutive part of the national psyche' (112). A host of problems are faced by those who, during apartheid, dreamed of political change: citizens are treated with condescension by petty officials, municipal services are poor, corruption and nepotism are widespread and communities lack cohesion and order. In Katlehong now, Dlamini says:

> Problems there are, aplenty. As I write this, I can look out of the main window in our lounge to see young men going in and out of the local drug dealer's house. I can walk up and down the street to see the many backyard shacks that have sprung up in my neighbourhood as unemployed homeowners use their properties to make ends meet and desperate homeless people pay whatever rent is demanded of them. I can also walk around the neighbourhood to see government schools [...] that have mastered the art of churning out educated illiterates: students who spend their entire careers being taught in English and yet would not know a verb if it cornered them behind a shack and offered them drugs at a discount. Then there are the invisible problems: people my age and younger rotting away in poorly lit bedrooms as HIV/AIDS claims their lives inch by inch [...]. (2009, 63)

Dlamini (2009) concedes that township populations were kept stable – and were thus able to foster strong communities – due to the apartheid state's severe restrictions on the freedom of movement of black South Africans; nevertheless, he avers, township communities *were* secure, with benevolent support characterising relationships. This is no longer so. Thus, nostalgia for his apartheid youth is a reasonable response to frustrated expectations and a deficient present. Dlamini quotes Mr Ntswayi, an unemployed man from Mandela's birthplace: 'My life was better during apartheid [...]. Freedom turned out to be just a word' (5).

David Cannadine notes that 'depression is the begetter of nostalgia' (cited by Samuel 1994, 261). Gordimer's rejection of nostalgia as sentimental and escapist (see Stoltz 2011) can be just, for some nostalgics undoubtedly indulge in mawkishness and idealisation, in ritualised commemorisation (Ricoeur 1999a, 9) which has little concern for verity. However, Dlamini repeatedly rejects the simplifications of *restorative* nostalgia; *reflective* nostalgia is not simply an 'exile [...] from the present' (Muller 2006, 748). Dlamini's reflective nostalgia is close to critical history. Unlike shared memory or closed memory, which seeks to establish fixed, authorised versions of history, '*History*, critical history, [is committed] to looking for alternative lines that connect a past event to its present historical descriptions' (Margalit 2002, 60–61). *Native Nostalgia* opposes the crude state-endorsed heroes-and-villains narrative which 'strip[s] difference of its mystique' (Dlamini 2009, 113) and falsifies so as to create opportunities for 'political entrepreneurship' (156). It contests the master narrative that homogenises all blacks as victims, that deploys 'racial nativism' (156) in the service of the few who have 'no [personal] history of [engagement in the liberation] struggle' but who nevertheless 'take advantage of the valorisation (or is it fetishism) of blackness to enrich themselves or gain positions' (156). Dlamini's reflective nostalgia is ethical remembering because it strives for a more complete, truthful account of the past; it evades neither joyful nor unpleasant memories, but uses these to enrich and supplement the historical record with personal memory and its inevitable 'interaction of memory and desire' (Muller 2006, 748).

Dlamini's fondness for his remembered past comprehends his love for his mother and admiration for her strength and integrity; it celebrates a sense of belonging and responsibility, human worth, *ubuntu* and the community's mutually respectful rituals; it commends the order of a social world which township inhabitants created *despite* apartheid's abuses. Ethical memory, whether it involves a wistful yearning or not, favours the good rather than the expedient or harmful so as to foster this in future.

Davis writes that 'nostalgia, despite its private, sometimes intensely felt personal character [...] derives from and has continuing implications for our lives as social actors' (1979, vii). When Dlamini and others offer their testimony it behoves those who seek to better understand the past to take seriously their right to recall the past as they see it since their views add new dimensions to that knowledge. Testimony 'constitutes the fundamental transitional structure between memory and history' (Ricouer 2004, 21). But this does not mean that we must overlook the inevitable limits to memory's reliability: memory is directed by motive (why is one remembering this now?), by audience (who is one recalling this for?), by occasion (when is the recall happening?) and by form (what generic form will the record take?). Furthermore, memory is incomplete, corruptible and fallible.[12] Thus, recollections will not have equal weight. Nonetheless, all voices should be heard in the continuing search for truth of what happened – a quest that is necessary for ethical as well as epistemological reasons (Ricoeur 1999b, 14–15). 'My memories', Dlamini (2009) concludes, will contribute to the appreciation of 'why apartheid suffered the kind of moral defeat that led to its demise' (152). Dlamini commemorates ordinary South Africans' triumphant defiance of the apartheid state's attempts to subjugate the majority. When 'ordinary South Africans cast their memories of the past in such a nostalgic frame', these are minor acts of resistance, a 'second wave' (Coan 2011) against the dominant discourse which denies 'ordinary' understandings of our past [... and refuses to concede] that South Africans are not agreed upon the meaning of their past' (Dlamini 2009, 6).

Nostalgia is a bitter-sweet emotion, but one in which pleasure predominates. We should not, in our focus on the ethical and political implications of memory, forget that there is 'an aesthetic value to memory. The pleasure of recall is real' (Levi 2001, 145). The pleasure Dlamini (2009) seems to experience in reminiscing does not amount to romanticisation of the past but counters manipulated narratives which arise from political expediency, denying the complexity of the human condition[13] and a fully engaged remembering of place and time, crucial to what Dlamini refers to as the 'imagination of alternative futures' (110).

Notes

1. Arguably this day elicits sentimental and patronising rhetoric from politicians who remain silent about hideous national rape statistics. 'One in three of the 4,000 women questioned [...] said they had been raped in the past year. [In a Soweto survey] a quarter of all the [schoolboys] interviewed said that "jackrolling" [i.e. gang rape] was fun. More than 25% of South African men questioned in a [Medical Research Council] survey admitted to raping someone [...]. It is estimated that 500,000 rapes are committed annually in South Africa [... which] has some of the highest incidences of child and baby rape in the world with more than 67,000 cases of rape and sexual assaults against children reported in 2000. Welfare groups believe that the number of unreported incidents could be up to 10 times that number' (http://www.thewordsmith.biz/how-can-this-be/); see Rape Survivor Journey (2011).
2. Afrikaans is usually conceived of the language of *baaskap*. *Baaskap* (literally, mastery over) refers to whites' – or, in some instances, specifically Afrikaners' – domination of South Africans of all other races. Consider the dedication in Antjie Krog's (1998) *Country of My Skull*: 'for every victim who had an Afrikaner surname on her lips'. It is the language of nostalgia for Dlamini because of the many colourful Afrikaans terms which township residents (including his mother) relished in everyday conversation.
3. See Wildschut et al. (2006, 975–976). Davis also gives a succinct account of the 'semantic deterioration' (1979, 5) of nostalgia. See also Hirsch and Spitzer (2003, 82–83).
4. Miyeni is a South African writer, actor, radio and television personality. He has published numerous books (non-fiction, poetry and fiction); see Madondo (2012).
5. Davis' distinction between orders of nostalgia predates Boym's (though she, surprisingly, does not mention Davis). Davis (1979) distinguishes between three non-hierarchical orders (simple, reflexive and interpretive) but insists that 'once past childhood, all of us [...] experience all three levels of nostalgic reaction' (27) and may move 'from one "level" to another' (28).
6. Recently, for instance, ANC leaders defended their right to continue to sing the struggle songs 'Dubula Ibhunu' (shoot the Boer) and 'Umshini Wami' (bring me my machine gun). Not all black South Africans agree with this practice of remembering. Jansen, for instance, argues that the sentiments expressed therein breed 'racial distrust and suspicion', laying the 'groundwork for racial retaliation' (2011, 10). The courts agreed in the case of the shoot the Boer song. Such songs, in seeming to fuel further violence in an already pervasively violent country, are thus seen as the abuse of memory in the service of melancholia, that is, obsessive repetition, which perpetuates anger and hatred.
7. The title of Don Mattera's autobiography, *Memory is the Weapon* (1987), is metonymic for the general trend which uses testimony to counter state deception.
8. Nodoba (2012), academic and spokesperson for AZAPO, deplores 'the arrogance of the ANC' and its attempts to suffocate the history of other liberation movements: the tour guide on Robben Island omitted mention of all non-ANC prisoners, and on the public holiday of 21 March 2012 (commemorating the Sharpeville massacre of PAC supporters), President Zuma, instead of reminding auditors about the courage of

those PAC-affiliated anti-Pass protestors, focused on the ANC's Freedom Charter. Nodoba refers also to the state's ongoing attempts to suppress access to information. Journalist Stephen Coan (2011) argues that scholarship is needed to counter the version of the past 'currently being punted by the governing elite. President Jacob Zuma has claimed the Soweto Uprising as an ANC event. It wasn't – in fact the youth of June '76 were castigated as irresponsible in an ANC monthly published in July of the same year'.
9. According to Jansen (2011, 4), rector of the University of the Free State, '"public service" does not exist'; and 'for most, being elected to a government position is a simple matter of personal enrichment and political egotism'. How, he wonders, can those who claim the high moral ground have supported the AIDS policies that led 'millions of the poorest among us to suffer and die needlessly'; how could they have vetoed votes in the United Nations 'against known tyrants from Burma to Zimbabwe'?
10. Ironically, Todorov (2010) himself refers to the ANC as 'the party that had struggled against apartheid' (50), thus appearing, by means of the definite article, to endorse its own distorted version of its singular role as liberator of the masses.
11. Jansen asserts that in current political rhetoric, the past is evoked so as to authorise the view 'that the high moral ground belongs to the [...] black victim laying material and symbolic claim and control over the impure [...] white perpetrator' (2011, 6).
12. Gladwell (2009, 250) reminds us of the retrospective interpretive powers of hindsight, as propounded by Baruch Fischoff: 'creeping determinism' is 'the sense that grows on us, in retrospect, that what has happened was actually inevitable'.
13. Todorov (2010) argues that memory can only be an effective weapon against the repetition of evil acts if we acknowledge that specific circumstances allow evil to flourish: 'the remedy we are seeking will not consist in merely remembering the evil to which our group or our ancestors were victims. We have to go a step further and ask ourselves about the reasons that gave rise to the evil. [We have to recognize] that inhumanity is a human thing' (80–81). And then, 'it is not individuals or groups of individuals who are bad but their deeds. The memory of the past could help us in this enterprise of taming evil, on the condition that we keep in mind that good and evil flow from the same source and that in the world's best narratives they are not neatly divided' (83).

References

Barrett, Frederick S., Kevin J. Grimm, Richard W. Robbins, Tim Wildschut, and Constantine Sedikides. 2010. "Music-Evoked Nostalgia: Affect, Memory, and Personality." *Emotion* 10 (3): 390–403.

Boym, Svetlana. 2001. *The Future of Nostalgia.* New York: Basic Books.

Chase, Malcolm, and Christopher Shaw. 1989. "The Dimensions of Nostalgia." In *The Imagined Past: History and Nostalgia*, edited by Christopher Shaw, and Malcolm Chase, 1–17. Manchester: Manchester University Press.

Coan, Stephen. 2011. "Waiting for the Second Wave." *The Witness*, July 6. http://www.witness.co.za/index.php?showcontent&global[_id]=63989

Davis, Fred. 1979. *Yearning for Yesterday: A Sociology of Nostalgia*. New York: Free Press.

Dlamini, Jacob. 2009. *Native Nostalgia*. Auckland Park: Jacana Media.

Dlamini, Jacob. n.d. "Resume of Jacob Dlamini." http://ccrri.ukzn.ac.za/docs/Jacob%20Dlamini%20Resume_1.PDF

du Plessis, Carien. 2010. "PAC Hijacked Sharpeville March – Malema." *Independent Online News*, March 23. http://www.iol.co.za/news/politics/pac-hijacked-sharpeville-march-malema-1.477188

Fanon, Frantz. 1963. *The Wretched of the Earth*. New York: Grove Press.

Gladwell, Malcolm. 2009. *What the Dog Saw and Other Adventures*. London: Penguin.

Hirsch, Marianne, and Leo Spitzer. 2003. "'We Would Not Have Come Without You': Generations of Nostalgia." In *Contested Pasts: The Politics of Memory*, edited by Katharine Hodgkin, and Susannah Radstone, 79–95. London: Routledge.

Jansen, Jonathan. 2011. *We Need to Talk*. Johannesburg: Pan Macmillan.

Krog, Antjie. 1998. *Country of My Skull*. Johannesburg: Random House.

Levi, Primo. 2001. *The Voice of Memory: Interviews 1961–87*, edited by Marco Belpoliti, and Robert Gordon. Cambridge: Polity.

Madondo, Bongani. 2012. "Eric Miyeni Blessed with a Tongue that Will Not Shut up." *Mail & Guardian*, August 3. http://mg.co.za/article/2012-08-03-00-miyeni-blessed-with-a-tongue-that-will-not-shut-up

Mapenzauswa, Stella. 2012. "Africa Money – Memo to South Africa: Economic Woes Begin at Home." *Reuters*, August 24. http://in.reuters.com/article/2012/08/24/africa-money-idINL6E8JNJAH20120824

Margalit, Avishai. 2002. *The Ethics of Memory*. Cambridge, MA: Harvard University Press.

Mattera, Don. 1987. *Memory Is the Weapon*. Johannesburg: Ravan Press.

McKaiser, Eusebius. 2009. "Remembering Apartheid with Fondness." *Politicsweb*, November 29. http://www.politicsweb.co.za/politicsweb/view/politicsweb/en/page71627?oid=152786&sn=Detail&pid=71627

Miyeni, Eric. 2011. "Defining Blacks by Past Misery Is Unfair." *Sowetan Live*, June 27. http://www.sowetanlive.co.za/columnists/2011/06/27/defining-blacks-by-past-misery-is-unfair

Muller, Adam. 2006. "Notes toward a Theory of Nostalgia: Childhood and the Evocation of the Past in Two European 'Heritage' Films." *New Literary History* 37 (4): 739–760.

Munyaka, Mluleki, and Mokgethi Motlhabi. 2009. "Ubuntu and Its Socio-Moral Significance." In *African Ethics: An Anthology of Comparative and Applied Ethics*, edited by Munyaradzi Felix Murove, 63–84. Scottsville: University of KwaZulu-Natal Press.

Murove, Munyaradzi Felix, ed. 2009. *African Ethics: An Anthology of Comparative and Applied Ethics*. Scottsville: University of KwaZulu-Natal Press.

Nodoba, Gaontebale. 2012. "ANC Hegemony on Robben Island." *Politicsweb*, April 2. http://www.politicsweb.co.za/politicsweb/view/politicsweb/en/page71639?oid=290482&sn=Detail&pid=71639

Orwell, George. 1990. *Nineteen Eighty-Four*. London: Penguin.

Rape Survivor Journey. 2011. "Rape Statistics – South Africa and Worldwide." http://www.rape.co.za/index.php?option=com_content&task=view&id=875

Republic of South Africa. 1996. "Constitution of the Republic of South Africa." http://www.info.gov.za/documents/constitution/1996/96preamble.html

Ricoeur, Paul. 1999a. "Memory and Forgetting." In *Questioning Ethics: Contemporary Debates in Philosophy*, edited by Richard Kearney, and Mark Dooley, 5–11. London: Routledge.

Ricoeur, Paul. 1999b. "Imagination, Testimony and Trust: A Dialogue with Paul Ricoeur." In *Questioning Ethics: Contemporary Debates in Philosophy*, edited by Richard Kearney, and Mark Dooley, 12–17. London: Routledge.

Ricoeur, Paul. 2004. *Memory, History, and Forgetting*. Chicago: University of Chicago Press.

Samuel, Raphael. 1994. *Theatres of Memory: Past and Present in Contemporary Culture*. Vol. 1. London: Verso.

Sartre, Jean-Paul. 1963. "Preface." In *The Wretched of the Earth*, by Frantz Fanon, 7–31. New York: Grove Press.

Smith, David James. 2010. *Young Mandela*. London: Weidenfeld & Nicolson.

Steinberg, Jonny. 2010. "I Say I Must Say This." *The Sunday Times*, February 7. http://www.timeslive.co.za/lifestyle/books/2010/02/07/i-say-i-must-say-this

Stoltz, Jacques. 2011. "Memory, Forgetting and the Creative Spark." *Archival Platform*, August 15. http://www.archivalplatform.org/blog/entry/memory_forgetting/

Todorov, Tzvetan. 2010. *Memory as a Remedy for Evil*. London: Seagull.

Wildschut, Tim, Constantine Sedikides, Jamie Arndt, and Clay Routledge. 2006. "Nostalgia: Content, Triggers, Functions." *Journal of Personality and Social Psychology* 91 (5): 975–993.

Excavating Tempelhof airfield: objects of memory and the politics of absence

Maria Theresia Starzmann

Department of Anthropology, McGill University, Montreal, Canada

Seeking to critically engage with German post-war politics of memory through a study of material culture, this paper examines the political implications of absence for archaeological work. More specifically, it confronts the problem of the lacuna of the archive of the Holocaust and explores how we can productively engage the archival absences that animate the present. Introducing first results from archaeological excavations at a former forced labour camp at Tempelhof airfield in Berlin, Germany, I discuss how archaeology, by investigating what remains after the Holocaust, may allow us to manifest absence, loss and historical silence. Analysing the role of objects of memory in storytelling and history writing, I also lay out how tender a task an archaeological study of the Nazi past is, pointing out where our work may risk to misappropriate history.

[A] fractured horizon looms in which to make one's way as a spectral agency, one for whom a full 'recovery' is impossible, one for whom the irrecoverable becomes, paradoxically, the condition of a new political agency. (Butler 2003, 467)

1. Introduction

Several years ago, the Jewish Museum in Berlin had on display a neatly folded linen towel that Margarete Kuttner had packed for her 16-year-old son Paul, who left Berlin in February 1939 as part of the *Kindertransport*. Margarete Kuttner was deported to Auschwitz where she was killed in late February 1943. Arrived in London, Paul Kuttner never unpacked his towel. The towel was part of the museum's permanent collection, but was removed to its depot for conservation reasons. There it rests folded as it was on the day when Margarete Kuttner placed it into her son's suitcase (Figure 1). What remains is what Assmann (1992, 20)

Figure 1. Linen towel with initials 'M.K.' for Margarete Kuttner (photo: Jens Ziehe, Jewish Museum Berlin, Paul Kuttner Trust).

calls '*[d]as Gedächtnis der Dinge*' (the memory of things) – an object that conjures up not only past lives, but also the irreplaceable loss of life. As a result of the ways in which the towel was attended to and sustained – in this case most importantly by a sort of non-practice, that is, by what was *not* done with it (it was *not* unpacked, *not* unfolded, *not* used) – the towel sits squarely at the limit between life and death, between past and present. Recognising it to be much more than a mere relic or an object of empty contemplation, the towel embodies an absence that can be felt as physically as any presence (Bille, Hastrup, and Sørensen 2003; Buchli and Lucas 2001).

Studying the Nazi past, archaeologically or otherwise, is a decision that impacts a number of subjects, ranging from the survivors of the Nazi Holocaust to the generations born after the Second World War. Importantly, it also concerns those who can no longer speak because they, like Margarete Kuttner, did not survive the Holocaust. Exploring the role of material culture in archaeological analyses of sites of Nazi crimes, this paper makes absence a focal point. Agamben (1999) has pointed out that the archive of the Holocaust, while containing numerous testimonies and eyewitness accounts, nevertheless forms around a lacuna, because there is no complete witness. Such witness would be the one who has encountered the whole truth, but she/he is also the one who did not survive the Holocaust ('the drowned' in Levi's [1996] account).

At pains to recognise the partiality of all perspectives, I find the intimation of a complete witness problematic, especially so because the absence of the complete witness may provide justification for those inclined to question the 'truthfulness' of the experiences of survivors. Yet, I believe that Agamben draws our attention to something of central importance. Taking a cue from Crossland's work, the absence that I trace throughout this paper does not inevitably imply the loss of life, but rather refers us in a more general sense to 'the seizure of people from networks of social and family relationships' (2002, 123). Forced labourers, such as the men and women deployed at Tempelhof, were pulled out of their familiar environments by coercion, leaving a void among those who stayed behind and themselves experienced painful and traumatic losses.

An archaeological project that deals with a history of loss, absence and trauma, as introduced in this paper, has to be politically accountable towards the subjects of our inquiry – those who were the targets of a brutal politics of racism, exploitation and industrialised genocide. Instead of trying to recover and represent that which has been lost, our goal should be to mark the losses we are confronted with, to summon the presence of the absence of the Holocaust archive. If absence were made manifest by that which remains, working with material culture could allow us to engage in a process of memory work that does not understand absence as lack. Rather, absence becomes the stipulation for an active politics – 'the condition of a new political agency' (Butler 2003, 467) – that resists trivialisation as well as saturation of memory (González-Ruibal 2008, 258), by which I mean an overabundance of social meaning that may entail commodification and alienation.

Against this background, the paper introduces some of the findings from archaeological excavations conducted in 2012 in the area of a former Nazi forced labour camp at Tempelhof airfield in Berlin.[1] Besides responding to a recognised need for a historical archaeology, which is thus far not an established discipline in the German university system, the project's main concern is an engagement with the Nazi history of Tempelhof airfield, which is often bracketed from public discourses. For Pollock and Bernbeck (Forthcoming), the excavations at Tempelhof are therefore *Sichtbarmachungen*, rendering visible those things that might otherwise have been left to neglect or decay. In addition, while the available historical sources are important documents that are integrated into the ongoing archaeological work, they do not typically speak of the daily life of the prisoners and labourers who were forced to work at Tempelhof for a growing military industry. Archaeology may then help us to better understand what I call, for lack of a better word, the quotidian aspects of life in the camp – 'from eating to personal hygiene to connections (if any) to families and communities back home' (Pollock and Bernbeck Forthcoming).

The *Sichtbarmachungen* at Tempelhof involved the recovery of a large amount of archaeological objects. The quality of these objects, as well as the fact that only a relatively small number of items can with certainty be assigned to the context of the forced labour camp, constitutes the analytical basis for my deliberations apropos the role of objects in engaging archival absence. Following Fowles (2010, 28), I argue that this absence is itself object-like, which is to say that it has its own 'distinctive affordances and material consequences that are not only prior to meaning but can, of their own accord, direct the process of signification'. In other words, we encounter the absence that is so palpable in the archaeological record at Tempelhof not as something immaterial or as an actual thing, but as the materialisation of practices and non-practices, of things that have and have not been done (cf. Meyer 2012).

HISTORICAL JUSTICE

As I demonstrate in this paper, recognising the vital role of absence in processes of signification will eventually unsettle the idea that the archaeological record must be complete and our memories of the past whole in order to be historically meaningful. This allows us to reconsider some foundational assumptions regarding historicity (*sensu* Trouillot 1995) and the temporality of the archive, thus conveying how memory gets reworked over time (cf. Moshenska 2006). However, I also recognise that there are limits to memory and narrative, and in the last section of the paper I address issues of power in the construction of historical narratives and personal recollections, which cannot be severed from ethical and political problems entangled with our archaeological praxis in the field.

2. Forced labour at Tempelhof airfield

Tempelhof airfield is publicly known as the 'gate to freedom' due to its role during the Berlin airlift in 1948 and 1949. The excavation project, however, focuses its attention on a much darker chapter of German history. On 1 May 1933, the Nazis celebrated a newly declared national holiday, the 'Day of National Work'.[2] Tempelhof airport was used for a massive propagandistic event with hundreds of thousands of participants (Assatzk 2012; Coppi 2012). The following day, in a cynical twist of its supposedly pro-worker ideology, the Nationalsozialistische Deutsche Arbeiterpartei (NSDAP; National Socialist German Workers Party) banned all unions, arresting union members and functionaries. On 10 May 1933, the Deutsche Arbeitsfront (DAF; German Labour Front) was founded as a surrogate union, with the aim of organising German workers as well as assuring their 'social hygiene' and the aesthetic appearance of the workplace (Aly, Chroust, and Pross 1994). In this function, the organisation provided the tableware for workplace canteens, which had to carry the uniform label 'Amt Schönheit der Arbeit' (Bureau Beauty of Labour) (Zentek 2009). A number of fragments of this tableware were found during our excavations (Figure 2), suggesting that these dishes belonged to the factory

Figure 2. Porcelain shard from the manufacturer Hutschenreuther (photo: Jessica Meyer, Landesdenkmalamt Berlin).

branches of the airplane manufacturers at Tempelhof. Not only German workers, but foreign and forced labourers too had to comply with the regulations of the DAF (Budraß 2001, 43).

Only two months later, in July 1933, the Gestapo established a detention facility in the former military prison Columbia-Haus, located at the north-western edge of the airfield. In December 1934, Columbia-Haus became a concentration camp under the control of the SS. Between 1934 and 1936, around 10,000 political and ideological opponents of the Nazi regime were imprisoned, tortured and killed there (Pollock and Bernbeck Forthcoming). By the end of 1936, most prisoners were moved to the newly built concentration camp Sachsenhausen in Oranienburg, north of Berlin. The Columbia-Haus was demolished in 1938 in the course of the construction work for the new monumental airport terminal designed by architect Ernst Sagebiel.

In 1939, before the new airport building was completed, the company Weserflug GmbH, under the supervision of the Reichsluftfahrtministerium (Ministry of Aviation), began using parts of the building complex for the maintenance, repair and refurbishment, and later also for the production of airplanes (Wenz 2000). By then, the company had already been closely cooperating with the airforce in the licensed production of the *Sturzkampfbomber*, a type of dive-bomber, at its headquarters in Bremen. The plant at Tempelhof accounted for 90% of the total production of this type of dive-bombers in Germany by October 1944 (Pophanken 2000, 116). It was not until after the beginning of the Second World War, however, that the Weserflug GmbH started using forced labour. Historical documents show that forced labourers began working at Tempelhof airfield in the autumn of 1940, most of them having been deported to Germany from Poland and other, mostly Eastern European countries. While Weserflug's Tempelhof plant employed about 1000 workers in late 1940, its workforce increased to more than 4000 by 1944. Half of these were foreign workers (a company directory lists 20 different nationalities), comprising both men and women as well as enlisted and conscripted civilians (including 86 Jewish civilian workers), but also French and Russian prisoners of war (Heisig 2012, 46). Due to the relatively high number of foreign labourers at the Tempelhof branch of the Weserflug GmbH, the company decided to build four camps on the airfield that housed the workers in simple wooden huts.[3] According to Heisig, each of these camps was for different groups of workers, who were spatially segregated based on their legal status (such as civilian, POW, foreign/German) (2012, 50).

A lesser noted, largely unpublished aspect of the history of Tempelhof airfield is the deployment of forced labour by Lufthansa, which was founded in 1926 and until 1933 was known under the name Deutsche Luft Hansa AG. The old airport at Tempelhof, opened in 1923 and located in the north-eastern part of today's airfield, was Lufthansa's home base. With the beginning of the Second World War, Lufthansa greatly reduced its civilian air transport activities and took over major maintenance and installation work for the Luftwaffe, which was carried out in the hangars of the old airport, where a control workshop was located, and in the new airport building in a maintenance workshop (Budraß 2001, 10; cf. Pollock and Bernbeck Forthcoming). Like Weserflug, Lufthansa used forced labour at Tempelhof airfield, mainly workers from Poland, the Ukraine and the Netherlands, as well as a number of conscripted Jewish workers from Germany who were later deported to concentration camps (Budraß 2001). The workers deployed in the Lufthansa control workshop were housed in a camp adjacent to the north of the old hangars. The camp (in the following 'Lufthansa camp'), which existed from 1942 to 1944, was made up of several *Wohnbaracken* (accommodation huts), a kitchen and a mess hall (potentially for use by Germans only), a privy, a lavatory and a boiler room. The Jewish workers, who were not living in the camp, had to use a separate toilet, called the '*Juden-Abort*' in Lufthansa documents, which was located at the eastern end of the old airport (Budraß 2001, 42).

3. Excavating the Lufthansa camp

During the 2012 archaeological campaign, nine trenches were excavated in five areas (Areas 1, 2, 3, 5 and 6), uncovering a total of 1220 m². My discussion focuses on the results from the excavations in Areas 1 and 2, where remains from the Lufthansa camp were uncovered, including an air-raid shelter running north to south that was located just west of the accommodation huts within the camp (Figure 3).[4]

In Area 1, Trench 1 and Trench 2 yielded material remains that date from the primary context of the forced labour camp, with Trench 1 cutting the western-most end of a hut that had a width of 12.5 m. Trench 2 cuts the northern wall of a second hut located slightly to the south and contained construction debris related to the Lufthansa camp. From a cost and construction report[5] dating from September 1942, it is known that the Deutsche Lufthansa AG functioned as the building contractor, planning a camp that would consist of three accommodation huts, measuring 12.5 m × 52.5 m each, as well as a somewhat smaller *Wirtschaftsbaracke* (utility hut), measuring 12.5 m × 41.25 m. The camp was originally intended to house 300 people, occupying a total area of approximately 2400 m².

A construction plan[6] also from 1942 indicates, however, that the actual 'residential' area of the camp consisted of four long huts and one slightly shorter hut (42.5 m in length), all intended for housing workers and oriented approximately in east-west direction. In addition, a *Wirtschaftsbaracke* (41.25 m in length) was located east of the accommodation huts and oriented in north-south direction. According to the construction plan, this building, designated *Ausländer-Wirtschaftsbaracke*, was intended specifically for use by foreign workers. An aerial reconnaissance photo[7] from March 1945, when the huts were already demolished, largely confirms this outline of the camp, clearly showing the foundations of the four long huts. The difference between the initial construction estimate and the finished project is proof that the building contractor cut costs by constructing more huts for the available money, resulting in a sparsely equipped camp.[8]

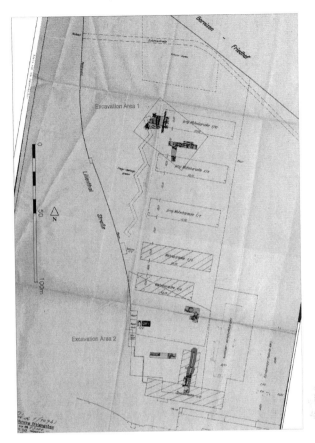

Figure 3. Construction plan for the Lilienthal camp from 1942 (source: Bundesarchiv).

In this context, it is noteworthy that some of the archaeological objects we unearthed can provide us with an idea of how the huts were constructed. Thus, we found a large number of nails measuring about 100 mm; the tips of the nails were bent over at about 80 mm. It is likely that the nails were used for constructing the walls of the huts. As far as we know from excavations at other forced labour camps,[9] the walls were typically built from wood and sometimes tarpaper was added as insulation. The nails we found suggest that the walls of the huts were not very strong, probably only about 80–90 mm thick; the protruding ends of the nails that were knocked over must have served to fasten the tarpaper (Figure 4).

The cost report also provides some information on the construction and design of the huts. It mentions, for example, concrete floors, heating, light, running water and sanitary installations. Our archaeological research indicates the presence of utilities (water, electricity and sewage) in the hut we excavated in Trench 1. Inside the hut, along the western and southern foundations, we found remains of ceramic sewage pipes that date to the original context of the

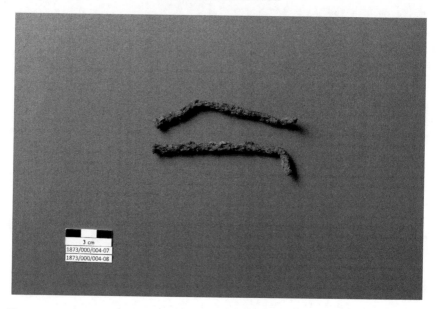

Figure 4. Two iron nails from Area 1 (photo: Jessica Meyer, Landesdenkmalamt Berlin).

camp. However, at this point we cannot provide any information on the distribution of utilities within a complete hut, their presence within the other accommodation units and ultimately whom the utilities served. Further, shattered remains of bricks as well as three small brick platforms were unearthed. While the bricks might predate the huts, perhaps belonging to the context of a nineteenth-century cemetery, it cannot be ruled out that the platforms served as foundations for posts that subdivided the interior of the buildings; indeed, a similar situation has been documented for the medical hut in the concentration camp Mauthausen (Dejnega and Theune Forthcoming).

Some artefacts provide us with information regarding interior installations. Among these are fragments of glazed tiles (mainly of light brown and yellow colour shades) that could be mantle pieces from ovens or *Kochmaschinen* (kitchen stoves).[10] Historical sources document that in concentration camps each hut was usually equipped with an oven (cf. Dejnega and Theune Forthcoming). Although no similar documentation exists for forced labour camps, the tiles we found suggest that some of the huts in the Lufthansa camp might have had an oven or a similar installation. Several pieces of large hollow bricks (measuring approximately 0.4 m × 0.4 m × 0.4 m) could also stem from an oven or chimney. However, because these building parts were not found inside the hut, but out of context in Trench 2, it is impossible to say whether these bricks actually belonged to the camp.

Approximately 10 m west of the hut, the excavations revealed parts of an air-raid shelter that ran roughly north to south. The air-raid shelter consisted of a zigzag slit trench lined with an approximately 2-m high, box-sectioned tunnel constructed from prefabricated, reinforced concrete beams. During the excavations, the air-raid shelter was cut in two places, the northern cut having exposed a shallower, horizontally built concrete structure that appears to be the entrance to the shelter.

The excavations in Area 2 in the southern part of the Lufthansa camp concentrated on three contexts, which include a waste pit (Trench 3), a fire-fighting pond (Trenches 4 and 5) and the kitchen hut with adjacent mess hall (Trench 6). While Trenches 3, 4 and 5 revealed a large volume of artefacts, most of which can with certainty be dated to the time of the US American occupation in Berlin, the findings from Trench 6 are linked to the Lufthansa camp and thus also to the huts in Area 1.

Trench 3 was a waste pit or dump, located roughly between the southernmost accommodation hut and the kitchen. Its stratigraphy reveals that the pit underwent at least two phases of deposition, separated by a layer of solid sandy loam. From preliminary analyses, it appears that these two phases indicate the use of the dump first by the occupants (maybe the kitchen staff) of the Lufthansa camp, mainly for kitchen waste, including a large quantity of animal bones and broken dishes. The later phase of usage can be attributed to US American soldiers, who disposed of waste there, including a high amount of sanitary items; many of these objects bore American brand names or labels designating them as belonging to a 'pro-kit' that was issued to each American soldier by the United States Medical Department during the Second World War.

The fire-fighting pond, which seems to have belonged to the eastern hangars of the old airport, was only built after 1940 and was not destroyed during the war. Our excavations cut the pond in two places, that is, on its western edge (Trench 4) and on its south-eastern corner (Trench 5). Based on the finds from Trenches 4 and 5 – not just tubes of toothpaste or shaving cream, aftershave bottles or tins of shoe polish with American labels, but also pieces of English-language newspapers and soldiers' identification tags – it appears that the pond was similarly used as a garbage dump by the United States Army stationed in Tempelhof after the end of the Second World War. In addition, the pond contained a considerable amount of building-material waste and old machine parts, such as shards of window and safety glass; scrap metal, including metal fittings, screws, nails and bolts; batteries; locks; and paint buckets.

The excavations in Trench 6 cut through two building complexes, a kitchen hut extending north to south and an adjacent mess hall that was built perpendicular to the kitchen hut. While these two buildings are not mentioned in the cost report from 1942, they were (or became) part of the Lufthansa camp too, as indicated by the construction plan in Figure 3, but they were not completely destroyed during the war. The mess hall apparently consisted of one storey only. The kitchen hut was cut lengthwise from north to south in the course of the excavations, revealing a basement. The walls inside this basement were completely stripped away at some point, likely indicating the reuse of building materials. It appears that during the building's demolition, the massive reinforced concrete slabs of an air-raid bunker that was part of the building collapsed into the basement. Further alterations were made once the building was demolished, when a large ceramic sewer pipe and smaller metal water pipes were laid through the southern part of the kitchen, cutting the building in east-west direction.

Based on the bomb-strike pattern on the aerial photograph from 1945, we must assume that the Lufthansa camp was severely damaged during air raids. As our excavations revealed, the remaining parts of the huts were stripped down to the foundations. Photographic evidence of the clean-up by the US Army at another camp on the Tempelhof airfield after the war suggests that some of the building materials were later reused (Ed Collins, personal communication). While the demolition must have been mainly a response to the air-raid damage, we cannot assume that the only reason the camp was not repaired was a lack of resources. Without arguing that this is proof of a sense of wrong among the perpetrators, the demolitions at Tempelhof could also have been an attempt at silencing history. In that case, if we consider what remains and what does not remain, the objects we encounter may present to us the things we cannot remember, which manifest in various kinds of absences that I trace in the next section of the paper.

4. Experiencing absence

The structures that were excavated at Tempelhof yielded a large number of archaeological objects.[11] As already mentioned, only a few of these artefacts were found in contexts that can with certainty be attributed to the Lufthansa camp. This refers us to the problem of what Bernbeck (2005, 113) has described as 'political taphonomy', suggesting that the processes by which cultural materials accumulate and preserve in the archaeological record can indicate past power differentials. As a result, 'people who are marginalised in life are often represented by only ephemeral traces in the material record, in notable distinction to the more powerful whose archaeological footprints are often gigantic in comparison' (Pollock and Bernbeck Forthcoming). In addition to constituting such ephemeral traces, many of the objects we found at Tempelhof appear themselves marginal, if not to say out-of-place, in the larger context of forced labour. Shards of window glass, bottle caps, buttons and leather fragments are archaeological objects that cite a seemingly familiar world now absent. Despite their everyday character – or rather, precisely because of it – these objects have a particularly strong ability to elicit affective responses in us. Found in contexts 'other than those in which the dominant cultural tradition would apply them' (Beaudry, Cook, and Mrozowski 1996, 277), the objects make manifest that which is missing from life in the camp as a result of a web of violence and terror (cf. Theune 2010).

In the following, I introduce a selection of finds from our excavations at Tempelhof and explain how they make present, in exemplary ways, an object-like absence. Importantly, absence is not just there, representing or symbolising a history of loss and trauma, but it results from materialised practice, and more specifically from the various ways in which humans interact or do not interact with things. Absence, I contend, conveys itself to us through experiences of void, forgetfulness and loss.

4.1. Absence as void

The experience of void refers us not to a loss of things that have once been there, but to things entirely missing, that is, a non-existence of things or what we may call 'non-things' (Fowles 2010, 25). Non-things are encountered as negative spaces where the presence of some objects marks the absence of others – a view that parallels Trouillot's (1995) notion of mentions and silences as co-constitutive parts of a historical narrative or archive. I argue that at Tempelhof, void was clearly defined by a relative lack of personal(ised) items that could have belonged to the forced labourers, which is, of course, also an issue of preservation and political taphonomy (see above).

We know of such items from other sites, where excavations yielded a series of artefacts that clearly display a makeshift character, indicating how things had been turned into personal objects. Among the finds from Buchenwald, for example, is a 'ruler-comb' – a comb someone had cut out for her/himself from a plastic ruler (Shalev-Gerz 2006). At the concentration camp Sachsenhausen, archaeologists excavated a small heart carved from a piece of wood; and a star that was cut from a thin metal sheet with a small hole in one tip, so that it could be hung up using a string or ribbon (Theune 2010, 6). For archaeologists, these finds convey not only a sense of everyday life, but they are also considered testimony to the self-determination of people who faced absolute physical and emotional deprivation. The resilience of those who endured life in the camp is maybe most immediately evidenced by improvised objects that were essential for a person's survival, like utensils for eating. Thus, at Sachsenhausen someone had used a discarded piece of plastic to fashion a knife, and a spoon had been forged from a broken metal handle (Theune 2011, 557–558; cf. Myers 2007).

Because the non-existence of certain things, such as personal(ised) items, is revealed only by the existence of other things, my discussion needs extension. After all, we did recover a large quantity of objects during our excavations at Tempelhof that looked quite impersonal to the unaccustomed eye, such as mass-produced bottles, porcelain dishes or fragments of tiles, most of which do not bear obvious traces of handling beyond their manufacture and their use in intended-for contexts. This observation builds the basis for my reflections on the forgetfulness[12] of things in the next section.

4.2. Absence as forgetfulness

As described above, we can well imagine that the personalised items from Buchenwald and Sachsenhausen might have given hope or comfort to a person in the past, but many artefacts from Tempelhof appear unnervingly neutral.

Building materials such as nails, screws and bolts are seemingly uninvolved things, while other finds, such as slag or pebbles, may not even be considered artefacts at all if we understand this term to refer to objects that have been manipulated by humans. They are, so to speak, characterised by a lack of traces of human practice. Yet, I argue that these things had a significant and active role to play in the historical processes we study.

This is not to say that the artefacts we found did something or made people in the past do something. In fact, I am far from a Latourian perspective that grants agency to material culture or understands things as 'actants' (Latour 1994, 33). I also find it futile to assign to an object the role of a co-culprit when we talk about the crimes committed by human agents. It is politically irresponsible to suggest that a thing – such as a gun – has the 'potential to take hold of passersby and force them to play roles in its story' (Latour 1994, 31). But it is true that we involve objects in our actions and that they can be enabling or disenabling for human practice, so that object and subject are linked in what Latour calls a symmetrical translation. As he writes, 'You are another subject because you hold the gun; the gun is another object because it has entered into a relationship with you' (Latour 1999, 179). Seemingly neutral artefacts can become alarmingly oppressive in a larger context of violent practice – the nails holding up the wooden walls of a flimsily built hut that can hardly protect against the cold of a harsh Berlin winter; the pebbles on the stony paths between the huts whose sharp edges cut into the insufficiently soled shoes of a prisoner.

The forgetfulness of things unfurls at the moment when this context changes and with it our experience of the objects. In other words, what is absent today is the social context of an object's deployment, including the motivations of those who decided to build flimsy huts. When we interpret the excavated artefacts as nothing other than unengaged things, their part in the story does not convey itself to us.

4.3. *Absence as loss*

Although it is true that very few personal items have been found at Tempelhof, a number of finds exhibit clear traces of having been manipulated by an individual. These objects, however, were later lost or forsaken and finally got buried in the ground. And while the life cycle of the lost or forsaken thing has been interrupted, the artefact, once unearthed, still bears conspicuous traces of past human practice. In a reversal of the circumstances encountered with the non-things and the forgetful things described above, it is now the existence of an object that manifests the absence of a person – an absence that we experience as loss.

At least one such item has been found during our excavations, although it cannot with certainty be assigned to the context of the Lufthansa camp because it was collected from the fire-fighting pond in Area 2. However, it is possible that this item was discarded from the camp. The object is a fragment of acrylic glass, in which someone had drilled a flower pattern and inscribed the name 'Ursula' twice, one time only half-completed. One edge of the glass shows additional traces of drilling, resulting in an irregular outline (Figure 5). A second name was scratched onto the back of the glass, suggestive of the signature of someone called '[J]ames', with a drawn-out 's'. This signature displays a different handwriting from the cursive of Ursula, maybe by a US soldier who found the glass fragment in Tempelhof, later adding his name to Ursula's.

The names on the glass are residues on a long gone object now recovered. We do not know who Ursula and James are (were), or whether they knew each other, and all they have left behind is merely a faint trace of their memory etched into the glass (cf. Olivier 2011). Just like the people in a photograph, they are there and simultaneously not there. This is the memory of loss – a memory of two 'absent makers who are remote in time and space, yet simultaneously active and present' (Latour 1999, 189).

5. Rethinking the archive

The agreed-upon focus in history and archaeology on those things that are present transmits to us, not unexpectedly, a notion of the archive as a storage place

Figure 5. Fragment of acrylic glass with drilled flower pattern and the name 'Ursula' (photo: Jessica Meyer, Landesdenkmalamt Berlin).

containing information on a series of events that have a clearly defined temporality, meaning each event happened prior, or subsequent to (and because of), another event. My proposed shift of focus towards absence allows me to reconsider this idea of temporality and reassess the associated understanding of historicity, according to which historical processes are best described by way of a more or less coherent narrative. Proposing instead that the archive forms around voids, losses and forgetfulness, the presence of absence in the archive makes itself felt through the lack of a stringent sequential temporality, through anachronisms, and through the shattering of direction in history (cf. Butler 2003).

In response to this insight, my reflections on the history of Tempelhof are an attempt to not reproduce the kinds of narratives that require consistency. Moreover, because the absence of the archive is found between recollection and oblivion – between what has and has not been said, between what is and is not remembered – absence is in quite fundamental ways also about what we can potentially say or remember. If the goal is, as I have suggested at the beginning of this paper, not to represent absence, but to make it manifest, the question to pose at this moment is how to engage the future possibilities of the archive in politically accountable ways? How do we speak about the losses we encounter, the voids we are confronted with and our own as well as others' forgetting?

This, of course, has every bit to do with the power of historical narration and storytelling (cf. Moshenska 2010). I am aware that 'historical traces are inherently uneven, sources are not created equal' (Trouillot 1995, 47) – no matter whether they manifest absence or document presence. As I cannot divest myself of agency, in this paper I undoubtedly favour some archaeological traces over others, foreground certain cultural meanings and not others, pick out some historical events as significant but not others. While I maintain that the archaeological objects we have excavated are indeed retrieved from the liminal space between remembering and forgetting, an overshadowing concern is nonetheless that my perception of what constitutes an absence in the archaeological archive of Tempelhof derives from my expectations of what we *should* have found during our excavations, that is, of my own imaginations of the past.

The presence of objects as documents or data that inform us about the past is always constructed and archaeological processes of recovering, collecting and classifying artefacts are always selective; inadvertently, such practices create a hierarchy of value among objects that is both ideological and authoritative (Hamilakis 2010). Yet, the arguments against the production of coherent historical narratives voiced by a growing number of archaeologists (especially among those who study the contemporary past) are not merely intended as source criticism. Their focus on what González-Ruibal describes as 'the inherently partial, fragmentary, and therefore uncanny nature of the archaeological record' (2008, 251) reflects a political desire not to overcome a painful history, but to conjure up its ghostly presence instead.

Here an imminent risk remains, however, having to do with the danger of political misappropriations of a history marked by loss, trauma and absence.

Indeed, to recognise the fragmentary nature of the archaeological record brings into focus the issue that there are always as many stories as there are storytellers. Can we recount every single story or should we collapse a diversity of memories? González-Ruibal (2008, 250) argues decidedly against the need for multivocality and the introduction of ever more voices, stories and perspectives. He is right to contend that stories as such are not empowering. Indeed, stories can have the opposite effect when the telling of a story has a heavier toll on its teller than on the listeners, especially when a story intensifies trauma through recall (cf. Srivastava and Francis 2006). What is more, when we deal with the history of the Nazi Holocaust, there is the imminent danger that the circulation of revisionist stories brings about further victimisation. While in both of these cases our concern is for the survivors of the Holocaust, yet another aspect of misappropriation pertains to those who did not survive, especially if our stories are merely externalised representations of a painful history – a history that is 'theirs' more so than 'ours'.

This being said, issues of power over representation loom particularly large in archaeology given that the discipline revolves around constructions of a scientific practice as objective and an object-driven research technique. Excavation is at the core of this, as of any, archaeological project. The project at Tempelhof airfield is nevertheless committed to go beyond 'what is there' and grapple with the problems of void, forgetfulness and loss that I have outlined above. The approach is multidisciplinary and includes the collection of oral histories from former forced labourers as well as an ethnographic study of processes of scientific knowledge production (cf. Davidovic 2009; Davidovic-Walther 2011).[13] In addition, students who are part of the project are encouraged to keep diaries, in which they record their personal reflections on our work at Tempelhof. These diaries in particular throw into sharp relief how on a personal and emotional level we may be deeply affected by the realisation that we excavate contexts marked by absences and voids, while as archaeologists we feel the need to continue to produce coherent historical narratives that centre on the presence of certain things and people. Thus, the diary entries criticise in particular how scientific techniques of sorting, counting and measuring the fragmentary vestiges we are left with create a false sense of presence, and that by doing so they transform past subjects, now absent, into objects (cf. Bernbeck 2010).[14]

This only demonstrates that if we want to engage in politically accountable practices of summoning the absences contained in the archaeological archive, we must be careful not to seize a painful heritage and repackage it as an archaeological commodity. As I have argued, objects that manifest absence are particularly important in this context, because of the negative spaces they embody – that is, they speak not to what happened but to 'what has been prevented from ever taking place [...] the sum of thoughts unthought, of unfelt feelings, of works never accomplished, of lives unlived to their natural end' (Gross 2001, xv). In manifesting that which has been denied to or taken from others in the past, such objects make it impossible for us to decouple recollections of the past from issues of oppression, exploitation and disenfranchisement in history. Consequently, the objects – and the absences they hold – have the potential to become points of reference for collective activism in the present and future, responding to political violence by turning privatised pain into a shared experience of struggle and survival (Crossland 2002; Eng and Kazanjian 2003; González-Ruibal 2007).

Acknowledgements

This paper has benefited considerably from discussions with a number of people, who have variously supported my interest in an archaeology of forced labour camps. Only able to mention some of them, I would like to thank Helga Vogel for engaged comments on an earlier draft of this paper; Reinhard Bernbeck and Susan Pollock, as well as two anonymous reviewers, for productive criticism and necessary revisions; John Roby for pertinent clarifications and, as ever, for invaluable extensions, such as his linking of memory and commodification. I also thank Nilufar Reichel for taking the time for several perceptive conversations, which contributed much to the last section of the paper. Ed Collins reviewed the parts of my text that describe the archaeological contexts in Areas 1 and 2, and he provided Figure 3. Jessica Meyer produced brilliant photographs, a small selection of which is published in this paper. Thanks is also due to the students, who worked with me at Tempelhof, for their sincere commitment to a difficult subject matter and field praxis.

Notes

1. The excavation project, which was initiated by Susan Pollock and Reinhard Bernbeck, is being conducted as collaboration between Freie Universität Berlin and the Landesdenkmalamt Berlin since 2012. The project is funded by the Berlin Senate and supported by the Senatsverwaltung für Stadtentwicklung und Umwelt. The first excavations at Tempelhof airfield were carried out over a period of eight months in the summer and autumn of 2012. Between June and December 2012, I participated in the project as a research associate, being primarily responsible for the documentation and initial analysis of the archaeological artefacts. The second season of archaeological work at the site began in the spring of 2013 and was still ongoing at the time of completion of this paper in September 2013.
2. A 'Labour Day' had first been advocated in 1919 by the Social Democratic Party (SPD), the German Democratic Party (DDP) and some members of the Center Party (Zentrum), but the relevant legislation did not find a majority in parliament.
3. Not all workers of the Weserflug GmbH were housed in the huts on Tempelhof airfield, however. Some foreign civilian workers, and otherwise mostly German workers, lived in tenement buildings in Berlin, mainly in the districts of Moabit and Neukölln (Heisig 2012, 50).
4. The contexts from Trench 2 in Area 1 are not discussed in detail here, because with the exception of a small piece of a foundation wall belonging to one of the accommodation huts, they seem to mostly predate the Lufthansa camp by about 70 years. The majority of remains uncovered in Trench 2, including the outlines of former graves, stems from a time when the area was used as a military cemetery, starting in around 1870.
5. Beate Winzer of the Berliner Geschichtswerkstatt e.V. has kindly directed our attention to the cost and construction report from the Bundesarchiv (federal archives) (BArchiv R 4606/4891, Akte III Rü d 1 [1073]).
6. In Figure 3, the AutoCAD plan that was generated during our excavations has been plotted over the original construction plan (BArch R 4606/4891, Akte III Rü d 1 [1074]).

7. The aerial reconnaissance photograph can be accessed through the historical imagery view of Google Earth.
8. The value of integrating different types of historical sources, including archaeological information, is particularly apparent here. In addition to the cost report and the construction plan (both documents dating from 1942), a plan of the whole airfield from 1943 exists (TU Berlin Architekturmuseum Inv.-Nr. 42544). This hand-drawn plan by Ernst Sagebiel on a scale of 1:4000 shows a total of six accommodation huts.
9. See, for example, the excavations at a former forced labour and external concentration camp next to the factories of the Dreilinden Maschinenbau GmbH, a subsidiary of the Robert Bosch AG in Kleinmachnow, southwest of Berlin (Antkowiak 2003). In Kleinmachnow, the wooden walls of the huts were constructed on top of a brick course, which was laid on concrete strip foundations.
10. *Kochmaschinen* were common features in German open-plan kitchen-living rooms until the 1950s. These were stoves that were clad with tiles, had two cast-iron cooktops of adjustable size and were heated with wood or coal; the ash could be removed through a hatch on the side of the stove.
11. Because the analysis of the recorded artefacts is ongoing, I cannot yet provide data on the exact number of finds or their distribution across the site. The estimated number of finds ranges around 18,000 objects and it is clear that the density of artefacts varies considerably between different excavation areas, with Area 1 yielding a relatively low number of finds compared to Area 2.
12. Reinhard Bernbeck, having read an earlier version of the paper, suggested this term to me.
13. The ethnographic project is carried out under the direction of Antonia Davidovic of Christian-Albrechts-Universität zu Kiel.
14. Moshenska, who excavated a Nazi POW camp in Silesia, had a similar experience when survivors of the camp who came to visit the site 'appeared to find the bagging and labelling of finds particularly discomforting and repeatedly challenged us about it' (2006, 63).

References

Agamben, Giorgio. 1999. *Remnants of Auschwitz: The Witness and the Archive*. New York: Zone Books.

Aly, Götz, Peter Chroust, and Christian Pross. 1994. *Cleansing the Fatherland: Nazi Medicine and Racial Hygiene*. Baltimore, MD: Johns Hopkins University Press.

Antkowiak, Matthias. 2003. "Struktur eines Rüstungsbetriebes: Barackenlager in Kleinmachnow, Landkreis Potsdam-Mittelmark." In *Jahrbuch Archäologie in Berlin und Brandenburg 2002*, edited by Archäologische Gesellschaft in Berlin und Brandenburg e.V., 165–167. Stuttgart: Konrad Theiss Verlag.

Assatzk, Mirko. 2012. "Die militärische Nutzung des Tempelhofer Feldes unter der nationalsozialistischen Herrschaft." In *Kein Ort der Freiheit – Das Tempelhofer Feld 1933–1945: Konzentrationslager – Luftwaffenstützpunkt – Rüstungszentrum*, edited by Berliner Geschichtswerkstatt e.V., 11–19. Berlin: Bunter Hund.

Assmann, Jan. 1992. *Das kulturelle Gedächtnis: Schrift, Erinnerung und politische Identität in frühen Hochkulturen*. München: C.H. Beck.
Beaudry, Mary C., Lauren J. Cook, and Stephen A. Mrozowski. 1996. "Artifacts and Active Voices: Material Culture as Social Discourse." In *Images of the Recent Past: Readings in Historical Archaeology*, edited by Charles E. Orser, 272–310. Walnut Creek, CA: AltaMira Press.
Bernbeck, Reinhard. 2005. "The Past as Fact and Fiction: From Historical Novels to Novel Histories." In *Archaeologies of the Middle East: Critical Perspectives*, edited by Susan Pollock, and Reinhard Bernbeck, 97–122. Oxford: Blackwell.
Bernbeck, Reinhard. 2010. "'La Jalousie' und Archäologie: Plädoyer für subjektloses Erzählen." *EAZ – Ethnographisch-Archäologische Zeitschrift* 51 (1–2): 64–86.
Bille, Mikkel, Frieda Hastrup, and Tim Flohr Sørensen, eds. 2003. *An Anthropology of Absence: Materializations of Transcendence and Loss*. New York: Springer.
Buchli, Victor, and Gavin Lucas, eds. 2001. *Archaeologies of the Contemporary Past*. New York: Routledge.
Budraß, Lutz. 2001. *Die Lufthansa und ihre ausländischen Arbeiter im Zweiten Weltkrieg*. Frankfurt am Main: Deutsche Lufthansa AG.
Butler, Judith. 2003. "Afterword: After Loss, What Then?" In *Loss: The Politics of Mourning*, edited by David L. Eng, and David Kazanjian, 467–473. Berkeley: University of California Press.
Coppi, Hans. 2012. "Für einen Gedenk- und Lernort auf dem Tempelhofer Feld: Erinnerung an Propaganda, Terror und militärische Mobilmachung." In *Kein Ort der Freiheit – Das Tempelhofer Feld 1933–1945: Konzentrationslager – Luftwaffenstützpunkt – Rüstungszentrum*, edited by Berliner Geschichtswerkstatt e.V., 7–9. Berlin: Bunter Hund.
Crossland, Zoe. 2002. "Violent Spaces: Conflict over the Reappearance of Argentina's Disappeared." In *Matériel Culture: The Archaeology of Twentieth-Century Conflict*, edited by John Schofield, William Gray Johnson, and Colleen M. Beck, 115–131. New York: Routledge.
Davidovic, Antonia. 2009. *Praktiken archäologischer Wissensproduktion: Eine kulturanthropologische Wissenschaftsforschung*. Münster: Ugarit Verlag.
Davidovic-Walther, Tonia. 2011. "Die Herstellung archäologischen Wissens: Praxen und Interaktionen." *Zeitschrift für Volkskunde* 107 (1): 49–64.
Dejnega, Melanie, and Claudia Theune. Forthcoming. "Das Sanitätslager in Wort, Bild und Objekt: Warum die Zusammenarbeit von HistorikerInnen und ArchäologInnen Sinn macht." In *Leben und Überleben in Mauthausen. Vol. 2: Mauthausen überleben und erinnern*, edited by Alexander Prenninger, Regina Fritz, Gerhard Botz, and Eva Brücker.
Eng, David, and David Kazanjian. 2003. *Loss: The Politics of Mourning*. Berkeley: University of California Press.
Fowles, Severin. 2010. "People Without Things." In *An Anthropology of Absence: Materializations of Transcendence and Loss*, edited by Mikkel Bille, Frieda Hastrup, and Tim Flohr Sørensen, 23–41. New York: Springer.
González-Ruibal, Alfredo. 2007. "Making Things Public: Archaeologies of the Spanish Civil War." *Public Archaeology* 6 (4): 203–226.
González-Ruibal, Alfredo. 2008. "Time to Destroy: An Archaeology of Supermodernity." *Current Anthropology* 49 (2): 247–279.
Gross, Jan T. 2001. *Neighbors: The Destruction of the Jewish Community in Jedwabne, Poland*. Princeton, NJ: Princeton University Press.
Hamilakis, Yannis. 2010. "Re-Collecting the Fragments: Archaeology as Mnemonic Practice." In *Material Mnemonics: Everyday Memory in Prehistoric Europe*, edited by Katina T. Lillios, and Vasileios Tsamis, 188–199. Oxford: Oxbow.

Heisig, Matthias. 2012. "Die 'Weser' Flugzeugbau GmbH auf dem Flughafen Tempelhof – Rüstungsproduktion und Zwangsarbeit für den Krieg." In *Kein Ort der Freiheit – Das Tempelhofer Feld 1933–1945: Konzentrationslager – Luftwaffenstützpunkt – Rüstungszentrum*, edited by Berliner Geschichtswerkstatt e.V., 43–61. Berlin: Bunter Hund.

Latour, Bruno. 1994. "On Technical Mediation: Philosophy, Sociology, Genealogy." *Common Knowledge* 3 (2): 29–64.

Latour, Bruno. 1999. *Pandora's Hope: Essays on the Reality of Science Studies*. Cambridge, MA: Harvard University Press.

Levi, Primo. 1996. *Survival in Auschwitz: The Nazi Assault on Humanity*. New York: Simon & Schuster.

Meyer, Morgan. 2012. "Placing and Tracing Absence: A Material Culture of the Immaterial." *Journal of Material Culture* 17 (1): 103–110.

Moshenska, Gabriel. 2006. "Scales of Memory in the Archaeology of the Second World War." *Papers from the Institute of Archaeology* 17: 58–68.

Moshenska, Gabriel. 2010. "Working with Memory in the Archaeology of Modern Conflict." *Cambridge Archaeological Journal* 20 (1): 33–48.

Myers, Adrian T. 2007. "Portable Material Culture and Death Factory Auschwitz." *Papers from the Institute of Archaeology* 18: 57–69.

Olivier, Laurent. 2011. *Dark Abyss of Time: Memory and Archaeology*. Walnut Creek, CA: AltaMira Press.

Pollock, Susan, and Reinhard Bernbeck. Forthcoming. "A Gate to a Darker World: Excavating at the Tempelhof Airport." In *Ethics, Archaeology and Violence*, edited by Alfredo González-Ruibal, and Gabriel Moshenska.

Pophanken, Hartmut. 2000. *Gründung und Ausbau der "Weser" Flugzeugbau GmbH 1933 bis 1939: Unternehmerisches Entscheidungshandeln im Kontext der nationalsozialistischen Luftrüstung*. Bremen: Hauschild H.M. GmbH.

Shalev-Gertz, Esther. 2006. *MenschenDinge = The Human Aspect of Objects*. Weimar: Stiftung Gedenkstätten Buchenwald und Mittelbau-Dora.

Srivastava, Sarita, and Margot Francis. 2006. "The Problem of 'Authentic Experience': Storytelling in Anti-Racist and Anti-Homophobic Education." *Critical Sociology* 32 (2–3): 275–307.

Theune, Claudia. 2010. "Historical Archaeology in National Socialist Concentration Camps in Central Europe." *Historische Archäologie* 2. http://www.histarch.uni-kiel.de/2010_Theune_low.pdf

Theune, Claudia. 2011. "Das Gedächtnis der Dinge." In *Politische Gewalt und Machtausübung im 20. Jahrhundert: Zeitgeschichte, Zeitgeschehen und Kontroversen*, edited by Heinrich Berger, Melanie Dejnega, Regina Fritz, and Alexander Prenninger, 543–560. Wien: Böhlau.

Trouillot, Michel-Rolph. 1995. *Silencing the Past: Power and the Production of History*. Boston, MA: Beacon Press.

Wenz, F.-Herbert. 2000. *Flughafen Tempelhof: Chronik des Berliner Werkes der "Weser" Flugzeugbau GmbH Bremen – Bau der Kriegsflugzeuge Ju 87-Stuka und Fw 190 1939–1945*. Lemwerder: Stedinger Verlag.

Zentek, Sabine. 2009. *Designer im Dritten Reich: Gute Formen sind eine Frage der richtigen Haltung*. Dortmund: Lelesken-Verlag.

Jewish Haifa denies its Arab past

Gilad Margalit

Department of General History, University of Haifa, Haifa, Israel

Haifa developed from a small Arab town in the late Ottoman period into a Jewish-Arab urban centre in British Palestine. Today it is a Jewish city with a small Arab minority. In April 1948, following the Jewish conquest of the city, most of its Arab population fled. Israel's Zionist leadership took advantage of their flight and decided to demolish much of the old city, founded in 1761 by the Arab ruler of the Galilee, Daher el-Omar. In 2011, the municipality of the City of Haifa, as well as the majority of the city's Jewish population, all but ignored Haifa's 250th anniversary. The article critically discusses and contextualises the official, Zionist memory of the city's past and explores alternative Jewish attempts to commemorate Haifa's Arab heritage.

In 1946, during the final years of the British mandate in Palestine, Haifa had a population of 145,430, of whom 48.9% were Arabs. From November 1947, growing tensions between Jews and Arabs prompted Arab residents to leave the city. Most of the remaining Arab population – about 65,000 people – fled after the Jewish victory and military occupation of Haifa's Arab neigbourhoods in April 1948, with only around 3500 Arabs remaining in Haifa (Goren and Ben Arzi 1998). As early as June 1948, the Israelis started to consolidate a policy that prevented most refugees from returning to their homes within the state of Israel (Morris 2004, 309–340). Since 1948, the population of Haifa has again grown, but most newcomers have been Jewish immigrants, with only a few thousand Palestinian refugees returning after 1948.

The local manifestation of the Jewish–Arab conflict and the consequences of the military victory in 1948 do not loom large in the public statements of the mayor of Haifa, Yona Yahav. He often refers to Haifa as 'a city of coexistence'. 'For over a hundred years, orthodox Jews, secular Jews, Christian and Muslim Arabs, Baha'i and people of other religions all lived in harmony, as good neighbors', he writes on the city's website (Yahav, n.d.). 'There is a history of coexistence, and there is almost no history of trauma here', he was reported as saying in 2006 (Kesler 2006). 'There were no religious wars here. It's no more than a fishermen's village that has evolved into a thriving town'.

Modern Haifa was founded in 1761 by the Arab ruler of the Galilee, Daher el-Omar. But in 2011, neither the mayor nor the local government saw the need to commemorate the city's 250th birthday. Only the local Arab community, and Zochrot, a small radical-left, mostly Jewish organisation, celebrated the anniversary: Palestinian community organisations staged an event at the al-Midan theater and curated a moving exhibition of paintings: 'Haifa Through The Eyes of Its Children'; Zochrot conducted a guided tour through the remains of the old city and erected signs commemorating the former names of the quarter.

In this article, I explore hegemonic local Israeli-Jewish memory politics and practices regarding the city's Arab past, on the one hand, and, on the other, attempts by Jewish radicals to promote 'an alternative memory to the hegemonic Zionist memory' (Musih 2005). In doing so, I wish to question the predominant image of Haifa as a city characterised by a unique Jewish-Palestinian relationship. The official and non-official promoters of this image use the term *Du–Kium* ('coexistence'), which has been borrowed from the vocabulary of the Cold War, as a synonym for an exceptional form of tolerance – one of the Jewish majority towards the Palestinian minority.

I am a professional historian, but my writing about the town where I was born, grew up and still live today is not impartial and emotionally charged. Nevertheless, I trust that my personal recollections are helpful for gaining a better understanding of collective memory-making against the backdrop of a national conflict in a contested territory.

The *damnatio memoriae* of Haifa's old city

The official silence about Haifa's 250th anniversary is symptomatic of Israel's political memory. The Jewish majority in Israel and its political representatives tend to regard Israel as an exclusive nation state of the Jewish people, and not as a state of all its citizens. Therefore, most government agencies and many other public bodies give preferential treatment to Jews, while at the same time deliberately neglecting, or even discriminating against, Palestinian citizens, whose concerns and memories are regarded as irrelevant. This practice contradicts the very promise of democratic equality for all citizens regardless of their ethnic origins, which was contained in Israel's 1948 Declaration of Independence (Smooha 1997; Yiftachel 2006).

The municipal government of Haifa regards itself as a custodian of the hegemonic Zionist narrative. It identified the 250th anniversary as a component of a competing, if not hostile, Palestinian narrative that needed to be suppressed. The local government perceives the city as a solely Jewish-Zionist entity in space and in time; therefore, only those events that pertain directly to Jews are inscribed in the official history of the city. When the mayor refers to 'coexistence', he, much like the majority of the Jewish population in Haifa and, for that matter, in Israel generally, means a form of coexistence that preserves the present state of power relations between a strong Jewish majority and a weak Israeli-Palestinian minority. The coexistence formula enables the Jewish majority to preserve and exercise their prerogatives as members of the dominant group and, at the same time, to feel enlightened and liberal regarding their Israeli-Palestinian fellow citizens who have been the object of their discrimination. According to this formula, the Israeli-Palestinian minority in Haifa should accept its subaltern status vis-à-vis the Jewish majority, even with respect to the history of the city's non-Jewish beginnings in the eighteenth century.

The local government may have wanted to ignore the city's anniversary also because it did not want to draw attention to what had happened to the historical nucleus of the city of Haifa during the 1948 war. In early May 1948, a local committee for Arab affairs, which had been established on 24 April, following the Arab defeat and the mass Arab exodus from Haifa, had produced a memorandum titled 'Urgent improvement works in Haifa'. In it, the committee observed that the 'evacuation' of the Arab neighbourhoods provided

> an exceptional opportunity to carry out preservation works involving destruction. [...] The expected waves of [Jewish] immigrants and the return of many of the Arabs who had left the city, should goad us to take all the required measures without delay. (Cited in Goren 1994, 61)

The memorandum strongly recommended to make use of the opportunity because it 'might not recur in our generation'.

In May 1948, David Ben-Gurion, Israel's first prime minister, visited Haifa and was briefed about the planned 'improvement works'. He told the Jewish mayor, Shabtai Levi, to execute them. However, Levi was reluctant to do so because he feared that the demolition would expose the municipality to claims for compensation. Therefore, Levi suggested to Ben-Gurion to follow precedents from the late Ottoman period regarding similar projects in Jaffa and Damascus, whereby the Ottoman central government was responsible for the implementation of developments that involved demolition (Levi 1978). Ben-Gurion accepted Levi's recommendation and, in his capacity as the Minister of Defence, ordered a unit of the Israeli army to carry out the demolition. The destruction took place between June and October 1948. Ben-Gurion instructed the Israeli army not to harm any house of worship, so the mosques and churches were spared. Ironically, six synagogues in the Harat al-Yahud, the Jewish quarter within the old city, were demolished (Khalfon 1978, 60–62). The Jewish inhabitants of this quarter had abandoned it in 1938 as a result of Arab violence during the Arab revolt.

The official excuse for the wide-ranging demolition was the allegedly urgent need to implement a town plan that had been designed by the British in 1943. It aimed to modernise Haifa by demolishing parts of the old city and building a central boulevard that would dissect the city centre from west to east. However, the destruction in 1948 by Israeli army units grossly exceeded the requirements of the 1943 plan. More than 220 buildings were razed to the ground, most of which had been abandoned by their Arab residents when they had fled the city. The destruction left an ugly scar in the middle of the city, which never healed; contrary to the initial plans, no new buildings replaced those that had been torn down. I would like to suggest that Ben-Gurion's decision to demolish part of the old city stemmed from his desire to seize the opportunity created by the flight of the majority of the Arab population in April 1948 and to prevent the return of the Palestinian refugees, rather than from a deep urge to modernise Haifa.

On 15 September 1948, the newspaper *Davar*, the organ of the trade union organisation Histadrut, praised the demolition as a positive contribution to the city's development and as an improvement of its residents' living conditions:

> [T]he farsighted could already envisage fully lighted and ventilated houses instead of the old city's current shady houses. Those listening attentively would recognize within the sounds of the detonations and the roar of the bulldozers demolishing dilapidated walls, the jovial sounds of new and healthy generations that would grow up in this neighbourhood. They would appreciate that one demolishes only to re-build in better conditions. (Menachem 1948)

The old and densely built Arab quarter would have represented to Ben-Gurion and Levi a backward Oriental urban space which did not suit the futuristic vision of Haifa as a Zionist city. In his 1902 novel *Altneuland*, Theodor Herzl had already envisaged Haifa as a modern, clean urban space in the spirit of European urban planning maxims of the last decades of the nineteenth century. Herzl wrote of a 'magnificent city [...] built beside the sapphire-blue Mediterranean' where '[t]housands of white villas gleamed out of luxuriant green gardens' (Herzl 1987, 58). In the sixth chapter of his novel, he described his protagonists' visit to Jaffa, the first oriental urban space that they had encountered in Palestine:

> Jaffa made a very unpleasant impression upon them. Though nobly situated on the blue Mediterranean, the town was in a state of extreme decay. [...] The alleys were dirty, neglected, full of vile odors. Everywhere misery in bright Oriental rags. Poor Turks, dirty Arabs, timid Jews lounged about – indolent, beggarly, hopeless. A peculiar, tomblike odor of mold caught one's breath. (Herzl 1987, 42)

Other national and local Zionist leaders shared Herzl's Central European aesthetic preferences, and adopted and internalised the orientalist rejection and scorn for the oriental urban space, which they regarded as ugly, filthy and backward (Raz-Krakotzkin 1993, 44–46, 1999, 44–48). Shabtai Levi, Haifa's first Jewish mayor, who was born and grew up in Istanbul, wrote about Haifa: 'As any other oriental town it consisted of a complex of dense and stinking alleys' (1978, 80). The disdain for the Arab heritage that national and local Zionist leaders shared did not necessarily result in wholesale destruction; in the 1960s and 1970s, the former Arab neighbourhood adjacent to the old city, Wadi Salib, was deliberately neglected, which led to the collapse of many of its buildings (Weiss 2011).

The idea that the Arabs and their culture were primitive and backward, however, was only one aspect of a highly ambivalent Zionist attitude towards the Arabs and the Orient. As non-modern native dwellers of the Holy Land, the Arabs served for the early Zionists, as well as for many Christian pilgrims, as living fossils who had preserved the way of life, clothing and agriculture of the Jews of antiquity. Raz-Krakotzkin (1999, 44–46) has argued that both aspects reflect an orientalist approach in the Saidian sense. While the Arab was objectified as an authentic relic of times gone by and even as a model for a brand-new native Hebrew identity that was meant to be distinct from anything in the Jewish diaspora (Berlovits 1996, 113–166; Eyal 2006, 33–61), the romantic mystification of a seemingly timeless Arab material culture led to the preservation of some elements of the oriental urban and rural landscape of Arab Palestine. The Zionists' ambivalence towards the oriental city is reflected in a statement made in 1952 by the Custodian of Absentees' Property, Mordechai Shatner, who suggested that parts of the former Palestinian cities be also preserved due to their historical and aesthetic value, even though he attributed these to a pre-Muslim past:

> We have to turn the abandoned cities into developed modern cities, places that we could achieve only if we build modern houses in all the vacant yards and empty lots in these cities. Over time, those place would acquire similar characters as the cities built by the Jewish *Yishuv* [the pre-state Zionist settlement in Palestine]. Certain parts such as the old city of Acre, a part of the old city of Jaffa and more, would remain in their current condition and would serve as a living museum in the state. (Cited in Berger 1998, 62)

In the first years of the young and poor state, Israel experienced a chronic lack of accommodation for the masses of Jewish immigrants, and many of them were therefore housed in abandoned Arab villages (Kadman 2008, 24–27). A suggestion raised in Cabinet in the early 1950s to adopt construction methods taken from the Arab vernacular architecture in order to lower the construction costs and also to accelerate the supply of viable accommodation solutions for the immigrants, instead of accommodating them in tents and tin shacks, was rejected. In a cabinet meeting in June 1952, the prime minister concluded the discussion on such alternative construction solutions to the problem of accommodation by saying: 'This is not a land for wooden houses, or for clay houses or for stone houses' (cited in Efrat 2001). By negating such alternative construction materials, methods and styles, Ben-Gurion articulated the hegemonic Zionist modernist architectural vision of the period, a modernist architectural vision of concrete and cement.[1] Apart from some exceptions, this vision sentenced most of the Arab vernacular architecture to demolition and neglect.

An interest in the vernacular architecture developed only gradually: first among Israeli bohemians and artists, and later among architects who criticised the vagueness and detachment of the modernist style that dominated local architecture from the 1930s and replaced the eclectic style of the 1910s and 1920s which had incorporated oriental elements. The Israeli architect Zvi Efrat correctly observed:

> [T]he fondness that the [Jewish] Israeli elites manifest for Arab property and landscape, reflects beyond the [involved] business intuition, a romantic longing for

anything that might represent an authentic nativeness – A yearning that has percolated beneath the official modernist press, in the Jewish [modern] *Yishuv*, since its very beginning. (Efrat 2001)

A very central figure in this cultural development was the architect and Dadaist artist, Marcel Janco (see Slyomovics 1998, 31–38). In 1953, as an official of the Ministry of the Interior, he happened upon the impending demolition of the Arab village Ein Khud by the Israeli army. Janco stopped the demolition and initiated the establishment of an artists' colony in the village which received the Hebrew name Ein Hod. Significantly, Janco justified his fondness for the vernacular Arab architecture of Ein Khud by attributing to it a pre-Arab, in fact European, antiquity. He claimed:

I could realize as an architect and an artist, that this was not just an ordinary Arab village, but an ancient historical settlement. There were huge stones there, stones that only the Romans had used for construction. (Cited in Yoffe 1982, 75–76)

In this respect, Janco was no exception; Benvenisti (2000, 169) claims that the invention of non-Arab 'glorious histories' for impressive Palestinian buildings which survived demolition is widespread in Israel.

Later Janco was involved in the protests against the plans to demolish the old Arab city of Jaffa and in attempts to preserve other old Arab quarters in Israel. The advocacy of Janco and others contributed not only to the ascent of Arab vernacular architecture but also to the appreciation of the modern Arab architecture of the 1920s, 1930s and 1940s. It became 'chic' – first among Jewish-Israeli bohemians, and then among other Jewish elites – to live in an 'Arab house'. This re-evaluation had an effect on the real estate market and led to the gentrification of quarters such as the former bourgeois Arab quarters of West Jerusalem (Talbieh, Bakaa and Katamon) where the well-heeled Jewish bourgeoisie replaced the former poor Arab or, more usually, poor Jewish residents who had been accommodated in the abandoned property of bourgeois Palestinian families after 1948. This development also reached certain parts of Haifa's former Arab neighbourhoods. It contributed to the development of public awareness in Israel about the value of old buildings, including Arab ones. I suspect that today a considerable portion of the Israeli intelligentsia would regard the demolition of Haifa's old city as a barbaric act. Most of them, however, due to their identification with the Zionist cause, might try *post factum* to justify it as an existential need of the young Jewish state in 1948.

The Zionist establishment initiated another symbolic expression of *damnatio memoriae* for the conquered Arab space, which transformed it into a Zionist space. In 1951 the municipal administration renamed about 40 streets in the centre of the Arab quarters of the city. For example, Khmra Square, named after a famous Arab family, became Paris Square; Mukhalis Street, named after the Palestinian educator, became I.L. Peretz Street (after the famous Yiddish poet); Salach A-Din Street became HaGiborim Street (the 'Street of the Heroes', referring to the forces that had conquered the Arab quarters of Haifa; see Azaryahu 1993, 102–104). These changes were not comprehensive: While today more than 300 streets in Haifa honour names and terms related to *Tkumat Israel* ('the Revival of Israel'), commemorating, for example, Zionist leaders or Israeli Defence Force units, 71 streets are named after Arab personalities. However, most of them are located in the predominantly Arab neighbourhoods of the city, such as Wadi Nisnas, or in other streets with mostly Israeli-Palestinians residents. Most of them were named before 1947. When representatives of the Arab community requested that Daher el-Omar be honoured by naming a street after him, the municipal naming committee acceded to their request but chose a small cul-de-sac in Haifa al Atika, an outer suburb, rather than a main street in the old city which he had founded in 1761.

All these practices were not unique to Haifa but were implemented in most of the so-called mixed cities which were occupied by the Jews in the 1948 war, including Jaffa (Rotbard 2005, 200–205) and Tiberias (where the destruction was more significant than in Haifa), as well as in occupied Arab towns such Lydda (Lod), Ramla and Magdal (Monterescu and Rabinowitz 2007, 15–17). These practices could also be observed in the former Palestinian rural space, where villages from which their inhabitants had been expelled or had fled received Jewish names (Kadman 2008, 50–63).

Nevertheless – and this is probably one of Haifa's peculiarities – more recently, the municipal administration named a few streets after prominent local and national Arab leaders, prominent anti-Zionists, such as the Greek Catholic Bishop of the Galilee during the first half of the twentieth century, Gregorios Hajjar, as well as national Communist leaders, such as the historian Emil Tuma and the author Emil Habibi. However, this is a marginal phenomenon – a handful of such names within hundreds of Jewish street names – and an exception that confirms the rule. In spite of their anti-Zionist stance, Arab Communists, as opposed to the nationalists, adopted in 1948 the Soviet position and supported the foundation of the Zionist state. Until the end of the Cold War, the state of Israel did not allow the establishment of an Arab nationalist party; under these circumstances, the Israeli Communist party Maki became the only legitimate anti-Zionist political party that appealed to Israeli Arabs. The honoured personalities were also mostly Christians. The Zionist establishment was aware that western public opinion was more concerned about Christian than about Muslim communities in the Holy Land; at the same time, some Zionist leaders erroneously assumed that due to the influence of European Christianity, Christian Palestinians had adopted a more moderate attitude towards Zionism than Muslim Palestinians.

A Haifa socialisation

I was born in 1959 in Haifa into an Ashkenazi Jewish family. At the time, the city had about 180,000 inhabitants, of whom only 5.1% were non-Jewish. Both my parents were members of the *Dor Tashach*, the generation of 1948; as students at Hebrew University, they had joined the Palmach, the elite fighting force of the Haganah, and participated in the 1948 war in the battles on the Jerusalem front. They sharply criticised Ben-Gurion's and his party's policies from a left-wing Zionist stance. However, by blaming Ben-Gurion for the lack of peace with the Arab countries, they exculpated the Socialist Zionist opposition to his government of their responsibilities and ignored the consensual policies and practices advocated by their own political circles.

Both my parents had working relationships with Israeli-Palestinians. At home, my father often talked about his Israeli-Palestinian colleagues and acquaintance. I knew that my parents attended their celebrations, but they never came to our own, and very seldom visited our house. I can recall only very few occasions when I accompanied my parents to visit their Israeli-Palestinian colleagues. Some of them I met for the first time during the *Shivaa* – the seven-day mourning period – for my father, when they visited my mother to comfort her. The only Arabs I personally knew as a child were our cleaning women and the handymen who occasionally carried out maintenance work at our house.

My mother, whose parents had emigrated in 1936 from Poland to Palestine, grew up in Haifa. But I do not recall her talking during my childhood about the old city, although recently she told me about going to the *casbah* in the old city in the 1940s, until a Jew was killed there by Arabs. During my childhood I knew nothing of the Palestinian history of my hometown. The circuses which then used to come regularly to Haifa erected their large tents in the expansive open space in the heart of the downtown area, where, unbeknownst to me at the time, much of the old city had been prior to its destruction in 1948. The only building I knew of the few that remained of the old city was the *kishle* (prison), which my mother pointed out to me as she had been imprisoned there in 1947 by the British for illegal activities.

Another memory I have is of schoolteachers reciting Levi Shabtai's plea to Haifa's Arab dignitaries in April 1948 after the Jewish conquest; he urged them to stay, but they did not want to sign a document of surrender and chose to leave the city. My teachers usually ignored the fact that since the summer of 1948, the state of Israel did not allow Arab refugees to return and that their houses – if they had not been demolished – were expropriated and handed over to Jewish immigrants.

In 1967, during my third year at school, we learnt about Haifa. I remember that I was excited about this part of the curriculum because it meant going for visits into town and doing excursions to the port and to factories. We used a textbook, *Haifa – Our City* (Brin, Gutman-Katz, and Palti 1970); reading it again 45 years later, and as a historian, I was struck by the fact that the non-Jewish presence and non-Jewish contributions to Haifa's development from a small fishing village to a prosperous city are obscured, if not omitted altogether. The idyllic portrayal of a fishing village at the foot of Mount Carmel, with which the booklet begins, does not mention that its inhabitants were Arabs. In a passage that tries to convey a sense of excitement about the momentous changes that had occurred in Haifa's history, the authors also credit a British initiative to the Zionists:

> No longer a small village on the slopes of Mount Carmel, but a big, beautiful and prosperous city that grows and flourishes between the sea and the top of the mountain; its citizens, mostly Jewish, have come back to their homeland as their great leader Dr. Benjamin Zeev Herzl had envisaged. They and their sons have built a marvellous city and a big port. (Brin, Gutman-Katz, and Palti 1970, 5)

The British plan to build a modern port in 1931 was implemented mostly out of strategic considerations (Stern 1981); Haifa was regarded as a central station on the way to the Empire's colonies in the Middle and Far East. Later it also functioned as a gateway for Iraqi oil, which arrived by pipeline at Haifa Bay. The port also served as the headquarters of the British army in the Middle East. At least half of the workers who built the new port were Arabs. Much like Haifa's mayor on the city's website (Yahav, n.d.), the booklet refers to Haifa's religious diversity, but it does not make reference to different national or ethnic groups.

In 1990 the booklet was updated and republished. The new edition (Katz 1990) mentions the non-Jewish past of the city and omits the false attribution of the building of the port to Zionism. A new chapter has been added that deals with the history of the city's inhabitants and their national identity. It also discusses the dramatic consequences of the 1948 war; but the occupation of the Arab neighbourhoods of Haifa is still considered part of the 'liberation of the city'. The students are still asked, as they had been in 1955, to mark in colour with arrows the main advance routes of the Jewish 'liberator-occupiers'. In spite of the changes, the overall narrative has remained intact. Haifa is still portrayed as an exclusively Jewish and Zionist city. The building of new neighbourhoods is attributed only to Jews, although several Arab neighbourhoods were created during the period of the British mandate. There is a reference to the small community of German Templars who were expelled in 1947 and a leading question about their contribution to the development of Haifa – as if they had become a part of the Zionist enterprise (see also Yazbak 1999). No similar question refers to the Arab population.

An alternative Jewish memory

Zochrot was founded in Tel Aviv in 2002 with the slogan 'Nakba in Hebrew'. While its founders were Jews, Zochrot defines itself as a Jewish-Palestinian organisation and has Palestinian members. Its aim has been to ensure that the *Nakba*, the Palestinian tragedy of 1948, becomes part of the Hebrew lexicon and to promote an alternative to the hegemonic Zionist memory that denies and silences the Palestinian tragedy. The Hebrew term *zochrot* means 'we remember' in the feminine plural form of the verb. On its website, the organisation explains:

> The masculine form of remembering [*zochrim*], as presented in the Zionist discourse, is violent and nationalistic. Zochrot aims to promote another form of remembering, an alternative form that will enable the expression of other memories that are often kept silent. In addition, Zochrot makes an effort to create a space for the memory of women in the Palestinian Nakba. (Musih 2005)

By organising tours to the sites of former Arab villages and quarters and by erecting signs to draw attention to the previous (Arab) names of streets or neighbourhoods, Zochrot aims to bring to the Israeli surface the country's suppressed Arab past. Zochrot's founders are convinced that reconciliation and peace will need to be grounded in knowledge of the suffering of the Palestinians and will require Jewish Israelis to take responsibility for the *Nakba* and support the return of Palestinian refugees. Most Israelis reject such a solution as both undesirable and unrealistic as the Palestinians' former homes have either been demolished or are inhabited by Jews.

Zochrot claims that it is not aspiring to create narratives and memories that replace and negate those of the Zionists, but rather that it is trying to build Jewish–Arab alliances that would foster the creation of a different, more open space where different narratives could co-exist. Contrary to its declared intention, however, Zochrot has uncritically adopted the nationalist Palestinian narrative about the Jewish–Arab conflict. For example, the organisation has published a booklet about Haifa (Zochrot 2004) that reproduces the Palestinian narrative, which in turn mirrors the hegemonic nationalist Jewish narrative. As the Jewish master narrative tends to obscure the non-Jewish – and especially the Arab – presence in Haifa, so does the Palestinian narrative, adopted by this Jewish-Israeli anti-Zionist radical group, ignore the Jewish presence in the Haifa of ancient times and downplay its presence today.

In a historical survey which opens the booklet, its author maintains that: 'In 1880 even before the Zionist movement, a settlement of Jewish inhabitants, mostly of East European origin started in the town, as well as a settlement of various European nationals who had arrived due to the developing trade' (Zochrot 2004, 9). The authors ignore that by then there were 55 Jewish families in Haifa, most of them of North African origin and some of them *Mustaaribun*, Arabic-speaking Jews who had lived in Palestine before the arrival of the first waves of expelled Spanish Jews in the fifteenth century. Why did the authors move the beginning of the Jewish presence to 1880 – one year before the first Zionist *Aliyah*? The narrative portrays the Jewish immigration to Palestine as a by-product of European colonialism and the result of Zionism; it ignores the pre-Zionist Jewish presence in Haifa and its influence on the city until 1948. The motives of oriental Jews to leave Morocco and settle in Haifa were religious and not Zionist; as such, they do not fit into the colonialist paradigm shared by Zochrot and Palestinian nationalists. The fact that these mostly Arabic-speaking Jewish communities had lived in the Muslim quarter of the old cities and usually maintained good relations with their Arab neighbours (Khalfon 1978, 60–63; Nathanson and Shiblak 2011, 186–188) does not fit with the nationalist Palestinian narrative, although it could serve as an inspiration for reconciliation between Jews and Arabs in Haifa and beyond (Nathanson and Shiblak 2011, 184–186). Also seemingly paradoxically, since the foundation of the Jewish state, the Palestinians are portrayed as objects rather than subjects who actively opposed Zionist immigration.

The booklet also ignores the Palestinian attacks on Jewish quarters in 1929, and during the Arab revolt 1936–1939 which was a reaction against the British pro-Zionist policy and the growth of Jewish immigration due to the anti-Semitic policies and practices in Nazi Germany and Poland. Until 1929, about 300 families, most of them descendants of Moroccan Jews who had settled in Haifa in the nineteenth century, lived in the Harat al-Yahud. Following the 1929 Arab riots against the Jewish *Yishuv*, and then again – and this time for good – in 1938, Jews living in Harat al-Yahud were evacuated to the modern Jewish neighbourhood of Hadar HaCarmel (Goldstein 1989). Remarkably enough, Zochrot's booklet does not discuss the demolition of the old quarter in 1948 and the deliberate neglect of the former Muslim neighbourhood of Wadi Salib; the only references are a couple of pictures of the current dilapidated state of some old Arab buildings.

Zochrot's demands for an official Israeli acknowledgment of the historical injustice done to the Palestinians potentially imply other political demands: for the return of the refugees, for the restitution of confiscated land and for a transformation of Israel into a bi-national state. They have frightened the moderate Israeli mainstream, including the Zionist left that had dominated Israeli politics from 1948 to 1977. While the moderates simply reject the positions of Zochrot, the nationalist right-wing organisation Im Tirzu attributes them to a highly sophisticated conspiracy of the Arab enemy. According to Im Tirzu, 'the Arabs' have lost all hope of defeating Israel militarily and therefore try to defeat the Zionist spirit by spreading false accusations and blood libels about the Zionist victory in the 1948 war. In order to achieve this goal, 'the Arabs' are helped by radical left-wing Jewish individuals and organisations such as Zochrot, which manipulate naïve, self-deluding and self-hating Jewish intellectuals. Im Tirzu speakers accuse such Israeli radicals of weakening and breaking the Zionist spirit and the belief that the Zionist cause is just. Im Tirzu has launched a counter-campaign with the publication of a booklet (Segal and Tadmor 2011) that claims to prove that the Jews were the victims of the Arabs in 1948, and that Zochrot's discourse on the *Nakba* is a revisionist Palestinian lie.

Conclusion

The story of Haifa brings to the fore the tragic history of the Israeli–Palestinian conflict. After 1948, only a small minority of Haifa's Arab population remained or was allowed to return. Most of the abandoned Arab property was looted, destroyed or officially confiscated. Then the local agents of the Zionist state embarked on an ambitious mission of memory politics, which aspired to turn the Arab space that had been cleansed of its original population into a Jewish-Zionist space. Seven decades after the *Nakba*, the local Zionist establishment and the Jewish majority still stubbornly refuse to acknowledge the Arab past and heritage of Haifa, and vehemently reject even symbolic gestures of historical justice towards a significant community within their city. This seems to suggest a deep sense of insecurity among the Jewish majority – as if not only the Palestinians themselves but also their past and memories are still haunting Zionist Haifa. Torrents of hatred towards the Jewish state and threats to expel its Jewish population, some of it coming from Islamist Israeli-Palestinians, function to legitimise such fears, a lack of confidence and an absence of good will on the part of the Jewish Israelis towards their Israeli-Palestinian fellow citizens.

Hopefully, the end of the Israeli–Palestinian conflict would mollify this stance, but it would not necessarily improve the tense relationship between Jews and Arabs in Haifa and in the state of Israel, more generally. Many Israelis who believe in a two-state solution want each of the two states to grant and guarantee rights exclusively to their own nationals and not to the members of the other nation. As any political solution of the conflict would involve territorial concessions in the West Bank, and thereby of land that religious circles consider to be part of the divine promise to the people of Israel, a two-state solution might harden the Israeli positions regarding Israeli-Palestinian demands for historical justice within the boundaries of the state of Israel.

Meanwhile, in Haifa, Jewish law and accountancy firms have purchased and renovated some of the typical Arab bourgeois houses in Wadi Salib and elsewhere. In the old city, except for the renovated and reconstructed mosques and churches, the few remaining buildings are decaying and will probably be targeted by developers. But I remain optimistic: I hope that the municipal government will embark on a project of reconstruction, in an act of homage to Daher el-Omar, in the part of the ruined old city that extends from the old Carmelite church of Elijah the Prophet to the Al-Jarina mosque and serves today as a parking lot.

I have a dream for Haifa in 2061, which probably only my young granddaughter will live to see. I hope that the 300th anniversary of my hometown will be officially acknowledged and celebrated by *all* its citizens, and that this civic festivity will create a local tradition that Jews and Palestinians alike will be proud of.

Note

1. This ideal was expressed also in one of the most famous Zionist poems, 'Shir boker' ('Morning Song'), written by Nathan Alterman in 1935. In the poem, Alterman compares the land of Zion to a woman whose lovers promise to adorn her with beautiful garments: 'We will dress you in a gown of concrete and cement, and lay for you a carpet of gardens'.

References

Azaryahu, Maoz. 1993. "Bein shtei arim: Hantzachat milchemet Haatzmaut beHaifa ve-beTel Aviv." *Cathedra* 68: 98–125.

Benvenisti, Meron. 2000. *Sacred Landscape: The Buried History of the Holy Land Since 1948*. Berkeley: University of California Press.

Berger, Tamar. 1998. *Diyonisus ba-senter*. Tel Aviv: ha-Kibuts ha-me'uh ad.
Berlovits, Yafah. 1996. *Le-hamtsi erets, le-hamtsi 'am: tashtiyot sifrut v e-tarbut ba-yetsirah shel ha-'aliyah ha-rishonah*. Tel Aviv: ha-Kibuts ha-me'uhad.
Brin, Hanan, Hannah Gutman-Katz, and Michael Palti. 1970. *Haifa irenu*. Choveret Le-Avoda Atzmit Le-Hakarat Haifa ve-Hasviva, Haifa: Sifriat Merchavim.
Efrat, Zvi. 2001. "Vernacular." *Studio – ktav et le-omanut*, 120. http://readingmachine.co.il/home/books/book_studio_120/chapter03_8515038
Eyal, Gil. 2006. *The Disenchantment of the Orient: Expertise in Arab Affairs and the Israeli State*. Stanford, CA: Stanford University Press.
Goldstein, Yakoov. 1989. "Meoraot 1929 beHaifa ve-trumatam shel Anshei Hashomer Hatzair leHaganat Ha'Ir." *Cathedra* 52: 149–180.
Goren, Tamir. 1994. "Ehalmut shel Ha'ir Haatika Minof Haifa." *Ofakim BeGeografia* 40–41: 57–81.
Goren, Tamir, and Yossi Ben Arzi. 1998. "Kechomer BeYad Hayotzer: Ytzuv Hamerchav Ha'ironi shel Araviei Haifa." *Mechkarim B'Geografia shel Eretz Israel* 15: 7–28.
Herzl, Theodor. 1987. *Old New Land (Altneuland)*. Translated by Lotta Levensohn. New York: Markus Wiener Publishing.
Kadman, Noga. 2008, November. *Be-tside ha-derekh uve-shule ha-toda'ah: dehikat ha-kefarim ha-'Arviyim she-hitrokenu be-1948 meha-śiah ha-Yiśre'eli*. Jerusalem: Sifre.
Katz, Hannah. 1990. *Haifa Irenu*. Haifa: HaReali HaIvri.
Kesler, Bruce. 2006. "Haifa, City of Peace." *FrontPageMag*, July 27. http://archive.frontpagemag.com/readArticle.aspx?ARTID=3376
Khalfon, Avraham. 1978. "Haifa Iri." In *Hefah Olifantveha-hazon ha-Tsiyoni*, edited by Joseph Nedava, 59–69. Hefah: Universitat Hefah ha-Katedra Le-Tsiyonut al shem Reuven Hecht.
Levi, Shabtai. 1978. "MeZichronoti." In *Hefah Olifantveha-hazon ha-Tsiyoni*, edited by Joseph Nedava, 78–174. Hefah: Universitat Hefah ha-Katedra Le-Tsiyonut al shem Reuven Hecht.
Menachem, Z. 1948. "Ytzuv Ha'ir Hachadasha." *Davar*, September 15.
Monterescu, Daniel, and Dan Rabinowitz. 2007. "Introduction." In *Mixed Towns, Trapped Communities: Historical Narratives, Spatial Dynamics, Gender Relations and Cultural Encounters in Palestinian-Israeli Towns*, edited by Daniel Monterescu, and Dan Rabinowitz, 1–34. Abingdon: Ashgate.
Morris, Benny. 2004. *The Birth of the Palestinian Refugee Problem Revisited*. Cambridge: Cambridge University Press.
Musih, Norma. 2005, August. "Learning the Nakba as a Condition for Peace and Reconciliation." http://www.zochrot.org/en/content/learning-nakba-condition-peace-and-reconciliation
Nathanson, Regev, and Abbas Shiblak. 2011. "Haifa Umm Al Gharib: Historical Notes on Inter-Communal Relations." In *Haifa Before and After 1948: Narratives of a Mixed City*, edited by Mahmoud Yazbak, and Yfaat Weiss, 185–205. Dordrecht: Institute for Historical Justice and Reconciliation and Republic of Letters.
Raz-Krakotzkin, Amnon. 1993. "Galut BeToch Ribonut: Le-Bikoret Shlilat Hagalut BeTarbut Haisraelit." *Teoria ve-Bikoret* 4: 23–55.
Raz-Krakotzkin, Amnon. 1999. "Orientalism, Madaei HaYehadut ve-Hachevra Ha'israelit: Mispar Heharot." *Jama'a* 3 (1): 34–59.
Rotbard, Sharon. 2005. *Ir levanah, 'ir shehorah*. Tel Aviv: Bavel.
Segal, Arel, and Erez Tadmor. 2011. *Nakba Harta*. Jerusalem: Im Tirzu.
Slyomovics, Susan. 1998. *The Object of Memory: Arab and Jew Narrate the Palestinian Village*. Philadelphia: University of Pennsylvania Press.
Smooha, Sammy. 1997. "Ethnic Democracy: Israel as an Archetype." *Israel Studies* 2 (2): 198–241.

Stern, Shimon. 1981. "Hamaavak al Hakamat Nemal Haifa betkufat Hamandat Habriti." *Cathedra* 21: 171–186.

Weiss, Yfaat. 2011. *A Confiscated Memory: Wadi Salib and Haifa's Lost Heritage*. New York: Columbia University Press.

Yahav, Yona. n.d. "Living in Haifa." http://haifahaifa.co.il/living-in-haifa/.

Yazbak, Mahmoud. 1999. "Templars as Proto-Zionists? The 'German Colony' in Late Ottoman Haifa." *Journal of Palestine Studies* 28 (4): 40–54.

Yiftachel, Oren. 2006. *Ethnocracy: Land and Identity Politics in Israel/Palestine*. Philadelphia: University of Pennsylvania Press.

Yoffe, A. B. 1982. *Marsel Yanko*. Ramat-Gan: Masadah.

Zochrot. 2004. *Zochrot et Haifa*. Tel Aviv: Zochrot. http://zochrot.org/sites/default/files/haifa.pdf

Ghosts and *compañeros*: haunting stories and the quest for justice around Argentina's former terror sites

Estela Schindel

Center of Excellence 'Cultural Foundations of Social Integration', Universität Konstanz, Konstanz, Germany

The policies adopted by the Argentine government since 2003 in favour of truth, memory and justice have resulted in the opening up of former clandestine detention centres (CDCs) to the public, and their transformation into sites of memory. The practices and discourses developed at such locations, however, produce their own silences and shadows. In this article, I explore narratives about ghosts and other supernatural phenomena that are attached to the remnants of former places of terror. I draw on the concept of haunting as a key to understanding the figure of the *desaparecido* (the 'disappeared'), who is neither dead nor alive and dwells in an intermediate realm, and who also signals a demand for historical justice. Unlike the official narratives told at the former CDCs, stories of haunting are told in low voices and tend to emerge in liminal spaces. I suggest that these stories are symptoms of an unease, and that they ought to be considered in relation to the difficulty of mourning or accepting loss. They draw attention to the latent legacies of the past that might not be completely accounted for within more ideologically informed, rational approaches to commemorating the past.

Entering the attic of the Officers' Club at the former navy school ESMA (Escuela de Mecánica de la Armada), one of the largest clandestine detention and torture centres of the Argentinean dictatorship (1976–1983), Victor Basterra remarked: 'I am an agnostic. But each time I come here – which I do often – I feel that this place is full of presences'. The kidnapped prisoners were held captive and tortured in this building before being secretly murdered on the so-called death flights. One part of the attic was known as Capucha ('hood'), a reference to the fact that the prisoners would always be blindfolded by a hood. The navy imprisoned Victor in Capucha from 1979 to 1983. Now he is helping to transform the ESMA into a site of memory and for the promotion of human rights. Victor was kidnapped for being a political and union activist; his interpretation of the horrors he witnessed and endured is lucid and politically informed. Like many Argentineans, including myself, Victor believes that the mass disappearances were designed to stymie political activism and paralyse the society at large. The systematic extermination of thousands by making them disappear was to guarantee that political activism be removed from the public sphere for generations. The presences mentioned by Victor, however, point to something that escapes the rational and coherent frameworks commonly used to make sense of the suffering endured at the ESMA. Even for someone who visits the site frequently as an engaged witness, there is a haunting quality attached to the attic that does not recede. Victor feels the *presences* of his former fellow detainees.

Victor's reference to haunting, while only an aside in his larger narrative, is symptomatic of a more generalised phenomenon: references to the supernatural that are circulating in hushed voices around and about the dictatorship's sites of terror, and appear at the margins of the politically informed practices and discourses that are currently being developed in several of Argentina's former clandestine detention centres (CDCs). These subterranean stories of haunting draw attention to the latent legacy of the past, which needs to be addressed in more complex terms than has so far been the case.

The stories of haunting that I discuss in this article were not at the centre of my original research project, but rather revealed themselves only in the course of my fieldwork. The interviews I did with relatives of the *desaparecidos* (the 'disappeared'), survivors, activists, officials and neighbours of former CDCs focused on the contiguity between the detention and torture centres, and the 'normal' urban spaces around them. Survivors, in particular, drew attention to the contrast between the physical proximity of, and the actual distance separating, the inside of the CDC and the outside life that went on as usual; one of them, Ana Maria Careaga, for instance, described being a disappeared as 'being so close and so far away from civilization'.

My fieldwork took place between February and April 2011 in and around eight former CDCs in Buenos Aires, Cordoba and Rosario. The interviews were filmed and used in the 2011 documentary series *Espacios de memoria* about sites of memory in Argentina. The pre- and post-production contact and the interruptions typical of a film shoot allowed for spontaneous conversations with the people involved with the CDC, and a more comprehensive, semi-participant observation of their interactions with each other and with the site itself. It was in this context that stories about haunting emerged and caught my attention. As with Victor's remark, they appeared as a by-product, a peripheral finding, of my main research. As I continued to listen and reflect on these stories, I wondered about their possible cause and meaning, particularly in contrast to the highly structured narratives that frame the policies aimed at transforming the former CDCs into sites of memory. What are these stories about ghosts and haunting telling us? Why are they linked to liminal zones or marginal figures? Is their emergence related to the *ghostly* condition of the disappeared? Are they a symptom of what is perceived as an unsolved past or a demand for justice from the dead? Could the haunting point to the legacy of their suffering, as Victor's comment suggests? Or do they point to other forms of knowledge of the past? After exploring these questions, I reflect on the methodological and epistemological challenges posed by stories of haunting and suggest that they are a potentially fruitful source of knowledge.

Recovery, memory policies and official narratives

Comprising 31 buildings in a 17-hectare area, the ESMA constitutes a miniature city inside the city. It is an adequate location for the creation of an effective space of exception (Agamben 1998): physically contiguous with the 'normal' urban fabric but juridically disentangled from it. Its streets and alleys are surrounded by dense vegetation, which seem to issue a strange, silent commentary; here, nature continues to flourish where human civilisation collapsed. The main buildings of the ESMA face busy Libertador Avenue, one of the main access roads into Buenos Aires, and are perfectly visible by those driving past.

When I first visited the ESMA in 2009, I did so as part of a three-hour guided tour. Our guide showed us the various places the prisoners would have gone through during their ordeal at the Officers' Club. She explained not only the meaning and use of each space, but also the role played by this detention centre in the context of the repressive structure, and the relationship between the network of CDCs and Argentine society at large. The infamous Capucha was the end point of our visit. It remains empty; the low, inclined ceiling sustained by iron girders, which feature in the first sketches drawn by survivors who were trying to denounce the place as an illegal detention and torture centre. Out of respect for the wishes of former detainees-disappeared and relatives of the victims, nothing in the attic has been renovated or modified, except for signposts that reproduce fragments of survivors' testimonies. Our guide provided lots of information, showed a deep level of historical knowledge and left sufficient space for reflection, respecting both the moments of silence and the questions of the visitors. The script of the visit was nevertheless stringent. It stressed a historical and political understanding of state terror and reflected on the social conditions that made disappearances possible. It did not appeal to the emotions nor did it indulge in details of cruelties.

This script is not an exception, but rather representative of the way in which the dictatorial past is constructed and narrated in contemporary Argentina, both by the state and by actors involved in the promotion of human rights. It conforms to a discourse born out of the resistance to the dictatorship and the denunciation of its crimes, and is thus based on certainties and a clear political positioning. Over several decades, this discourse has developed into a compact narrative that leaves little space for questions and may serve to obturate mourning or the acknowledgment of loss.

For 20 years after the end of the dictatorship, the human rights movement continued to act in opposition to the state (see Crenzel 2011; Malamud

Goti 1996). In 2003, the official policies towards the past changed decisively. When Nestor Kirchner assumed the presidency, he declared himself to be a member of the generation of the disappeared and his government to be inspired by the ideals that motivated them. His administration publicly acknowledged the victims as idealistic activists who fought for a better society, and implemented measures towards recovering historical memory and securing justice for the crimes of state terror. The so-called *leyes de impunidad* (impunity laws) were declared unconstitutional by the parliament and the Supreme Court, and cases against the military were reopened, the dictatorship and the disappeared were included in primary and secondary school curricula, and the anniversary of the military coup became a national holiday and a remembrance day. Kirchner's government and that of his successor, Cristina Fernández (since 2007), worked hand in hand with human rights organisations and fulfilled many of their long-standing demands regarding the search for truth, memory and justice.

It is in this context that many former CDCs were *recuperados* ('recovered'); this term is used by human rights organisations to describe a form of symbolic reparation whereby CDCs are transferred from the security forces to other sectors of the state and/or civil society and converted into sites of memory. Argentina's largest and most iconic CDC, the ESMA, was opened to the public by President Kirchner in a highly emotive ceremony on 24 March 2004. This event is remembered by survivors and relatives of the disappeared as an extremely significant moment. Most of them had never dared to imagine that the navy would be obliged to vacate the premises and that this symbol of suffering under state terror would be dedicated to the memory and to the promotion of human rights.

More than 500 places used as clandestine detention and torture centres during the dictatorship were distributed throughout Argentina. Their location alongside the 'normal' city allowed them to operate as a highly effective disciplining tool by permeating everyday life with terror. Their opening up as sites of memory contributes to neutralising and reversing their function as disseminators of terror. They now often act as nodes of cultural, social and political action that bring neighbours, activists, survivors and relatives of the disappeared into dialogue with each other and help them to understand themselves and each other as part of the same damaged social fabric. The organisations running these sites usually offer guided visits, cultural activities, workshops, acts of remembrance and pedagogical programmes – all of which play a crucial role in undoing the effects of terror discharged by these places (see Schindel 2012). Their administrative structures vary; usually they are managed by boards that include representatives of NGOs and of local, provincial and/or national governments. Not only are NGOs and state institutions working together in the management of these sites, but many members of human rights organisations also play a role within their administrative structures. Often survivors or relatives of the disappeared are employed in the administration of the former CDCs. The resistance discourse that originated under the dictatorship has thus converged with an official rhetoric that draws on the political ideology of the activists of the 1970s as a way of legitimating the government.

In line with the presidential human rights policy implemented since 2003, the official discourse enunciated at these sites, such as the guided visits, recovers and exalts the political ideals and the revolutionary spirit of the disappeared, tracing a genealogy between their political engagement and the memory work carried out today. This discourse has the potential to be reparative, in that it symbolically embraces the disappeared, welcoming them back into the social fabric after decades of isolation suffered by their relatives and friends. A keyword used to indicate this (re)connection, like a shared code across time and generations, is *compañeros*. This term is deeply rooted in the tradition of the Peronist movement, but also used more broadly to denote social and political activists; a *compañero* is one of our own, a figure at once anonymous and yet closely related and affectively charged. Speaking about the disappeared as *compañeros*, as is increasingly being done in official documents and during ceremonies, is an explicit acknowledgment of the political engagement of the victims of state terror and at the same time a declaration of one's own dedication to the revolutionary ideals that animated them. The term has, however, also become part of a self-celebratory, triumphalist rhetoric, which risks turning the victims of the dictatorship collectively into a sacred, reified figure, as in the much-used formula *30.000 compañeros detenidos-desaparecidos* ('30,000 detained-disappeared compañeros'). Like the script of the guided tour to the ESMA's Officers' Club, this rhetoric presents itself as a truth with no fissures.[1]

Ghost stories, haunted spaces

It is in the interstices of official discourse, with its seemingly solid certainties, at the margins of daily activity and in the liminal zones of the recovered detention centres, that other narrative registers emerge and stories of a different kind are told. These stories emerge when the cameras and microphones are off and the official activities have concluded. They allude to supernatural incidents, ghostly apparitions or haunted spaces. Recalling his initial weeks working as a security guard at the former CDC Virrey Cevallos in Buenos Aires, Gabriel Suarez told me:

> It was shocking ... I had nightmares and those things. There are strange noises. The house is very big so you don't know, there are winds everywhere, doors that slam, or open, (you think) it can be the noise of anything. But then you go to see and everything is closed, there is no draught. I already got used to that; at the beginning I was quite scared but I'm over that now.

Gabriel's account of his own experience is intermingled with the experience of others: 'The boy of the kiosk next door once heard his keys fall down without anyone being there', he said. 'He just heard it. Neighbours see people walking, they hear noises, see shadows, or cars driving in, even today. Sometimes, with the elderly, it is a suggestion'.

Similar incidents were reported by construction workers renovating the building that now houses the Museo de la Memoria in Rosario. During the dictatorship this mansion had served as the headquarters of the 2nd Army Corps.

While there is no evidence to suggest that prisoners were held captive or tortured there, it was the operative centre for the political repression in six provinces: the place where decisions concerning disappearance and assassination were taken and transmitted. After it had been used for some time as a venue for the theme bar Rock & Fellers, the local council acquired the building in order to accommodate the museum, which had been operating provisionally at another site. Its director Ruben Chababo remembered how during the renovations the workers came to him highly distressed about supernatural incidents they were experiencing, and that some of them never returned to work afterwards. Chababo spoke to me frankly about this episode and recalled how, before the opening, he engaged persons from various religious or spiritual backgrounds to 'clean the energy' of the house.

Similar stories of workers troubled by supernatural incidents circulate on the Internet. According to one, an old mansion in a rural location close to Mar del Plata, which had served as a detention centre, was bought by a businessman, who converted it into a disco. During the renovations, the workers complained that some rooms had 'bad energies' and that they had observed 'strange stains' appearing in certain parts of the building. There were rumours about 'strange voices' coming from the swimming pool and about strange 'shadows and sounds'. Similar stories circulate about the soccer stadium built for the 1978 World Cup in Mar del Plata, whose foundations are rumoured to have been built atop the bodies of *desaparecidos*. Ghost stories have also been told about the Parque Acuático in the same city, which has been used as an illegal detention and torture centre; here, several janitors quit their job because they could not cope with the ghosts (Soto Roland 2011). At the site of the Casa SIN on the outskirts of Buenos Aires, a former navy-run CDC which was sold in 2011 to make way for an office building, construction workers complained of strange incidents, such as inexplicable noises or beams that changed position from one day to the next without plausible cause. A neighbour was reported to have said:

> Workers are quite frightened, and even more since they heard what this place was. One bricklayer saw the figure of a military man dressed in his gala uniform, and a painter told me that he heard screams and harangues from the other side of the wall, but when he looked there was no one. We know these persons, we see them every day, and they have no reason to lie. Some of them quit the job and others have asked for leave. (Zanetto 2012)

As in Gabriel Suarez's account, the incidents are not narrated as a consistent story but are referred to in disarticulated terms. The stories of haunting I heard were mostly fragmentary and inconsistent and were not told by those who had witnessed the incident themselves but retold second-hand. The dynamics of such stories resembles that of rumour or gossip. Ghostly rumours proliferate rhizomatically – underground and horizontally – and the stories have neither concrete authors nor clear beginnings and endings. The official narrative, by contrast, is univocal, rationally founded and has little room for ambiguity or nuances. It circulates in the electronic and print media and is articulated prominently in public commemorations; it is enunciated by a strong, well-defined subject (the President, the *compañeros*, the relatives of the disappeared) and has a clear narrative structure organised in terms of a historical teleology (the fight for social justice, liberation, revolution).

As alternative carriers of information, rumours and gossip have received attention from scholars working on situations of extreme violence. In her analysis of vampire stories in East and Central Africa, Luise White considers rumours to be a rich historical source, as reports of the violence of the colonial extractive regime, not in spite but because of their uncertainty. Their inaccuracy, she argues, offers historians 'a way to see the world the way the storytellers did, as a world of vulnerability and unreasonable relationships' (White 2000, 6). What they might reveal, then, is not information about an external fact but knowledge about the deep conflicts that trouble society, for 'even though (oral accounts) do not depict actual events, conversations, or things that really happened, they describe meanings and powers and ideas that informed how people thought and behaved' (White 2000, 89). According to Feldman, in contexts of violence and death the rumour emerges as a narratological form capable of expressing a 'crisis of facticity', such as the one triggered by enforced disappearances (1995, 230). Rumours and their dissemination are characterised by fluctuation, randomness and variability, and thereby, according to Feldman, reproduce the peculiar structure of the violence through the defacement of authorship and agency: 'Through systematic disappearances, terror transforms the state of personhood into rumor, into dream' (1995, 231).

Tello Weiss, an anthropologist, a staff member of the former CDC La Perla and the daughter of a disappeared has been collecting ghost stories that circulate around former sites of terror. In a conversation with me, she suggested to interpret these accounts in relation to the state of fear and uncertainty created by mass disappearances, and argued that in fact the figure of the *desaparecido* itself engenders anxiety. In her interpretation, these stories relate to the tension between what is said and what remains unsaid, between the seen and the unseen, the known and the unknown. It is out of the anxiety created by the impossibility of finding consistent narratives for what has been seen or heard that such haunting stories emerge. It is as if a deeper layer lies underneath the official explanations offered at guided visits, challenging the attempts made by official policies to tame and frame the past horror in an intelligible, coherent, tranquilising narrative.

Watchmen, dogs, children: the symbolic mediators of haunting

Daniel Schiavi was the coordinator of the first group of guides that worked at the ESMA after it passed into civilian hands. During a seminar in 2008, he spoke openly about rumours of haunting at the former Officers' Club: 'Impossible to be alone in the building. Screams and whispers in the corridors. Doors slamming. Apparitions on the stairways. A girl prowls about in the park at night. Animated buildings' (Schiavi 2008, 486). All this, he added, was 'seen and heard by diverse persons, those called *pobres de espíritu* ['the poor of spirit'] by Christianity and the humble or *descamisados* ['shirtless'] by Evita [Perón]. Or by those well instructed but sensitive to the great beyond'.

When we interviewed him for our documentary, Daniel again attributed certain characteristics to those who perceive the hauntedness of the space, recalling the reaction of a tradesman:

> A boy came to fix some lights, or some electric stuff in Capucha. And suddenly he suffered a collapse and we had to take him out, he was feeling really bad. So for the common people, who are not informed, as soon as they get a hint of the place where they are, they just panic, they are so intensely moved, it affects more strongly those persons who generationally or for some other reason are further removed.

The protagonists of the ghost stories mentioned above – security guards, workers and janitors – are people with no or little formal education, who do not necessarily subscribe to an informed political discourse. According to Daniel, they are less aware of the place's history and lack the interpretative frameworks that would allow them to understand its somber atmosphere in rational terms. While all this is probably true, there is another factor related to these figures that can explain not only why they may be more likely to experience haunting, but also why other, better educated and more politicised members of the former CDCs' staff see them as being particularly prone to such experiences.

As workers, they must stay late at the sites, when no one else would like to be there; they spend time in areas where no one likes to go alone, such as the not yet renovated zones, abandoned ruins or the external borders of the site. The role played by caretakers, security and cleaning personnel, technicians and unskilled labourers at the memorial sites has not yet received the attention it deserves: beyond official and public activities, they have the closest contact with the dense affective energy of the space and must face the very concrete challenges of their daily maintenance. They receive the often disturbing testimonies of first-time visitors or the sometimes aggressive comments of passers-by. And it is they who support with their physical presence, with their bodily and affective work, the possibility of keeping the former torture centres open and who therefore sustain political decisions that are taken elsewhere. Unlike the members of the pedagogical teams, the guides, or the survivors and relatives like Victor or Daniel, who are active at the CDCs, these people do not always link the place to a politically articulate discourse: they just do their job. This might increase their anxiety, but at the same time it allows them to develop a less normative, more spontaneous affective contact to the materiality of the place. In this context, other interpretative frameworks may appear: spiritual or religious explanatory patterns arise at the margins of official discourses that are replete with admonitions and certainties. Their stories coexist with the public rhetoric about the place without necessarily disputing or contradicting it; they could not do so because they respond to a different narrative logic. But the ghostly rumours do propose alternative ways of explaining the unexplainable, or dealing with the uncanny, and thus highlight the inevitable voids of any official storytelling.

These workers are perceived to be particularly sensitive to haunting because they operate as liminal translators between the surface of the visible and the realm of the unknown. The liminal refers here to a threshold (from the latin *limen*), a stage between cultural transitions or a 'contact zone', as in Lotman's (1990) notion of a semiotic borderland, an in-between area that allows a connection between different cultural spheres. In this case, the contact is between the 'normal' city and the CDC as a space of exception, between the alleged civilisation of everyday life outside and the barbarism of torture and cruelty inside.

This could explain why the inhabitants of such peripheral zones act as 'translators' between the two separate spaces. It could also explain why references to the supernatural are sometimes projected onto animals or children, as if they were symbolic mediators between the two realms. At the ESMA, whose large area had for a long time been difficult to administer and keep under control, wild dogs had taken over sections of the grounds and become the subjects of urban legends. Dogs were said to be a menace and an unmanageable plague, often in connection to ghostly appearances. At the former CDC La Perla, located in a rural area of the province of Cordoba, staff members recount that when the security guards patrol the place where the torture room used to be, their dog will bark and refuse to go any further.

Children have also been credited with a secret ability for perceiving the haunted quality of a particular site. Having served as one of the biggest torture and detention centres of Cordoba, the CDC La Ribera was initially re-purposed as a kindergarten and school. The staff at the school collected many stories told by children, who would hear voices or screams and see ghosts or apparitions wandering around the courtyard, or who were afraid of going to the toilet because they would hear weeping there. Concrete elements would nourish the rumours, such as the discovery of electric wiring believed to be related to torture devices (Ratti, n.d.). But the fantastic narratives were also fed by what their parents had seen and heard during the dictatorship. Jessica Rosenkovich, a member of the pedagogical staff of this memory site, told me:

> I don't know if the children knew exactly where they were, but they had listened to things at home or from neighbours, because here the neighbourhood could see what happened [...] and that had created a lot of myths and stories among the children [...] and knowing the history of this place, or at least feeling or perceiving it, aroused in them a lot of stories and anecdotes. They used to call that part (of the courtyard) 'the dead zone', that means that there was something generated in them between reality and the intense aspect of the place. We don't have any testimony about people being hanged or executed there. But the wall is marked with bullet holes and hooks, and we think that is what led this to be 'the dead zone' for them and provoke all these thoughts and fantasies around the place.

Whether projected onto dogs, children or persons considered to be less informed or politically engaged, the haunting revealed by these stories is suggestive of an unease that other approaches cannot completely grasp. Supernatural approaches to the drama of enforced disappearances have been largely taboo among human rights organisations and the relatives of the disappeared. A recently published testimonial book by Tarnopolsky (2012), whose parents, brother and sister were disappeared, is an exception. He writes frankly about his visits to clairvoyants (according to whom his sister might still be alive) and states that many relatives had made similar consultations, only that they would not publicly acknowledge it. Letting these troubling narratives appear at liminal zones of the former detention and torture centres – or projecting them into those spaces – might be a way of coming to terms with a haunting quality that not everyone can name.

Buildings and haunting: 'a radioactive zone'

The second time I visited ESMA's former Officers' Club, I was able to spend some time there alone. Usually, the building can only be accessed through the guided tours. However, when we were shooting the documentary, we were granted permission to stay there by ourselves with a reduced team. Having filmed the interview with Victor, we stayed with the cameraman and the sound technician in order to capture silent pictures of the empty building. A granite staircase connects the basement, where the torture rooms were located, and the attic where the victims were held captive. The steps still show the damage left by the shackles as the prisoners were taken to the cellar to be physically tortured and then back upstairs to the continuing torment of life under a *capucha*. The floors between the cellar and the attic housed the bedrooms of the officers, who would live there 'normally', among the horror, and had to necessarily hear the hideous noise of the chains. Those involved in the crimes committed at the ESMA are currently being tried and convicted, but they refuse, even in court, to reveal what they know about the whereabouts of the disappeared. The fact that the perpetrators do not speak may be part of what renders their empty habitations so uncanny, as if the walls would talk in their stead, but in a language we do not understand.

The only exception to this reticence among the naval personnel was the confession of Retired Navy Officer Adolfo Scilingo, who broke the Argentine military's pact of silence by talking to journalist Horacio Verbitsky about his participation in the so-called 'death flights'. This murderous practice consisting of pushing political dissidents alive out of airplanes over the South Atlantic had been previously mentioned in survivors' testimonies and was now publicly acknowledged for the first time by a former officer. In his long confession, Scilingo mentions the four things that still torment his conscience: the two death flights in which he participated, witnessing a torture session and the noise of the chains and shackles of the prisoners which, he says, he cannot forget (Verbitsky 1995, 29). Except for this brief mention by Scilingo, who has been convicted for his participation in the 'death flights' and is now serving a sentence in Spain, there are practically no accounts about the military or naval personnel who also inhabited the torture centres. There are, again, rumours. 'We know that before our arrival there were stories circulating among the marines about women in nightgowns and covered in blood penetrating the walls. Babies crying. Suicides in the sentry boxes by night', writes Schiavi (2008, 486). And there is the silent testimony of their former rooms.

It is difficult to imagine what it must have been like to live in the Officers' Club. José Luis Maqueda was the caretaker of the building when I visited in 2011. A man in his sixties and a former Peronist activist who had once studied theology, he used to spend more time there than anybody else. He referred to himself as someone with 'a special talent for coping with other people's pain'. 'But it is not easy', Maqueda said while showing us his work room, including the surveillance monitors, which, the urban legend goes, have recorded dogs barking at ghostly appearances at night. To me, walking along the corridors and seeing the navy personnel's bedrooms, closets and bathrooms made an even more sinister impression than seeing the places where the captives had suffered. The idea that for the naval officers these premises were something like a home made the sight of the otherwise banal furniture even more uncanny. I did not see or hear anything strange nor did I witness any paranormal incident. Nonetheless, a dense, extremely oppressive energy made it almost unbearable to remain there for long. It was not haunting in the sense of a ghostly apparition, but an evolving feeling, something unbearable and unspeakable, a malign atmosphere beyond rational explanation. Without a figure onto which to project this unease, as was often the case with the haunted stories described above, this disturbing energy seemed to be discharged by the very physicality of the place.

In descriptions of the haunted condition of the former CDCs, ghostly or supernatural anecdotes appear interwoven with expressions of anguish or distress. It is not about seeing or hearing phantasms, but about acknowledging the emotional effort of entering these sites. As Gabriel, the guard at Virrey Cevallos, told me: '(There are) people who cross themselves, I don't know why, they start to cry, they are impressed by the place, you get a lump in your throat'. Others, 'religious people', say that 'the place must be exorcised'. Norma, the woman in charge of cleaning there, told me how:

> a woman came in and blessed me. She said to me, 'May God help you, may God take care of you'. And then she went to the former torture room, without knowing what this room had been, and said, 'There are many souls suffering in here'.

Testimonies like these do not give an account of ghostly incidents but instead refer to an ominous feeling: of a supernatural force that, while going beyond what is positively seen or heard, is still perceivable and still produces effects. These are not ghost stories but stories of haunted spaces, where the buildings themselves seem to trigger visitors' emotions. Speaking about her difficulty to attend to the cultural activities that take place at the former ESMA, Mariana Eva Perez, the daughter of *desaparecidos* told us, 'For me the whole area is radioactive'. Schiavi, during our interview, said: 'it still emanates (this strange feeling), it affects each person in a different way (but) the clandestine centre, the historical site ESMA is still active, it still has this irradiating power'. The vocabulary used by them (emanating, irradiating) seems to attribute agency to the very materiality of the ESMA. But where does the haunting quality of the place actually reside? Does it lie in the substance, in the material remnants or is it actually projected onto it by the visitors? The anthropologist Navaro-Yashin (2012) dealt extensively with the tension between the agency and emotionality of things, and the role of the subject who feels and speaks, while analysing the haunted effect of the houses abandoned by the Greek-Cypriots forced to leave Northern Cyprus. Distancing herself both from the approach of the actor-network theory conceived by Bruno Latour that emphasises the role of 'non human' objects and from the philosophy of the subject that privileges the agency of human beings above all things, she prefers to speak of 'complex assemblages' or an 'embroilment of subjects with objects' (2012, 162). She does, however, ascribe a certain affectivity to non-human entities and recognises 'the emotive energies discharged by properties and objects', which are not only an expression of the inner worlds of her informants, but also the mark of 'the affect discharged upon them by the dwellings and environments' (2009, 4).

In a post-war context, according to Navaro-Yashin, the ghostly appears entangled with the materiality. It is the environment that discharges (haunted) affect, as an agent exerting affective forces or energies in its own right. Navaro-Yashin is drawing on Thrift's (2007) spatial theory of affect in the search for an affect which is not tied to subjectivity and discursivity, but can be read in many other things, such as space and the environment: in this case, the non-discursive sensation which a space or environment generates, or the affect discharged by the ruins, before this perception can be articulated.

Standing alone in a corridor at the Officers' Club generates a form of anguish which is too overwhelming to be conveyed narratively. Narratives, as Koschorke puts it, operate through reduction and selection: 'Only a fraction of the world's issues makes its way into the language. Only a fraction of that which one is able to articulate linguistically is a potential object of narrative' (2011, 6). Haunting affect cannot be organised discursively but, following Thrift, can be itself a form of thinking: an 'often indirect and non-reflective, but thinking all the same', a 'different kind of intelligence about the world' (2007, 175). If that is true, the haunted affect discharged by the ominous spaces of the former CDC, even if it cannot be completely represented or translated into a coherent narrative, could still be transporting *knowledge*. In Thrift's words, this knowledge amounts to 'a different model of thinking' that 'lies on the assemblages and relations of bodies, minds and affects' (2007, 62): not a rationally structured narrative nor a compact political interpretation, but another way of acknowledging and accounting for the traumas of the past.

Living with the specter: the ghosts as *compañeros*

In recent decades, following Derrida's conceptualisation of hauntology in *Specters of Marx* (1994), the specter has been readmitted into cultural and sociological inquiry as a cipher of the past that continues to affect the present of the living (Buse and Stott 1999; Davis 2005). Ghosts have been a subject of exploration in, for instance, literary theory, psychoanalysis and philosophy, both regarding our relation to the dead (why do they return? do they lie? what is their function? do we want to keep them with us?) (Davis 2007) and as a key to understanding how the effects of mass murder, genocide, slavery or colonial oppression extend far beyond the horrific moment, engendering trauma that echoes for generations, both on the side of perpetrators and on the side of victims (Schwab 2010).

Haunting has emerged as a key category for thinking about the effects that an unsolved past exerts on the present. Writing about the cultural memory of the Soviet terror, Alexander Etkind argues that Russian civil society is haunted by the 'unquiet ghosts' of the unburied Soviet past. Inspired by Derrida's hauntology, he develops a theory of cultural memory consisting of what he characterises as hardware (monuments, sculptures, memorials, historical sites), software (texts, films, guided tours, etc.) and *ghostware*: 'ghosts, spirits, vampires, dolls, and other man-made and man-imagined simulacra that carry the memory of the dead who were not properly buried' (2009, 195). In his study of the imaginary of wandering souls in post-war Vietnam, Kwon sustains that ghost-related stories account for the persistence of war memories in today's Vietnamese everyday life. Although marginal, ghosts are 'constitutive of the order of social life' and ideas about them are 'instructive to understanding wider moral and political issues' (Kwon 2008, 3).

In her passionate claim in favour of the haunting as a key to understanding broader social issues, Gordon (2008) draws on the case of the Argentinean disappeared and, specifically, the way they are conveyed in the work of Luisa Valenzuela. The mothers of the disappeared, like the protagonist of Valenzuela's novel *He Who Searches*, 'make a special contact with loss and with what was missing but overwhelmingly present' (Gordon 2008, 112). If disappearance is 'a state-sponsored method for producing ghosts' (125–126), in order to understand and resist state power, we should confront the haunting or 'touch the ghost' (134). Gordon suggests that the spectral or ghostly is a category that can help us to grasp that which exceeds a traditional scholarly approach and to detect haunted legacies that continue to exercise effects on the present even if, as with Argentina's disappeared, this happens in invisible, less apprehensible ways. Haunting thus becomes a useful concept for overcoming the limitations of a scholarship that has a 'restrictive commitment to an empiricist epistemology and its supporting ontology of the visible and the concrete' (Gordon 2008, viii). Gordon claims that scholarship ought to preoccupy itself with what has been lost but is only 'apparently' absent because – albeit disappeared – it continues to shadow social life: the past haunts the present. Haunting, for Gordon, designates the effect of all those forces which, while excluded from scholarly 'knowledge', still affect our lives; an animated state in which a repressed or unresolved social violence is making itself known, thus enabling a knowledge of 'the things behind the things'.

Gordon considers haunting legacies to be 'a constituent element of modern social life' (2008, 7): the phantoms of modernity's violence, as in the injuries of race, class and gender domination. Within this broad definition of haunting, to speak about the disappeared, the victims without grave, creates a sort of duplication or a redundancy, a ghostly figure inside a larger picture of the haunted effects of power. As the dweller of an intermediate realm, neither dead nor alive, and related to 'a peculiar dialectic of certainty and doubt' (Gordon 2008, 74), the *desaparecido* is a quasi-redundant ghost:

> For disappearance is a state-sponsored method for producing ghosts [...] It is a form of power, or maleficent magic, that is specifically designed to break down the distinctions between visibility and invisibility, certainty and doubt, life and death that we normally use to sustain an ongoing and more or less dependable existence. Disappearance targets haunting itself, targets just that state of being vulnerable, and also alert, to the precariousness of social order. (126)

The disappeared as a ghostly figure brought about by state terror is not to be confused with the specter as conceived by Derrida. For Derrida, the specter is the conveyor of legacies and demands from the dead, and acquires an emancipatory, almost messianic resonance in his claim for justice. As Quintana and Monteserín (2011) note, a differentiation must therefore be made between the sinister use of the phantasmatic in the figure of the disappeared by a repressive state, and the ethical and political potential posed by the specter – as an opening to justice and to the other – according to Derrida. In the first case, the production of specters is an efficient strategy of authoritarian power, a political re-appropriation of the spectral consisting in 'the reduction of persons to ghosts by way of a policy of punishment, social disciplining, disappearances' (Quintana and Monteserín 2011, 208).

For Derrida, on the other hand, to 'live with' ghosts suggests an invitation to account for the possibility of justice and accountability. It is, in this sense, a form of emancipating, messianic promise and a claim for justice. This other function of the specter, not as the unsettling haunting of former terror sites, but as the ethical command of the dead on the consciousness of the living, can be detected as an underground presence in Argentinean contemporary culture. At least two examples of this come to mind here, neither of which stem from the city's public space. The first takes place in the virtual realm of the Internet. In their blogs and online conversations, some children of the disappeared (now young adults) often share, and write about, their dreams. In those dreams, the figure of their parents is present as a phantom presence, as a ghost. Although not acknowledged as such, these digital platforms are also sites of memory where an intense memorial activity is taking place. The fact that some children of the disappeared tell each other about the ghosts of their parents appearing in dreams is more than an isolated circumstance and may reveal a major symptom concerning post-dictatorship Argentinean society at large: the haunting of a troubled past that is not yet pacified, despite all attempts by the state to 'recover' the past.

My second example relates to the imaginaries being produced on stage. In the southern winter of 2011, six versions of Shakespeare's *Hamlet* were being staged simultaneously in Buenos Aires. A journalist commenting on that fact asked: 'Is it blasphemous to relate the juxtaposition of ghosts with the presence of local spirits in Argentinean recent political life? It is certainly tempting' (Viola 2011). The large number of productions of *Hamlet* testifies to a deeper collective trauma or, at least, to the fact that something related to the father phantom's plea for justice seems to be pervading the country's cultural space. In both examples, we are dealing with narratives that exceed the structured scripts of museums and official pronouncements.

How can one version of the disappeared as a ghost – the fixation and immobilisation of the specter by way of terror – possibly be linked to this other figure of the specter that embodies an appeal of justice from the past and poses the ethical commandment of living with the ghosts or, as in Davis' reading of Derrida, occupies the place of the Levinasian other 'whose otherness we are responsible for preserving' (Davis 2007, 9)? Can these two images of the specter be reconciled? How to live with the ghosts that wander around and haunt the former detention sites?

What I heard and saw at the recovered CDCs in Cordoba seems to suggest that such a coexistence is possible. At the sites I visited in this province, ghostly presences are not treated as something alien to political and pedagogical work, or perceived as a threat to them, but are incorporated naturally into the daily routine. At the former detention centre D2, which now houses a memorial museum and provincial archives, staff members told me that no one stays alone after 8 o'clock at night or, if they must stay after hours, they see to it that a second person stays on as well. Ghostly presences or noises (rumours mention typewriter sounds in the night coming from the cell where an inmate had been forced to type) seem to be accepted as part of the dense emotional charge linked to the place. The haunted presences are not silenced nor minimised; they deserve the respect of the working staff, but are ultimately something one can live with. With the relaxed sense of humour for which this province is renowned, the staff working at Cordoba's former terror sites seem to be accomplishing what Derrida refers to as 'learning to live with ghosts', to live:

> in the upkeep, the conversation, the company, or the companionship, in the commerce without commerce of ghosts. To live otherwise, and better. No, not better, but more justly. But with them. [...] And this being-with specters would also be, not only but also, a politics of memory, of inheritance, and of generations. (1994, xviii)

For the management of the recovered terror sites, this means that the task might be less one of exorcising the ghosts of recent history, and more about offering tools to listen to their request; not excluding the stories of haunting from the former CDCs, but incorporating them into the larger political narrative as symptoms of the social unease still provoked by a traumatic past. It is about paying attention to what the specter wants to say, not as a contradiction, but as part of the legacy left by the failed revolutionary projects of the past.

The psychoanalyst Kersner wrote: 'We Argentines did not have 30,000 disappeared. We live with 30,000 disappeared' (1986, 134). Living with the disappeared can thus mean assuming their inheritance as a constitutive part of Argentinean identity. But it can also mean a very literal coexistence with their effect as both specters *and* ghosts. This does not mean that ghosts are not feared: people continue to avoid being alone at certain hours at the site, but their disturbing presence is perceived as part of the experience of recovering the CDCs. The quest for justice in the courtroom and pedagogical work done at the site are not detached here from the perception of a haunting legacy of the past. And the subscription to a rational, politically informed interpretation of state terror goes together with the acknowledgement of the voids and mysteries brought about by the disappearances. As the director of the former CDC La Perla, and son of a disappeared, Emiliano Fessia puts it: 'Yes, we know that there are ghosts around here. But as we always say, we are not afraid of them because they are *compañeros*'.

What can we learn from ghostly stories?

In the last days of 2012, the ESMA was on the front page of Argentinean newspapers because the Ministry of Justice had organised its New Year celebration at the former CDC. Many survivors and relatives of disappeared were genuinely offended. They were particularly outraged by the fact that the festivities included a barbecue. In the CDCs, the word *parrilla* ('grill') referred to the metal bed where prisoners were tortured with electric prods, while *hacer un asadito* (grilling; literally: 'making a grill') meant burning the bodies of those who had perished under torture. The objections of survivors raise the issue of moral or ethical limits – what can and what cannot be made at the ESMA? Is it right to eat there? Is it right to eat grilled meat? Many survivors and relatives of the disappeared were also deeply troubled by the triumphalist spirit of the ministry's reception. While it is indeed a political victory or a 'conquest' to have 'recovered' it from the navy, the ESMA is still a place where there is, in the end, nothing to celebrate.

Practices and discourses that emphasise the occupation of the ESMA often stress the importance of 'bringing life' into the space and 'exorcising the ghosts of the past'. These rhetorical constructions, which usually go together with a reified glorification of the disappeared, may expose the difficulty of accepting the losses and especially the defeat of that political project, while obstructing critical reflection on its possible failures. Such critical reflection would by no means relativise or justify the atrocities of state terrorism, but, on the contrary, it would help to understand why the exterminated activists had become so isolated and vulnerable to state repression (see Calveiro 2005). Reati (2004) warns that the processing of historical trauma takes longer than political institutions might be willing to accept, and that accepting loss, pain and defeat are a necessary part of the process. Many former militants find it difficult, for instance, to speak about their fears, present and past (Tello Weiss 2006). According to Reati, a collective consciousness of the void left by the failure of the revolutionary project of the

1970s is a precondition if Argentine society is to be able to 'exorcise' the traumatic aspects of the past in such a way that it 'does not irrupt as a specter, the return of the repressed, the absented presence in a Freudian sense' (2004, 124). Warning that memory generally frames the facts of the past in fixed narratives and implies stylised and simplified representations of historical events, Vezzetti (2002, 204) also sees in such 'self-celebratory' narratives a reluctance to admit failure or loss. As a 'narrative fetishism' they act as a sort of Freudian denial, aiming consciously or unconsciously to erase the traces of trauma, in what would actually be a refusal to mourn or even acknowledge the need to mourn.

A discourse that does not admit trauma, defeat or loss can develop into a self-sealed rhetoric and close off the possibility of learning from history. Ghostly stories destabilise and question such triumphalist discourses and practices. Stories of haunting are not crystallised narratives aimed at disputing the master interpretations of the past; an exaltation of the memory of the disappeared can coexist with the acknowledgement of the haunting, as the case of Cordoba shows. Rather, these stories are symptoms of an unpacified 'remainder' that cannot be completely apprehended by the official explanatory and at times even celebratory narrative. As with the African vampire stories analysed by White, the purpose of gossip and rumour:

> is not to deliver information but to discuss it. Stories transmitted without regard for official versions, stories that are amended and corrected and altered with every retelling, are indeed rumours, but they are also a means by which people debate the issues and concerns embodied in those stories. (White 2000, 176)

The ghost stories seem to be indicators of voids, silences or failures in other approaches to knowledge; they might not provide factual information, but they alert us to that which emerges in the cracks of the knowable. Rather than producing knowledge understood in a positivistic way, as empirically proven data, they provide evidence of an unease that official narratives cannot convey.

Chilean and Argentinean psychologists had warned early on about the long-lasting effects of enforced disappearances on the individuals and the societies affected (Kordon 2005; Kordon, Edelman, and Equipo de Asistencia Psicológica de Madres de Plaza de Mayo 1986; Riquelme 1990; Rojas Baeza 2009). In recent years, philosophers (Quintana and Monteserín 2011) and literary critics (Drucaroff 2011; Mandolessi 2012) have been attentive to the presence of ghosts and specters in the Argentine cultural sphere and to their possible meaning. Gatti (2008) convincingly confronts the 'narratives of the meaning' that try to 'make sense' of the disruption brought about by enforced disappearances as a 'catastrophe of meaning' (those of archaeologists, forensic experts, human rights activists) with the 'narratives of the no meaning' that, especially in the generation of the children of disappeared, pose the possibility of inhabiting the very ruins of meaning, the 'non-sense', the landscapes of waste. However, among other scholars the symptoms of unease that relate to the specific haunting qualities of the disappeared – as distinct to the dead – have either not received close examination or been dismissed altogether. In the copious research dealing with the collective memory of the disappeared, there is also little or no account of haunting as a social symptom. Authors who focus on understanding state terror in the context of a long-term class and political struggle (Izaguirre 1994) or as an exemplary form of modern 'reorganizing genocide' aimed at transforming social relations (Feierstein 2007) do not sufficiently account for the specific, haunting traits of the enforced disappearances as a repressive system based on the long-term effects of haunting.

Rational, coherent and comprehensive narratives can play an important role in shaping cultural memories; however, they operate in reductive and selective ways, and are therefore 'less a vehicle than a filter of communication' (Koschorke 2011, 6). The stories about ghosts that are told by the workers at former CDCs do not constitute coherent narratives, but they challenge and destabilise official attempts at normalising the past and can deliver valuable knowledge about the ways in which the trauma of the disappearances is still haunting Argentina's everyday life. They do not convey any truth per se but are symptoms of an unease. They reveal a state of anxiety in a society that, in spite of active reparative policies by the state, has not yet been pacified. They convey that the 'official script' told during the guided visit does not contain the whole story because the whole story is unknowable. This is something that the at times celebratory official rhetoric is not always willing to admit. An acceptance of loss, defeat and mourning could be a way of coping with this haunting legacy.

Ghosts stories are told by janitors and cleaners, security guards and tradesmen because they are in direct contact with the very materiality of the former sites of terror. This raises the question: who exactly must bear – on an everyday basis – the burden of historical traumata that concern society as a whole?

Stories of haunting have a vanishing, slippery quality. They draw on hints and rumours. Informants will tell them casually during breaks, may be unwilling to recount them afterwards and may be unable to identify the person who originally experienced the incident. Ghost stories also proliferate in the inherently ghostly, de-localised virtual space of the World Wide Web. Their rendering here, thus, cannot be separated from the difficulties inherent to the ghostly narratives as a research 'object'. But ghosts, as Gordon argues, demand a different kind of knowledge: researchers need to pay attention to the significant silences and the blind angles of their empirical material to see what is emerging in those obscure zones.

The ability to successfully meet the methodological challenge posed by haunting for research is rewarded by the epistemological benefits of welcoming back into social science all that an exclusively positivistic approach had paradoxically banned, as if – magically – it would then cease to exist. The assertion that the irrational is part of social life, which has been addressed here as haunting, is not new. Mythical narratives are a particular form of intellect; they contain and transmit knowledge, while mythicised, reified scientific approaches undergo the risk of leaving so much aside that they can no longer fulfil their own epistemological ambitions. Horkheimer and Adorno argued in a similar vein in the

Dialectic of Enlightenment, when they wrote that 'Myth is already enlightenment, and enlightenment reverts to mythology' (2002, xviii). Their quest for a rational acknowledgement of the irrational is often forgotten, but continues, nonetheless, to haunt the core of western mainstream scientific research.

Acknowledgements

Ideas presented here have been discussed with members of the research group 'Narratives of Terror and Disappearance' of the University of Konstanz. I am grateful to my colleagues for their input and suggestions and to the editor and anonymous reviewers for their insightful comments on earlier versions of this article.

Funding

The research leading to this article was funded by the European Research Council under the European Union's Seventh Framework Programme [(FP/2007–2013)/ERC Grant Agreement n° 240984].

Note

1. Particularly unsettling is the already institutionalised ritual of reading out aloud the names of the disappeared one by one, with the audience responding, after each name, with: *'Presente!'* ('Here!'). I find this disturbing for two reasons: because it is reminiscent of ceremonies enacted in Nazi Germany to commemorate the 'martyrs' of the National Socialist movement (Connerton, 1989, 42) and because the martial tone of this homage has traditionally been associated with the military, that is, with the persecutors of those whose suffering is being commemorated.

References

Agamben, Giorgio. 1998. *Homo Sacer: Sovereign Power and Bare Life*. Stanford, CA: Stanford University Press.

Buse, Peter, and Andrew Stott, eds. 1999. "Introduction: A Future for Haunting." In *Ghosts: Deconstruction, Psychoanalysis, History*, 1–20. Basingstoke: Palgrave Macmillan.

Calveiro, Pilar. 2005. *Política y/o violencia: Una aproximación a la guerrilla de los años 70*. Buenos Aires: Norma.

Connerton, Paul. 1989. *How Societies Remember*. Cambridge: Cambridge University Press.

Crenzel, Emilio. 2011. *The Memory of the Argentina Disappearances: The Political History of Nunca Mas*. New York: Routledge.

Davis, Colin. 2005. "État Présent: Hauntology, Spectres and Phantoms." *French Studies* 59 (3): 373–379.
Davis, Colin. 2007. *Haunted Subjects: Deconstruction, Psychoanalysis and the Return of the Dead*. London: Palgrave Macmillan.
Derrida, Jacques. 1994. *Specters of Marx: The State of the Debt, the Work of Mourning & the New International*. New York: Routledge.
Drucaroff, Elsa. 2011. *Los prisioneros de la torre. Política, relatos y jóvenes en la postdictadura*. Buenos Aires: Emecé.
Etkind, Alexander. 2009. "Post-Soviet Hauntology: Cultural Memory of the Soviet Terror." *Constellations* 16 (1): 182–200.
Feierstein, Daniel. 2007. *El genocidio como práctica social: entre el nazismo y la experiencia argentina. Hacia un análisis del aniquilamiento como reorganizador de las relaciones sociales*. Buenos Aires: FCE.
Feldman, Allen. 1995. "Ethnographic States of Emergency." In *Fieldwork Under Fire: Contemporary Studies of Violence and Survival*, edited by Carolyn Nordstrom, and Antonius C. G. M. Robben, 224–252. Berkeley: University of California Press.
Gatti, Gabriel. 2008. *El detenido-desaparecido: narrativas posibles para una catástrofe de la identidad*. Montevideo: Trilce.
Gordon, Avery. 2008. *Ghostly Matters: Haunting and the Sociological Imagination*. 2nd ed. Minneapolis: University of Minnesota Press.
Horkheimer, Max, and Theodor W. Adorno. 2002. *Dialectic of Enlightenment: Philosophical Fragments*. Stanford, CA: Stanford University Press.
Izaguirre, Ines. 1994. *Los desaparecidos: Recuperación de una identidad expropiada*. Buenos Aires: CEAL.
Kersner, Daniel. 1986. "El modelo mitológico como recurso para la inscripción histórica social." In *Efectos psicológicos de la represión política*, edited by Diana R. Kordon, Lucila I. Edelman, and Equipo de Asistencia Psicológica de Madres de Plaza de Mayo, 129–135. Buenos Aires: Sudamericana/Planeta.
Kordon, Diana. 2005. *Efectos psicológicos y psicosociales de la represión política y la impunidad de la dictadura a la actualidad*. Buenos Aires: Editorial Madres de Plaza de Mayo.
Kordon, Diana R., Lucila I. Edelman, and Equipo de Asistencia Psicológica de Madres de Plaza de Mayo. 1986. *Efectos psicológicos de la represión política*. Buenos Aires: Sudamericana/Planeta.
Koschorke, Albrecht. 2011. "In Praise of the Undefined: Toward a General Theory of Narrativity". Lecture at the Institute for Advanced Studies, Berlin.
Kwon, Heonik. 2008. *Ghosts of War in Vietnam*. Cambridge: Cambridge University Press.
Lotman, Yuri. 1990. *Universe of the Mind: A Semiotic Theory of Culture*. New York: I.B. Tauris.
Malamud Goti, José. 1996. *Game Without an End: State Terror and the Politics of Justice*. Norman: University of Oklahoma Press.
Mandolessi, Silvana. 2012. "Historias (de) fantasmas: Narrativas espectrales en la postdictadura argentina." Lecture presented at the 4th International Seminar on Policies of Memory, Centro Cultural de la Memoria Haroldo Conti, Buenos Aires.
Navaro-Yashin, Yael. 2009. "Affective Spaces, Melancholic Objects: Ruination and the Production of Anthropological Knowledge." *Journal of the Royal Anthropological Institute* 15 (1): 1–18.
Navaro-Yashin, Yael. 2012. *The Make-Believe Space: Affective Geography in a Postwar Polity*. Durham, NC: Duke University Press.
Quintana, María Marta, and Héctor Eduardo Monteserín. 2011. "Diapositivias espectrales: fragmentos para una interpretación de las desapariciones (o de lo siniestro fantasmático)." *Pasado Por-venir. Revista de Historia* 5: 199–217.

Ratti, Camilo. n.d. "Debate por el destino de un ex centro clandestino de la dictadura donde hoy funcionan un jardín y dos escuelas para mil chicos." *La Fogata*. http://www.lafogata.org/05arg/arg8/ar_17-9.htm

Reati, Fernando. 2004. "Trauma, duelo y derrota en las novelas de ex presos de la guerra sucia argentina." *Chasqui. Revista de literatura latinoamericana* 33 (1): 106–127.

Riquelme, Horacio, ed. 1990. *Zeitlandschaft im Nebel. Menschenrechte, Staatsterrorismus und psychosoziale Gesundheit in Südamerika*. Frankfurt: Vervuert.

Rojas Baeza, Paz. 2009. *La interminable ausencia. Estudio médico, psicológico y político de la desaparición forzada de personas*. Santiago de Chile: LOM.

Schiavi, Daniel. 2008. "La experiencia de la llegada de los Guías a la ex ESMA. Proposiciones despeinadas." Proceedings of the 1st International Seminar on Policies of Memory, Centro Cultural de la Memoria Haroldo Conti, Buenos Aires, CD Rom, 481–487. http://www.derhuman.jus.gov.ar/conti/_pdf/seminario1-08/Publicacion_1SIPM.pdf

Schindel, Estela. 2012. "Now the Neighbors Lose Their Fear': Restoring the Social Network Around Former Sites of Terror in Argentina." *International Journal of Transitional Justice* 6 (3): 467–485.

Schwab, Gabriele. 2010. *Haunting Legacies: Violent Histories and Transgenerational Trauma*. New York: Columbia University Press.

Soto Roland, Fernando Jorge. 2011 "Villa Joyosa, los fantasmas del pasado." *Falsaria*, December 20. http://www.falsaria.com/2011/12/villa-joyosa-los-fantasmas-del-pasado

Tarnopolsky, Daniel. 2012. *Betina Sin Aparecer: Historia íntima del caso Tarnopolsky, una familia diezmada por la dictadura militar*. Buenos Aires: Norma.

Tello Weiss, Mariana Eva. 2006. "'Vivimos al límite. Al límite entre la vida y la muerte, entre el bien y el mal'. El miedo en las memorias sobre la lucha armada en los '70." In *Miedos y Memorias en las Sociedades Contemporáneas*, edited by Héctor Schmucler, 27–43. Córdoba: Comunicarte.

Thrift, Nigel. 2007. *Non-Representational Theory: Space, Politics, Affect*, London: Routledge.

Verbitsky, Horacio. 1995. *El Vuelo*. Buenos Aires: Planeta.

Vezzetti, Hugo. 2002. *Pasado y presente: Guerra, dictadura y sociedad en la Argentina*. Buenos Aires: Siglo XXI.

Viola, Liliana. 2011. "Los fabulosos calavera." *Pagina/12*, August 28. http://www.pagina12.com.ar/diario/suplementos/radar/9-7288-2011-09-02.html

White, Luise. 2000. *Speaking with Vampires: Rumor and History in Colonial Africa*. Berkeley: University of California Press.

Zanetto, Guillermo. 2012. "Hacen oficinas en el ex búnker de Massera y los empleados ven fantasmas." *Conurbano*, August 29. http://24con.infonews.com/conurbano/nota/72888-destruyen-el-bunkerde-masserayvenfantasmas/

The desire for justice, psychic reparation and the politics of memory in 'post-conflict' Northern Ireland

Graham Dawson

School of Humanities, University of Brighton, Brighton, UK

The expression 'desire for justice' is commonly used to describe the demand for redress made by victims of violence within 'post-conflict' transition. This article addresses the subjective and psychic aspects of this *desire* for justice, as these articulate with the politics of memory, discourses of victimhood, and questions of recognition, reparation and reconciliation in the Northern Ireland peace process. It explores how psychic and emotional currents percolate into public discourse and politics, and how the traumatic effects of past violence affect the emotional dynamics of victims' involvement in truth and justice issues, in the context of devolved government and the controversies surrounding the work of the Eames–Bradley Consultative Group on the Past. The first part of the article develops a case study of one grass-roots organisation campaigning on behalf of victims of 'terrorist violence' during the Troubles, West Tyrone Voice (WTV). By examining the discourse of justice in WTV's public statements, and in interviews with members, it explores what justice means for the group and individuals in it, how others are represented in relation to this and how the emotional structure of WTV discourse shapes its responses to the British Government's reconciliation agenda. In the second part, the article reflects on this case study in the light of theories about the meaning of justice, its psychic roots and dynamics, developed within object-relations psychoanalysis. Emphasising the reciprocal effects of object relations in the internal world and the experience of social relations with external others, these theories suggest the emotional basis of a practice of historical justice based on mutuality and reparation. They also enable insight into the emotional dynamics at work in the continuing war over memory in Northern Ireland, centred on conflicting ideas about justice and how to achieve it.

The 'desire for justice' is an expression commonly used to describe the demand for redress made by victims of violence within 'post-conflict' transition. My argument in this article is that more attention must be paid to understanding the subjective and psychic aspects of this *desire* for justice, as these articulate with the politics of memory, discourses of victimhood and questions of recognition, reparation and reconciliation. The article explores how psychic and emotional currents percolate into public discourse and politics, affecting representation of and by victims and the ways in which others relate themselves to victims' expressed desires for justice. It focuses on the Irish peace process since the establishment of devolved government in Northern Ireland in 2008, a period characterised by stalled efforts towards engagement with the historical legacies of the conflict. As Smyth (2007, 12–14) and Hamber (2009, 221–222) have argued, contradictions arise in post-conflict society between the wish to secure forward-looking political arrangements based on negotiated compromises and the desire for justice (including retributive justice) that is often *felt* to be urgent, paramount and non-negotiable. These contradictions are especially acute for the victims of violence who, confronted by amnesty and other arrangements designed to draw perpetrators into a negotiated political settlement, may be forced to choose between the pursuit of justice and the securing of a peace settlement or the securing of information about the death of a loved one. According to Smyth (2007) and Hamber (2009), contradictions are likely to open up between the justice that is emotionally desired or felt to be psychically necessary, and what is realistically attainable in the world of political expediency, legal procedures and the loss and degradation of evidence. How, in the light of these contradictions, are we to think about, understand and relate to victims' desire for justice?

In what follows, I will develop two main propositions, each of which sets in train a distinct line of enquiry, to be developed in turn. First, the desire for justice is intrinsically connected to questions of memory and voice, is constructed by discourse, debate and policy in the public domain as well as in the intimacies of the private sphere, and involves complex relations between personal and collective memories. I explore the implications of this proposition through a case study of West Tyrone Voice (WTV), a grass-roots victims' support group that articulates a desire for justice in campaigning on behalf of mainly Border Protestant victims of terrorist violence during the Troubles. My interest here is in understanding the collective memory constructed through the public discourse of WTV and its relation to personal life stories, in order to establish what justice means for the group and its members, and to tease out the emotional states and psychic dynamics expressed in these representations.

Second, the desire for justice is relational and dialogic, formulated in relation to those who are responsible for the injustice – the perpetrators of violence – and to those who are perceived to help or hinder the pursuit of justice. These others are both real and imagined, involving object relations in the internal world of the psyche, which influences perceptions of social relations with real others. In this line of enquiry, I consider the value of thinking and insight from the object-relations tradition of psychoanalysis, grounded in Kleinian concepts of 'splitting' and 'reparation' within the inner world of the psyche, for understanding the desire for justice as a response to the trauma generated by political violence. Here I draw on psychoanalytic theory informed by clinical practice, which explores two main ideas: justice as fairness and mutuality, and justice as grievance and revenge. In the final section of the article, I reflect on how these two lines of enquiry might be brought together, and draw some provisional conclusions. Before turning to the two main sections of the article, the context in transitional or 'post-conflict'[1] Northern Ireland must first be established.

The desire for justice in the Irish peace process

With over 3700 people killed and an estimated 50,000 injured in Troubles-related violence – most occurring within Northern Ireland itself – the desire for justice has animated both nationalist and Unionist campaigns. However, justice has had different meanings across the political divide and become deeply enmeshed in the 'war over memory' fought over the moral and political significance of the Troubles (Dawson 2007, 15). A politics of victimhood developed from the very beginning of the peace process, centred on local and grass-roots victims' support groups and campaigns pursuing truth and justice in particular cases (Dawson 2007, 27). While Irish nationalist groups have mostly campaigned on cases of 'unlawful killing' by British state forces, Unionist and pro-British groups, including WTV, have campaigned on unresolved cases of 'terrorist violence', focusing especially on that of the Provisional Irish Republican Army (PIRA or IRA) and other Republican organisations. The very category of 'the victims of violence' has been contested, with Unionist and British victims' groups and politicians laying claim to the status of 'real victims' and 'forgotten victims' in a challenge to a perceived governmental bias towards nationalist victims (said to be demonstrated by the £195 million cost of the Public Inquiry into Bloody Sunday). A hegemonic narrative, government-led, about the road to peace and the terms on which this is to be established have framed victims' issues within a discourse of 'reconciliation'.[2]

Issues of truth recovery and justice with respect to victims of violence were only tangentially addressed in the 1998 Belfast Agreement, which was primarily concerned with securing an end to armed hostilities by reaching political accommodation between the parties. Since the Agreement, and under pressures from below including the campaigns mounted by the grass-roots victims' organisations, the British Government and, since 2008, the devolved Northern Ireland administration have launched a number of initiatives addressing the needs of victims (Mourlon 2012), but a coherent approach to questions of historical justice did not come about until the establishment of the Consultative Group on the Past (CGP) in 2007, known as Eames–Bradley after the two men appointed to lead it, with a remit 'to seek a consensus across Northern Ireland on the best way to deal with the legacy of the past' (Northern Ireland Office 2007; for the context, see Lundy and McGovern 2008b). Following an extensive consultation process in 2007–2008, the Eames–Bradley Report was presented to the British

Government in January 2009 (CGP 2009). It made 31 recommendations on how to address questions of memory, truth and justice in a fair and inclusive manner, within a framework designed to promote 'reconciliation' between 'communities that have been in conflict for a long time, each as likely as the other to be in denial of the wrong that has been done in its name and of the goodness of the other' (CGP 2009, 56). While recognising the pain of the past and the need for specific kinds of acknowledgement – for example, the importance of Republicans facing up to the damaging effects of the IRA's armed campaign upon Unionists (CGP 2009, 183–184) – the Report calls for 'a strategy of remembrance in which, instead of each community continuing to tell its own story to itself, the two should come together [...] so that each can tell its version of their common story to the other' (57). Reconciliation 'emerges from working together' to build new relationships, free from violence, and involves 'society as a whole [...] tak[ing] collective responsibility for the past instead of attributing blame and avoiding responsibility' (50).

In addressing unresolved matters of justice in the transition out of violent conflict, the Eames–Bradley Report acknowledges the 'desire for penal justice' as a key demand emerging from consultations: 'Many families [...] still have an understandable desire to see someone prosecuted for causing or contributing to their relative's death' (CGP 2009, 127). On this basis, it concludes that 'the possibility of bringing prosecutions should remain open and there should be no amnesty'. At the same time, it identifies a contradiction between this desire for retributive justice and the project of reconciliation: 'the very demand for justice can militate against the main goal of reconciliation, in ways and degrees that range from postponement to virtual rejection' (58). Instead, in its proposals for a Legacy Commission (2009, 16–20, 134–158), the Eames–Bradley Report leans away from retributive justice and towards the South African model of restorative justice.

As defined by Archbishop Desmond Tutu, Chair of the Truth and Reconciliation Commission (TRC) established in South Africa in 1995, '[T]he central concern [of restorative justice] is not retribution or punishment [...] but] the healing of breaches, the redressing of imbalances, the restoration of broken relationships and a search to rehabilitate both the victim and the perpetrator' (quoted in Hamber 2009, 132). There is no consensus about the merits of this shift, and in South Africa itself the TRC's amnesty provisions (granting freedom from judicial prosecution for perpetrators of human rights violations who testified before the Commission) were deeply controversial and bitterly opposed by some victims and survivors. Hamber endorses Diane Orentlicher, a legal advisor to the United Nations, when she writes that across cultures, 'human rights victims thirst for justice in the form of prosecutions' (2009, 119); in South Africa, argues Hamber, 'most victims' harboured 'desires for retributive justice' – that is, to 'get even' and 'make the offender pay' – through 'punishment of perpetrators' in a judicial process (117–119). He is critical not only of the 'ethically and morally problematic' denial of justice by the TRC's amnesty provisions (136), but also of a dominant national narrative in whose terms victims' rights are denied while 'those [victims] wanting justice are largely seen as anti-reconciliation' (137) and 'an obstacle to pragmatic political change' (136).

While the Eames–Bradley Report rejected the amnesty option for Northern Ireland, its emphasis on reconciliation at the expense of retributive justice opens up a similar danger: that those who refuse to be 'realistic' (CGP 2009, 37, see also 127, 186–187) in renouncing their right to judicial process and retribution thereby put themselves at risk of disapproval and condemnation. This danger manifests explicitly in the Report's expression of impatience with 'some victims groups' which are blamed for obstructing reconciliatory progress and charged with an inappropriate 'politicisation' of victimhood – with 'compounding the divisions and suspicions' (87), and using 'a long and determined pursuit of penal justice [. . .] as a means of continuing the conflict' (58). This echoes the argument advanced by Smyth (2007, 29) that victims' 'unrealistic and [. . .] unrealisable' desires contribute to 'a wider social tendency towards preoccupation with past grievances', to the detriment of more forward-thinking and constructive social and political initiatives.

The psychic and emotional currents that flow through public debates about transitional justice and reconciliation in the Irish peace process can be gauged from responses to the Eames–Bradley consultation. Throughout, from the announcement of its establishment and the conduct of the consultation process to the Report and subsequent discussion about what the British Government intended to do with it, the CGP was a focus of intense anxiety, hurt and anger. Amongst a number of issues sparking especially emotive controversy were the discussions about whether or not to offer amnesty to perpetrators; whether the conflict was, and should be described officially as, a war; and the recommendation for a 'recognition payment' of £12,000 payable to the closest surviving relative of every individual killed in a 'conflict-related' incident, which was widely regarded as offensive 'blood money' (see, for example, *Derry Journal*, January 30, 2009). Anger erupted at the public launch of the Report in January 2009 in Belfast. Unionist victims of terrorism, protesting against the proposals, launched verbal attacks on Republicans attending the event, including the President of Sinn Féin, Gerry Adams. They focused on atrocities committed by the IRA, while Republicans reciprocated with taunts about atrocities by loyalist paramilitaries. According to one press report, 'At one point the gathering threatened to descend into violence amid the welter of jabbing fingers and virulent insults' (Burns 2009). The event provoked wide public concern and reflection in the media about its significance that meshed with debate about the merits of the Report's various proposals, leading some commentators to concur with the *Irish Times* (January 31, 2009) that:

> It is simply too soon to ask Northern Ireland to set about an official and systematic exploration of the history of the Troubles. Even now [. . .] the wounds are still too sore, the divisions too deep and the past too hotly contested. Just talking about how

Northern Ireland might deal with the conflict's legacy generated scenes of anger and bitterness of a type many dared to hope were themselves in the past.

Evidently, the British Government agreed with this assessment: the Report was parked (see Northern Ireland Office 2010). As Suzanne Breen noted in March 2011, 'Since the controversial Eames–Bradley report was effectively binned two years ago, the entire victims' issue has dropped off the political agenda'. Consequently, progress in addressing the legacy issues of truth, justice and memory continues to be stymied.

WTV and the desire for justice

Among the Unionist protesters at the launch of the Eames–Bradley Report was Hazlett Lynch, the Director of WTV from the founding of the group in 1999 until 2011. Holding an enlarged portrait photograph of his brother Ken, a Royal Ulster Constabulary officer who was shot dead by the IRA in an ambush in 1977, Lynch was reported to have said, 'When IRA men died while launching cowardly attacks on this community, they actually received justice. The families of those murderers should not be consoled with a single penny today' (Burns 2009). For Lynch, the Eames–Bradley proposals were 'nauseating and offensive' in drawing 'moral equivalence between innocent victims [like his brother] and terrorists'; the Report 'is repugnant to decency, and is yet another futile attempt to re-write history in such a way that it sanitises everything that terrorists have visited on our country and its people' (Donnelly 2009).

WTV was one of the most uncompromising and assertive among the victims' support groups in its critique and rejection of Eames–Bradley. In its local leaflets and newsletter and on its website,[3] the group describes its mission as: 'Speaking and acting for the innocent victims of paramilitary terrorism in West Tyrone'. It serves an area along the western border between Northern Ireland and County Donegal in the Irish Republic, experienced as marginalised at the very 'edge of the Union' and with a significant legacy of violence: 132 people killed – 'in Co Tyrone, 26 of every 10,000 lost their lives', some 1200 physically injured and an estimated 13,000 people 'injured psychologically, emotionally and mentally'. WTV was formed to address a widespread sense of injustice in the Unionist communities in this Border region as across the whole of Northern Ireland, sparked by the Belfast Agreement, particularly the early release scheme for 'prisoners with conflict-related convictions', a measure that proved to be 'a catalyst for the formation of a tranche of Protestant and Unionist victims groups' (Dawson 2007, 277, see also 237–243). Lynch explains:

> [T]here was the feeling that these people who plunged many people in Northern Ireland into bereavement, into loss, into trauma, suffering and pain, were now getting out, they were being in a sense rewarded by the Government for what they had done, whereas those of us who have carried the wounds and the scars of their activities have been left, still with the pain. And there didn't seem to be any justice

or ... fairness of any kind, shown to those of us whose lives had been traumatized by the activities of these guys. (Quoted in Dawson 2007, 277)[4]

The WTV group's core aims are to:

> Be a voice for the victims of paramilitary terrorism, and their families; seek justice for these victims; seek formal recognition of their suffering; provide support and advice for our members; ensure the story of our pain and loss is never forgotten. (WTV 1999)

The group provides a safe, private space in which personal memories can be narrated and shared, and also constitutes a collective voice and agency that speaks about these experiences in wider public arenas, representing the many different personal memories of their members as a singular, collective narrative that tells of 'our experience'. The desire for justice voiced by WTV, then, is articulated in stories that are told in both private and public arenas, and has both a personal and a collective dimension (Dawson 2007, 237). These are considered in turn.

Personal memory and the desire for justice

In 2009, WTV had over 200 members and worked with hundreds more beneficiaries,[5] each of whom has their own particular historical experience of violence, their personal conception of justice and ideas and feelings about the significance of injustice in their own lives. To provide an indicative sense of these personal memories, ideas and feelings, I consider here two particular examples, making no claims as to their typicality or representativeness. Ramsey Turner and Gamble Moore were both members of WTV's Steering Committee when I interviewed them, together with two other members and the group's director, in November 2009.[6] In these interviews, each man has a distinctively different story to tell in response to my questions about the personal meaning of justice in the context of his own and his family's experience of violence, about the feelings underlying his desire and quest for justice, about his perception of those responsible for the violence and about how he thinks justice would best be served in his particular case.

Ramsey Turner, a retired foreman for a construction firm, was subjected to violence in 1997, during a period of tension three years into the peace process, after he had sold some land to a Roman Catholic. 'Our own people then set upon me and my wife' by throwing a stone though the living-room window of their home and delivering a live bullet in an envelope with a threatening note: 'It was pure hatred of me selling the site'. Turner's assailant(s) remained unknown, a faceless and sinister presence bearing a permanent sense of threat: 'I didn't sleep for weeks after it'. The incident badly affected Turner's wife and daughters as well. The family moved house, but the sense of threat from the unidentified perpetrator still remained 12 years later: 'They could be there watching your functions and what you're at [...] You don't feel safe, because a tribe of clients could gather round you, and you're never sure'. A further ramification was that

Turner felt he became the focus of suspicion within the local Unionist community precisely because he had been targeted in this way:

> I've done nothing wrong [...] but my pride is hurted [...] People think that I would be a traitor [...] I'd feel that if I was in company at a dance or some function, that people were looking at me and thinking, because I sold a site – a bit of Ireland – that I let people, let myself down, or let my country down.

His reputation as a leader in his community was damaged with no means of clearing his name:

> In Ireland [...] people are talking about you, but they don't talk to your face. That'd be your own people, people going to your own church [...] The dogs in the street knew what was happening [...] but it was never mentioned to any of us, any of the family.

Reliant on those responsible for upholding justice to discover the identity of his assailant, Turner recalls:

> There was never anybody brought to justice for what was done to me. It was never brought up in court at all. I'm sure there was plenty of evidence there if the police had have looked hard enough but there was nobody ever convicted.

The police 'didn't seem interested'. They lost the bullet. They lost the letter:

> Justice is very low in my case, very far down the line. [...] Nobody ever come to say that they'd done anything for me, and they had no suspects in mind. I had no suspects, or I wasn't going to point the finger at anybody.

Corroborating Herman's (2005) argument that victims place great emphasis on having the seriousness of the violent event and its impact acknowledged, Turner questions the readiness to play down the importance of his experience: 'Although I didn't look on it whenever it happened as to be the worst thing that could have happened to me, looking back on it I think it *was* the worst thing that could have happened'. Yet for the police, 'It's long forgot about, my incident'.

In these circumstances, for Turner justice is entirely dependent on the perpetrator making a confession:

> Unless someone goes into a police station and admits it, there'll never be any come back on it. I'm hoping that some day somebody will say to me, 'I'm the client that threw the stone through your window and left a bullet' – maybe dying of cancer or something and looking for forgiveness.

Imagining what he would desire of the perpetrator should this scenario arise, Turner dismisses retributive punishment, legal or otherwise, as unimportant: 'I wouldn't want to see him jailed [...] I wouldn't hit him a punch in the face'. Instead, he identifies two factors that would suffice for redress. First, he would need to discover the identity of his assailant(s): 'It would be enough for me to know who this client was [...] That boy was maybe forced to do it, but [...] if he did come to me I would know exactly who sent him, or who were the boys behind the scenes'. Second, he would want the truth of the matter to be revealed in public: '[I]f the name came forward ... It would ease my problem if it was brought to court and made him as public as I was, that he was the perpetrator, and let people decide as to who was at fault or wrong'. For Turner, then, discovering the truth about what was done to him, establishing the identity of the perpetrator and the harmfulness of his actions in public knowledge and securing the possibility of fair judgement in the court of local opinion are what matters in order to undo the unfairness of his treatment: 'That would give me and my wife great satisfaction [...] and that would be justice to me done'.

While Turner's story challenges a number of preconceptions about the experiential legacies of political violence in Northern Ireland, in representing an experience of intimidation from within his 'own' community, my second example testifies to the complexity of subjective responses to injustice and of the desire for justice even in cases that correspond more closely to politicised collective memories of the conflict. Gamble Moore, then a factory maintenance fitter and a part-time member of the locally recruited Ulster Defence Regiment (UDR) of the British Army, was targeted as a UDR soldier by the IRA in Strabane in 1973, at a time when 'it was really bad [and] there were bombings, shootings nearly every day'. Returning home from work with his wife and two workmates, his car was ambushed and he was shot three times, in the neck, chest and shoulder. Moore saved his own life by noticing the gunman as he stepped out to shoot and running the car into him – 'a terrible thing to do' – thereby disturbing his aim. Afterwards, Moore realised that the attack had been set up by a workmate seen talking earlier to a man dressed in black, and passed on the workmate's name to the Army. The police 'picked him up the next day, and let him go again'; Moore believes that the Army 'knew that I was going to be shot that day' but had decided not to intervene or to prosecute afterwards, because 'they had an informer somewhere'. One of the men involved absconded to Canada, while the other escaped over the Border into the Irish Republic. Moore had heard that 'the two of them are back in town again now', but thinks it unlikely he would recognise them after more than 30 years.

The effects of the shooting were profound. Moore suffered pain and needed to adjust to a permanently disabled arm, which cost him his job. The effects of the shooting on his internal world were also damaging and long-lasting. The attack 'changed my personality altogether. I was very hard to live with after it, I was [...] very impatient [... and] short tempered, it was eating away at me'. The sense of injustice preyed upon him: 'It was always on my mind to think that anybody should be my judge, jury and executioner. Who authorized them to do that? Why did they take it upon themselves to do that? Who gave them the right?' The shooting also had powerful emotional effects on his family: 'It changed my wife's personality altogether too', and 'badly affected' his teenaged daughter and his son, who 'joined the UDR [... partly] because of what had happened to me, that he'd be there to protect me'. Like Turner, Moore was left with an enduring sense of uncertainty and threat: 'I've been living under a cloud these last 36 years. I'm always waiting, it's always there in my mind that somebody could have a pop at me again, it's always there. It never leaves you'.

Unlike Turner, Moore's desire for justice does involve retribution: 'Justice means to me [...] that the perpetrators, those who injured me, be brought to justice and punished for what they did'. But Moore is careful to specify the kind of judicial retribution he considers appropriate:

> I don't mean to be physically hanged or anything like that, or shot, or whopped [...] I wouldn't want anybody to suffer pain [...] To me, the worst way you can punish a person is to take away his freedom [...] Deprive them of the company of their family, just as they tried to deprive my family of me. [...] They'd be suffering the same as I suffered.

Retribution through the criminal justice system, then, functions as the means by which Moore might realise a desire similar to Turner's, to establish equity between, on one hand, the intended effects of the violent attack and the 'punishment' suffered by the victim ('they tried to deprive my family [...] they were punishing me for not agreeing with them, with their political outlook'); and, on the other, the punishment to be meted out to the perpetrators by judicial process (to 'deprive them [...] of their family'): 'Justice would mean that they would be [...] made to feel the same way I felt when they attacked me'.

Redress for Moore also encompasses a measure of restorative justice. He expresses a wish that the perpetrators might 'realize what they have done, the enormity of what they have done', and acknowledge 'in their own minds that they had done wrong and they should atone for it'. Imagining an encounter with the perpetrators, he envisages that: 'If I met those people now, I would just say one thing to them: why? I wouldn't be out for striking them [...] or shooting them or anything like that, no'. However, Moore does not imagine the perpetrators engaging with him in any transformative way: 'I know these people, they're like a leopard, it never changes its spots, they'll never apologize. On the surface they may appear to apologize but deep down they don't'. Moore's lack of trust in any imaginable gesture of apology from those responsible for his shooting extends into the political domain and shapes his perceptions of Republican motives in the peace process:

> I can't ever see Republicans reconciled any way unless they get what they want – a united Ireland, and they want all the loyalists and Protestants all out of the country, they don't want us here at all. [...] I would love to see reconciliation [but] it depends on them being honest. You can see there with Gerry Adams and [the Sinn Féin Deputy First Minister] Martin McGuinness in parliament, they're still involved, they're still [...] Army Council men in the IRA, they'll never change their spots.

This wider context dampens any expectation that Moore might ever achieve the justice he desires for himself:

> I can't see it ever happening, oh no, that'll never happen, not at all. To me its just pipe dreams [...] because of the political situation in Northern Ireland [...] They'll get away with it, oh there won't be a thing done [...] Maybe you'll get a few people convicted if there's court cases for murder [... But] the like of me being shot [...], it'll not even be looked at and I know that ... It'll never change.

WTV's public discourse and the desire for justice

The public discourse of WTV is grounded in personal and familial experiences and stories such as those of Turner and Moore. The group's leaders emphasise the importance of WTV's outreach work to provide support for often isolated individuals and families,[7] building relationships through the exchange of stories. Identification with others who have undergone similar or comparable experiences leads to the formation of what Ashplant, Dawson, and Roper (2004, 17–21) call a 'shared and common memory' with distinctive narrative themes that connect people across their different experiences and understandings. WTV provides a focal point around which intersecting local memories are able to coalesce. It represents the group's collective experience in the form of a public discourse fashioned to intervene on behalf of group members in the public debates about the victims of violence and associated questions of truth and justice within post-conflict Northern Ireland.

The WTV public discourse on justice has a number of key characteristics (WTV 1999, 2008a; Dawson 2007, 233–287). First, the group's ethos is rooted in Protestant Christian moral principles and analysis of the Troubles. Lynch has argued that, 'as country people and as people who were brought up within a broad Christian ethos, we do know the difference between right and wrong [...] And we try to take that high moral ground' (quoted in Dawson 2007, 236). Second, these moral categories are associated with the ideological categories deployed in defence of the Unionist state of Northern Ireland, producing a distinction between the lawful and morally righteous violence of the state security forces and the criminal and morally repugnant violence of the terrorists. While opposed to all terrorism including that of loyalist paramilitaries, WTV's public focus has concentrated on PIRA and other Republican groups whose activities in the border areas were largely responsible for the harm inflicted on WTV's members, especially through targeting the locally recruited UDR and police (Dawson 2007, 214–223; Patterson 2010). Third, WTV's interventions in post-conflict culture and politics demonstrate a strong continuity with loyalist discourse before the paramilitary ceasefires of 1994. Its discourse emphasises these absolute moral distinctions (between terrorists and security forces, and between terrorists and their innocent victims). It demands retributive justice for terrorist crimes, in opposition to the restorative justice advocated within the peace process, and it critiques the 'betrayal' by government and state in their failure to pursue judicial retribution for hundreds of terrorist murders and other violent incidents with sufficient vigour both historically and currently (WTV 2008a, 17–18). Finally, these considerations of justice – 'the underlying and most pressing demand of victims in our group' (WTV 2008a) – underpin an oppositional stance towards the terms of the Belfast Agreement and the peace process constructed on its basis, articulated by WTV as a fundamental objection to allowing 'terrorists in government' (WTV 2009a, see also 2008a, 20).

HISTORICAL JUSTICE

These established principles and characteristics of WTV public discourse over a 10-year period, 1999–2009, provided the basis for the group's submission to the CGP's consultation process and critique of its conclusions (WTV 2008a, 2008b, 2009b).[8] Responding to the Eames–Bradley Report, WTV condemns its inclusive agenda in adopting the official definition of victims: 'all the surviving injured and those who care for them, together with those close relatives who mourn their dead' (Bloomfield 1998, 14), as a result of 'a conflict-related incident' (UK Parliament 2006; CGP 2009, 67–68). This definition is considered by WTV to be objectionable because it fails to exclude the agents of paramilitary violence (and their supporters) who are held to be perpetrators rather than victims, and 'refuses to differentiate between victims of terrorism and terrorists', giving rise to an 'implied "moral equivalence" between "terrorist" and "victim" [which] is totally unacceptable'. The 'language of inclusion' adopted in the Report, according to WTV, fails to establish these clearly defined and demarcated categories. Instead, the Report's writers have 'been taken in by' and reproduce 'the "double speak" of republicans', resulting in an 'attempt at re-writing history in such a way that all reference to "terrorism" is removed'. The Report in its entirety is rejected on these grounds: 'Hence, every other recommendation is tainted and seriously flawed, and ought to be rejected in toto by government and parliament, and by all groups working with the victims of terrorism' (WTV 2009b, 1). In a context where the Sinn Féin leaders, Adams and McGuinness, appeared to many victims to be unapologetic and unrepentant about the harm caused by IRA actions in the past, and where the present-day threat from Republican terrorism in the form of the Real IRA and the Continuity IRA continued to grow (WTV discourse recognises no distinction between the so-called 'dissident Republicans' and PIRA), Eames–Bradley was denounced by WTV for promoting the British Government's agenda of 'appeasing' terrorists to secure a flawed peace (WTV 2008a, 10). For WTV, the peace process as such, and all of Northern Ireland's new institutions including the power-sharing Assembly and Executive, the Victims Commission and the Commission for Human Rights, are considered to be compromised on this basis.[9]

At the core of this critique is an argument that justice has been foregone in the interests of political expediency, and a flawed notion of reconciliation adopted in its place (WTV 2008a, 13–16, 21–23). While the individual membership of WTV cannot be assumed to be homogeneous in its support for the group's public position on these issues – and, as Turner's story demonstrates, personal experiences of violence may be more complex and multifaceted than, or even diverge from, its public discourse – the uncompromising collective memory of the Troubles articulated by WTV speaks to profound discontents with post-conflict Northern Ireland amongst Unionist victims of terrorism. Furthermore, it establishes a subjective stance that refuses accommodation with, or co-option by, the hegemonic project of reconciliation. Where the Eames–Bradley Report (CGP 2009, 23) speaks of overcoming 'division and mistrust' through 'the desire for true and lasting reconciliation' – requiring 'acknowledgement of the moral dignity of our common humanity' coupled with 'mutual forgiveness' and with a willingness to recognise the multiple truths about the past (25) – WTV discourse speaks of moral absolutes and demands that politics and social relationships be conducted on the basis of a fundamental distinction between the harmers and the harmed. Where the discourse of reconciliation warns that the '[societal] process of addressing conflictual and fractured relationships' is fraught with 'paradoxes and [...] contradictions' (Hamber and Kelly 2005, 38), WTV discourse insists on avoiding any ambiguity. Where advocates of reconciliation promote a transformation in the 'culture of suspicion, fear, mistrust and violence' by 'engaging with those who are different from us' (Hamber and Kelly 2005, 38), WTV discourse grasps the social world as irredeemably bifurcated between good people and evil people, and sees terrorists as unrepentant sinners from whom nothing short of full and abject remorse will suffice, who remain dangerous and likely to revert to violence if their political demands are not conceded ('a leopard never changes its spots') and whose gestures of reconciliation are highly suspect and designed to fool people (WTV 2008b, 4). A third category is reserved for those who are fooled – 'do-gooders' (WTV 2008a, 8) and people who should know better (like Eames and Bradley) – and who are drawn into 'appeasing terrorists' rather than judging them on the basis of their past actions and future intentions. Standing in this way against the whole logic and thrust of the peace process, WTV's mobilisation of the desire for justice is not 'realistic' in currently practical, political terms, but rather expresses a utopian critique of politics as now conducted in Northern Ireland, while holding open the future possibility of attaining judicial redress within a properly 'rights-based approach to the needs of victims' (Hamber 2009, 136).

The desire for justice in object-relations psychoanalytic theory

I take my bearings in psychoanalytic theory from the object-relations tradition derived from the work of Melanie Klein (Segal 1973; Greenberg and Mitchell 1983; Dawson 1994, 27–52, 2007, 57–85). This offers ways of thinking about emotional and psychic life as a dynamic process occurring within a person's inner world, largely unconscious, peopled by imagined objects or 'imagos' with which the self interacts to establish various kinds of internal object relations. These imagined objects partly take their character from, and in turn function as imaginative templates that determine, perceptions of social others and relationships with these external objects. For Garland and her contributors (2002), this model enables a distinctive approach to trauma – including that generated in the context of political violence – understood as disturbance in the internal world stemming from an external event that breaches the defensive or protective 'envelope' of the psyche, and the psychic strategies developed in response to this breach. Crucially for Garland and colleagues, the traumatic event is mediated by pre-existing, internal object relations. Emotions generated by the (external) traumatic situation come to be associated with, and experienced in terms of, unresolved conflicts in the inner world. Defensive splitting of the self occurs in order to restore the defensive envelope and protect the self against what may be felt to be overwhelming emotions, which are projected outside the self into an 'other'. This internal state affects perceptions of external objects and situations, which are experienced according to internal psychic reality and coloured by it, such that behaviours and relationships in the social world become vehicles for 'acting out' internal object relations, managing internal disturbances and conflicts, and controlling emotions.

In traumatic splitting, the external, social world appears to confirm what is already known and believed about it; so, for example, the terrifying and devastating experiences produced in reality by paramilitary or state combatants confirm the presence in the internal world of a sinister and petrifying imago felt to have power to threaten or destroy the self. This imago, in turn, shapes the phantasies through which the social world is encountered, as can be seen in the testimony of a survivor of the Republican atrocity at Darkley Church in 1983, who for long afterwards was haunted by 'nightmares that [Republican gunmen] were going to come and take over the estate', and imagined 'where we could hide if they came to the house and sprayed it with gunfire' (Dawson 2007, 250). For object-relations theorists, recovery from trauma and the nurturing of psychic health depend upon capacities for 'reparation' being mobilised to think about the meanings and emotions attached to internal objects, to undo defensive splitting and to integrate contradictory emotions and conflicting aspects of the self within a less polarised inner world. The work of reparation is strengthened by the 'introjection', or taking in, of such capacities where they are encountered in social life: this enables 'something new to happen' within psychic reality (Greenberg and Mitchell 1983, 134).

Psychoanalysts within the object-relations tradition have reflected on the complex emotions and psychic conflicts involved in the desire for justice. Their work focuses on ideas of what is just and unjust, and the feelings and affect attached to those ideas in the internal world where the self relates to imagined internal objects, and in its social relations with real others. Here I draw, in turn, on studies that consider justice in relation to the concepts of fairness and grievance.

For Rayner (1999), the psychic significance of justice is underpinned by the experience of fairness, a commonly held and deeply felt idea recognised and utilised even by very young children, and one that is fundamental to our social well-being. The practice of fairness in our everyday lives centrally involves three elements. The first and most fundamental is mutuality. Fairness is felt to be owed to others as well as due from others; we wish to be fair and just in our actions as well as expect to be treated fairly by others, and thereby recognise our mutual dependence on one another (Rayner 1999, 479, 481). The second is 'equality of consideration' (483). To act fairly is to recognise the validity of the other's expectation of being treated fairly, and to recognise this as equivalent to one's own expectation of being fairly treated by the other. Third, acting fairly involves a complex amalgam of thought and emotion in evaluating an issue, including evaluation of one's own relation to others. It requires a capacity for introspection, to scrutinise one's own actions for fairness and unfairness; a capacity for reappraising one's own actions in the light of what others say, through dialogue and exchange of views; and a capacity to develop a balanced view of others as complex human beings rather than seeing only particular sides or aspects of them. Thus, the practice of fairness involves undoing splitting and projection in our dealings with others, and is intrinsically aligned with psychic integration and reparation.

According to Rayner, the importance of fairness in our psychic and social lives can be gauged by examining the feelings engendered by the experience of unfairness (and injustice), when relations of mutuality and equality are felt to have been broken:

> Reactions to their rupture or absence are often deep and intense, even full of violence [...] Many different emotions, sometimes dangerous ones, can emerge. Violent outrage, fury of accusation, vengeance, bitterness and disgust [...] Bafflement and being aggrieved or sad [... and] pain of indignation [... Such feelings are] particularly acute at moments of a ruptured basic trust. (Rayner 1999, 478–479)

For Rayner, this emotional intensity indicates the impact of unfair treatment upon the inner world where it damages the ability of the self to trust in mutually beneficial relationships with its internal objects. Uncertainty replaces trust, and where the experience of unfairness is repeated, a predisposition to expect unfair treatment may be established. This internal predisposition is brought to relations with real others and acted out there, as an expectation of receiving unfair treatment in reality. Rayner's notion of 'ruptured basic trust', then, enables us to understand the profound significance of unfairness in undermining the self's confidence in relations with others based on mutuality, equality and reciprocity – and indeed, in the very possibility of a justly ordered social world. Conversely, the desire for justice can be understood as the yearning for a world governed by fairness, and for the experience of the self in beneficial relations with others that would be possible in such a world.

This account of the rupturing of basic trust by unjust treatment is developed further in studies that examine the relationship between justice, the desire for revenge and the development of a sense of grievance (Steiner 1996; Young and Gibb 2002). For Steiner, unfairness is felt in the inner world as 'a deep sense of hurt, injustice and betrayal', the result of being let down by the internal objects (based on introjections of parents or other carers) from whom help, support and protection are expected; leaving the self exposed and vulnerable (1996, 435). These feelings may be too intense or overwhelming to acknowledge, and instead become split off and projected into an object felt to be needy and vulnerable. In this situation, the inner world is experienced as a hostile place coloured by anticipations of further traitorous betrayal, distrust of any offered help or support and a determination to rely only on oneself (Young and Gibb 2002, 86).

The experience of injustice also generates proportionally intense feelings of anger and wishes for revenge. According to Steiner (1996, 433), 'when such injuries are felt to be unfair they give rise to a wish for revenge that is accompanied by extreme hatred and destructiveness'. These feelings and impulses may also be too intense to acknowledge and bear, and again, through denial and projection, become invested in an object that is felt to be angry and vengeful towards the self. Here, the inner world becomes 'suffused with danger' and fear of attack by 'threatening hostile forces' (Young and Gibb 2002, 81). These are felt to exist in the social world as well, where others become the bearers of destructiveness and violence, while one's own anger and desire for revenge is disavowed and unconscious, and its psychic reality cannot be acknowledged (Steiner 1996, 440). Instead, Steiner argues, 'the destructiveness is controlled and expressed in indirect and often hidden ways' (443). The sense of injustice and these attendant affects may also be relieved through the actions of real others in the social world, by means of acknowledgement, apology, atonement and reparations; however, in some cases, 'a sense of injustice [...] cannot be assuaged' without 'some kind of attack seen to be equal to the original injury' (Young and Gibb 2002, 82). Steiner suggests that 'Revenge is the antithesis of forgiveness [...] the object cannot be let off the hook until it has been forced to confess and atone for the injury done' (434). Like Herman's analysis of the 'righteous anger' of victims of injustice (2005, 576), Steiner's account understands victims themselves to be subject to anger and have a capacity for violence (real or symbolic) to exact retribution from the perpetrator of harm. For Steiner, though, the desire for revenge is not always openly acknowledged, and then becomes disavowed anger and violence. As he puts it, 'the quest for vengeance begins as a demand for justice, but it seems to be taken over by a more malignant destructiveness of an insatiable kind', which cannot be assuaged (1996, 434).

Steiner's argument is that, in scenarios where the desire for revenge cannot be acknowledged, and anger in response to injustice is disavowed and remains unconscious, a deeper state of grievance develops. In this, an individual pursues 'claims of being treated unjustly in one form or another, in a way that seems driven and unassailable', and may 'remain stuck in an aggrieved state' (Young and Gibb 2002, 83), or 'impasse' (Steiner 1996, 434), whatever others do in the social world to address the injustice. This 'unconscious grievance structure' establishes a self-perpetuating 'psychic vicious circle' (Young and Gibb 2002, 84, 94) in which the sense of grievance becomes a psychic defence against the unacknowledged feelings – of loss, hurt and betrayal, of anger and the desire for revenge – provoked by the injustice, and has to be maintained continually in their place. The grievance is held onto 'like a precious object that can't be given up' (88). The internal world structured by grievance in this way has a number of key characteristics. First, it is pervaded by an atmosphere in which helpful interventions from others, whether attempting to address the injustice or to relieve the emotional burden of the injury, are made difficult, refused or rebuffed (94). Second, considerable psychic energy and work is invested in asserting 'the veracity of the grievance' (86), and maintaining 'in an active state' the narrative that defines and accounts for it (94), a narrative with a 'moralistic unforgiving quality' (Steiner 1996, 438) that attributes responsibility to others and blames them from the assumed position of the moral high ground (Young and Gibb 2002, 93). Third, the reality of the inner world requires continual renewal by the incorporation of fresh events that establish 'further cause for feeling [aggrieved]' and thereby 'sustain [...] existing internal structures' (Young and Gibb 2002, 88).

The subject of injustice turned to grievance, then, may become stitched into a scenario which is both self-perpetuating and resistant to further transformation: a condition of stuckness in which the desire for justice must be forever proclaimed but remain forever unfulfilled, its goal an ideal and unattainable object. The possibility of acting fairly towards others is reduced or precluded, since grievance undercuts the fundamental sense of mutual dependency necessary for a fair and just relationship to thrive. Real others in social reality are not experienced in their full complexity, but positioned in their allotted roles according to the narrative of grievance, thereby sealing them into the structure of perpetual and irredeemable injustice, either as perpetrators or as colluders. Those who are positioned by an unconscious grievance structure are likely to feel a range of emotions as a result. They may experience frustration and hopelessness at the stuckness and negativity that confront them in a situation in which nothing helpful can be given. They may also be provoked to blame the 'intransigence' of those who appear to be 'stuck in the past' and would not 'let go' or 'move on' (but such a reaction only reinforces the grievance narrative by confirming its expectations of a hostile world). Furthermore, what Steiner terms the 'disguised hatred' of disavowed anger 'is often felt to be vengeful by the object on the receiving end', for example in moralistic blaming (1996, 433). According to Steiner, it is difficult to describe how emergence from such a state occurs (441), and how 'a move towards reparation' begins (438). He suggests, however, that 'reconciliation is not based on denial [of anger] but on a recognition of psychic reality; it is not just an act of acknowledgement of wrongs done but also of difference and dependence' (444). Requiring the re-establishment of trust in mutuality, the reparation of grievance is necessarily a matter of object relations, as well as renewed relationship to real others in the social world.

The desire for justice: psychoanalytic insight and the writing of history

How, then, might insight into the desire for justice and its vicissitudes within psychoanalytic object relations theory contribute to understanding the complexities, contradictions and conflicts centred on the desire for justice in the histories of the Irish peace process and WTV? It is not my intention here to offer any kind of psychohistory, nor life-story analysis involving interpretation of the psychology of individuals. Bearing this caveat in mind, in the following, I argue that psychoanalytic thinking can aid our understanding of the historical experience of injustice and responses to it, and consider how psychoanalytic insights might be used to investigate the psychic and emotional structuring of public discourses, exchanges and interactions concerning these highly charged political issues.

Turning first to the narratives of Turner and Moore, both evoke a 'rupture of basic trust' stemming from acts that violently negate the principle of fairness in Rayner's sense and produce internal worlds characterised by uncertainty, lack of safety and distrust. In each case, the unjust actions to which they were subjected are described in terms of a fundamental loss of psychic equality, or 'equity' (Hamber 2009, 123). Where Turner feels himself to be exposed and vulnerable to attack, both physical and moral, his faceless assailant remains invisible and beyond moral scrutiny or punishment. The lack of equity between the assailants who take it upon themselves to be his 'judge, jury and executioner', and his own powerlessness to call them to account, 'eats away' at Moore. Both men feel let down or betrayed by those who fail to meet expectations of mutuality by offering acknowledgement and support: the police who have no care for Turner's distress or allow Moore's assailants to go free and the church communion that ostracises Turner. Both men are left to deal with what Rayner terms the 'pain of indignation' and a range of other difficult feelings that manifest in their internal worlds and in their family relationships. While as victims of violence they suffer in many ways and over long periods of time, those responsible for the violence 'get away with it' and never have to face the consequences of the harm they have caused.

Turner and Moore each describe their personal desire for justice in terms of a wish to restore the psychic equality lost within the internal world. Turner wishes that his faceless assailant could be made equally visible to himself in the local court of opinion, enabling fair judgement about whose action was most wrongful. Moore would like his attackers to not only be punished but also to 'be made to feel the same way I felt' and to 'suffer the same as I suffered'. Both men also demonstrate a desire that they themselves should act fairly in their imagined encounter with the perpetrator, by thinking through the various possibilities open to them, and considering which actions would feel right as a means to secure just satisfaction. Each comes to his own internal resolution of this question. In both cases, a desire to restore fairness in the internal world is matched by a corresponding wish for the restoration of a justly ordered social world – while acknowledging the political realities that appear to militate against any such possibility in their own cases and more generally in Northern Ireland. Turner sees that his 'incident' (like so many others) has been forgotten, and finds himself dependent entirely on a change of heart by his faceless attacker for the restoration of justice to the world. Moore would 'love to see reconciliation' in Northern Ireland but cannot believe it possible because of his distrust of Republicans.

WTV discourse speaks to these kinds of unfulfilled and perhaps unfulfillable desires. Its unambiguous call for the restoration of judicial retribution for 'terrorist crimes' past and present, as the necessary basis for both a functioning democracy (WTV 2008a, 17–18) and 'true reconciliation' (23), imagines a means to restore a justly ordered social world. However, the transformation in relations to others signalled by concepts of democracy and reconciliation involves more than judicial retribution alone. As Assefa (1999, 44) has argued:

> The central question in reconciliation is not whether justice is done, but rather how one goes about doing it in ways that can also promote future harmonious and positive relationship between parties that have to live with each other whether they like it or not. Justice is a necessary but not sufficient condition for reconciliation.

According to Assefa, the punishment of offenders in itself does nothing to transform conflictual group relations or prevent the 'desire to retaliate' for such punishment, which may be reproduced within social groups across generations. For Assefa (1999), 'the essence of reconciliation', and the source of its potential transformative power, lies in going beyond the 'present[ation] of grievances' and the demand that 'the adversary [...] should make amends', and depends upon 'self-reflection' about one's own role 'in the creation or perpetuation of conflict and hurtful interaction' (42–43). This argument need not imply a dubious moral equivalence between those responsible for harming others by their practice of violence, and those harmed by such violence. But it does prompt questions about the ways in which self and others are constructed through articulations of the desire for historical justice. Existing social relations and interactions, as well as their potential transformation, always involve, and depend reciprocally upon, object relations between the self and its others within the internal world. Psychoanalytic thinking about justice, then, may aid understanding of the psychic positionings that underpin current disputes over dealing with the past. Specifically, the psychoanalytic concept of grievance may illuminate the state of impasse or stuckness in Northern Ireland's politics of memory, while ideas linking justice to the rebuilding of basic trust in mutuality may help in formulating historical narratives and other public discourses that open up possibilities for 'something new to happen'.

To consider first the question of stuckness: psychoanalytic observations about the internal world and its object relations following a rupture of basic trust and the development of a grievance structure suggest ways of understanding the psychic world produced by WTV public discourse and its roots in the collective experience of Border Protestant communities. WTV discourse represents a world of unresolved injustices, characterised emotionally by hurt and loss, fear of continuing violence and persecution, and a sharp sense of betrayal and distrust. It structures relations with others on the basis of moral absolutism and an unwillingness to tolerate contradictions and ambiguities, and establishes a mode of Unionist subjectivity predicated on taking the moral high ground. This underpins political suspicion of Republicans and a hostile stance towards the mainstream Unionist leadership insofar as it is engaged in a search for political and moral accommodation with Republicans. The 'veracity of grievance' is reproduced in a narrative of moralistic blaming that draws on a wider loyalist collective memory of the Troubles: violence is represented as entirely the responsibility of the IRA, making no acknowledgement of the injustices perpetrated by the Unionist-dominated Northern Ireland state since its inception in 1921–1922, or by the armed forces of the state following the deployment of the British Army in 1969. This narrative of historical grievance is reinforced with reference to new events – the activities of anti-Agreement Republicans (McGonagle 2009), the appointment of a Victims Commissioner from a Republican family (*News Letter*, January 29, 2008) – that serve to confirm what has been argued all along about the duplicity of Republicans and the spuriousness of a peace process about which there is little or nothing positive to say. A 'moralistic unforgiving quality' permeates many of WTV's own public interventions, confronting others with unyielding and punitive moral standards that position them as uniquely blameworthy, or regard with suspicion those whose own interventions are intended to be constructive, such as Eames–Bradley and other 'do-gooders'.

Psychoanalytic considerations, then, may illuminate the psychic characteristics of a 'world of meaning' and reflect on the object relations of self and other that are structured through and by a specific public discourse. However, an analysis of this kind remains limited if it concentrates exclusively on a sole discursive agent rather than attending to the object relations and interactions constituted by the wider field of public discourse in which this agent participates. Protestant and Unionist perceptions of the peace process are also partly an effect of the particular way conflict transformation and notions of reconciliation have been designed and instituted politically (Lundy and McGovern 2008a). Stuckness is a result of the wider political situation rather than the responsibility of any one group. One important determining factor is the stasis in implementing a comprehensive approach to the issues of truth, justice and the legacy of the conflict – including a commitment to rigorous pursuit of the retributive justice desired by many victims of conflict-related violence – that results from British state policy. Another is the reinforcement of understandable feelings of injustice and grievance in Border Protestant communities due to the fear of renewed Republican terrorism, which has increased in intensity, capacity and political significance in the period since the restoration of devolved government in 2008, and gives the lie to calls for victims to 'let go' of grievance on the grounds that political violence is 'now in the past' in a post-conflict society.

A psychoanalytic interpretation of WTV discourse that neither attends to the way it is positioned and engages within these wider structures of power and contestation, nor reflects on the psychic dimensions of this positioning would be not only limited but also problematic. The interpretation itself may then perform a kind of aggression towards its object, be read as 'blaming the victims' and risk reinforcing the very grievance structure that it seeks to understand. It is precisely in its capacity to illuminate the psychic structuring of public exchanges, and to develop insight into the positioning of self and other on the basis of various kinds of object relations within one's own representations as well as in the discourse of the other, that psychoanalytic thinking about the desire for justice is most useful in a post-conflict scenario. Since perceptions of being treated unfairly generate such complex and destructive emotions, including an underlying anger that tends to remain unconscious, unacknowledged and liable to be projected into others, reciprocal provocations readily develop and draw people into the kind of exchange that erupted at the launch of the Eames–Bradley Report. Recognising these psychic dynamics, and making conscious and explicit both the hurts of injustice and potentially aggressive wishes to attack and blame others, is a necessary condition for unlocking grievance structures and restoring fairness and mutuality in relations with others.

Psychoanalytic thinking about the desire for justice in terms of fairness, mutuality and moral equality offers a touchstone for considering the reparation of object relations marked by historical injustice and grievance. It enables us to ask: how is the experience of mutuality weakened or strengthened according to the ways in which judicial procedures are organised and political opponents react to each other? What kind of response to expressions of anger or enactments of revenge would be most constructive and least damaging? How might perceptions of fairness be restored in exchanges concerned with the legacies of violence? What role could public organisations play in facilitating this? The paradoxes and contradictions that manifest in any transformative process must be confronted and assessed in these terms. The paradox of the Eames–Bradley Report – a developed exercise in fairness that attempts to establish a balanced and inclusive framework for addressing the unresolved past, including recognition of Unionist victims' desire for justice and a clear call for Republicans to acknowledge the depth of hurt in the Unionist community – is that it was rejected as *unfair* (by WTV amongst others) precisely because of its inclusivity in extending to Republican victims an equivalent recognition and call for acknowledgement. The challenge posed to the dominant discourse of inclusivity and reconciliation in Northern Ireland is how to deal fairly and justly with those who are fundamentally opposed to its own premises and goals, and who refuse to write terrorism out of history.

Acknowledgements

This article could not have been written without the assistance of leading members of West Tyrone Voice. I am grateful to Leslie Finlay, Raymond Finlay, Hazlett Lynch, Gamble Moore and Ramsey Turner for sharing with me their personal experiences and understandings; to Lynch for arranging the interviews, for providing access to documents and for critical discussion of my ideas and writing; and to Hazlett and Margaret Lynch for their warm hospitality. I have also benefited from discussion of earlier versions with colleagues at the 'Beyond Reconciliation' conference, University of Cape Town, 2–6 December 2009; the 'Ireland and Victims' conference, University of Rennes 2, 9–11 September 2010; the Psychoanalysis and History seminar series, Institute of Historical Research, University of London, 30 March 2011; 'Narratives of Victimhood in Post-conflict Northern Ireland', in the ESRC Seminar Series 'The Politics of Victimhood', Department of Politics and International Relations, University of Leicester, 9 December 2011; and the 'Historical Justice and Memory' conference, Swinburne University of Technology, 14–17 February 2012.

Notes

1. Neither of these terms is unproblematic; both may imply unhelpful normative interpretations. I use 'post-conflict' to signify a society and culture emerging from a period of intense political violence, engaged in efforts towards conflict transformation but overshadowed by a still unresolved past and subject to ongoing conflict which might include – as in Northern Ireland – further resort to political violence; see, for example, Lederach (1995).
2. For my critique of this strategy, see Dawson (2007, 60–61, 233, 254).
3. WTV leaflets dating back to the group's launch in 1998–1999, and copies of the newsletter, are archived in the Victims boxes at the Northern Ireland Political Collection, Linen Hall Library, Belfast. The website www.westtyronevoice.bravehost.com/ (accessed November 23, 2009) is no longer online.
4. In transcribed quotations from interviews, the following conventions have been used: ... denotes a pause; [...] denotes an editorial cut.
5. Hazlett Lynch, conversation with author, November 9, 2009; see also WTV (2008a, 1).
6. Steering Committee members Leslie Finlay, Raymond Finlay, Gamble Moore and Ramsey Turner were interviewed by the author in Newtownstewart, County Tyrone, on November 10, 2009; and Hazlett Lynch, Director, was interviewed by the author in Magherafelt, County Londonderry, on November 11, 2009.
7. Raymond Finlay, interviewed November 10, 2009; and Hazlett Lynch, interviewed November 11, 2009.
8. WTV (2008b) responds to the interim keynote speech delivered by Lord Eames and Denis Bradley on 29 May 2008 in Belfast and later published in CGP (2009, 180–190). WTV (2009b) responds to the Report. In 2011, funding difficulties and the departure of Hazlett Lynch curtailed this kind of public engagement by WTV.
9. Hazlett Lynch, conversation with author, November 9, 2009.

References

Ashplant, T. G., Graham Dawson, and Michael Roper. 2004. "The Politics of War Memory and Commemoration." In *Commemorating War: The Politics of Memory*, edited by T.G. Ashplant, Graham Dawson, and Michael Roper, 3–85. New Brunswick: Transaction.

Assefa, Hizkias. 1999. "The Meaning of Reconciliation." In *People Building Peace: Thirty-Five Inspiring Stories from Around the World*, 37–45. Utrecht: European Centre for Conflict Prevention.

Bloomfield, Sir Kenneth. 1998. *We Will Remember Them: Report of the Northern Ireland Victims Commissoner*. Belfast: TSO Northern Ireland.

Breen, Suzanne. 2011. "Time to Take Care of Unfinished Business." *Belfast Telegraph*. March 2. www.belfasttelegraph.co.uk/opinion/news-analysis/time-to-take-care-of-unfinished-business-15101049.html

Burns, John F. 2009. "Payment Plan for Northern Ireland Reconciliation Provokes Outrage." *New York Times*. January 29. www.nytimes.com/2009/01/29/world/europe/29ireland.html

CGP (Consultative Group on the Past). 2009. *Report of the Consultative Group on the Past*. Belfast: Consultative Group on the Past.

Dawson, Graham. 1994. *Soldier Heroes: British Adventure, Empire and the Imagining of Masculinities*. London: Routledge.

Dawson, Graham. 2007. *Making Peace with the Past? Memory, Trauma and the Irish Troubles*. Manchester: Manchester University Press.

Donnelly, Rosetta. 2009. "Victim's Brother Slams Eames-Bradley Proposals as 'Offensive'." *Ulster Herald*. January 29. www.nwipp-newspapers.com

Garland, Caroline, ed. 2002. *Understanding Trauma: A Psychoanalytical Approach*. London: Carnac.

Greenberg, Jay, and Stephen Mitchell. 1983. *Object Relations in Psychoanalytic Theory*. Cambridge, MA: Harvard University Press.

Hamber, Brandon. 2009. *Transforming Societies After Political Violence: Truth, Reconciliation and Mental Health*. New York: Springer.

Hamber, Brandon, and Gráinne Kelly. 2005. *A Place for Reconciliation?* Democratic Dialogue Report no. 18, Belfast.

Herman, Judith Lewis. 2005. "Justice from the Victim's Perspective." *Violence Against Women* 11 (5): 571–602.

Lederach, Jean Paul. 1995. *Preparing for Peace: Conflict Transformation Across Cultures*. Syracuse, NY: Syracuse University Press.

Lundy, Patricia, and Mark McGovern. 2008a. "A Trojan Horse? Unionism, Trust and Truth-Telling in Northern Ireland." *International Journal of Transitional Justice* 2 (1): 42–62.

Lundy, Patricia, and Mark McGovern. 2008b. "Truth, Justice and Dealing with the Legacy of the Past in Northern Ireland, 1998–2008." *Ethnopolitics* 7 (1): 177–193.

McGonagle, Suzanne. 2009. "Dissidents Behind 400 Real Security Alerts in Two Years." *Irish News*. July 28. www.saoirse32.dreamwidth.org/4332144.html

Mourlon, Fabrice. 2012. "Assessing the Achievements of Assistance to the Victims of the Conflict in Northern Ireland." In *Ireland and Victims: Confronting the Past, Forging the Future*, edited by Lesley Lelourec, and Gráinne Kelly, 189–207. Oxford: Peter Lang.

Northern Ireland Office. 2007. "Hain Announces Group to Look at the Past. Press Release on Behalf of Peter Hain, Secretary of State for Northern Ireland." June 22. http://cain.ulst.ac.uk/issues/politics/docs/nio/ph220607.htm

Northern Ireland Office. 2010. "Dealing with the Past in Northern Ireland: The Recommendations of the Consultative Group on the Past." Belfast: Northern Ireland Office.

Patterson, Henry. 2010. "Sectarianism Revisited: The Provisional IRA Campaign in a Border Region of Northern Ireland." *Terrorism and Political Violence* 22 (3): 337–356.

Rayner, Eric. 1999. "Some Functions of Being Fair and Just: Or Not, in Clinical Psychoanalysis." *International Journal of Psychoanalysis* 80 (3): 477–492.

Segal, Hannah. 1973. *Introduction to the Work of Melanie Klein*. London: Hogarth Press.

Smyth, Marie Breen. 2007. *Truth Recovery and Justice After Conflict: Managing Violent Pasts*. London: Routledge.

Steiner, John. 1996. "Revenge and Resentment in the 'Oedipus Situation'." *International Journal of Psychoanalysis* 77: 433–443.

UK Parliament. 2006. *Victims and Survivors (Northern Ireland) Order*. Northern Ireland Statutory Instrument no. 2953 (N.I. 17). www.legislation.gov.uk/nisi/2006/2953/contents

WTV (West Tyrone Voice). 1999. *Voice of the Victims*. Bi-annual newsletter, Newtownstewart.

WTV. 2008a. "Submission of Our Group to the Eames-Bradley Consultation.", (Unpublished). Prepared by J. E. Hazlett Lynch, January 17.

WTV. 2008b. "Eames/Bradley Consultation (sic) Group on the Past." (Unpublished). Submitted by J. E. Hazlett Lynch, June 10.

WTV. 2009a. "IRA Murder Squads Still Active in Northern Ireland." *Voice of the Victims* 11 (1): 4 (12 pp.).

WTV. 2009b. "Consultative Group on the Past: Victims of Terrorism – No Strangers to Hurt.", (Unpublished). April 8.

Young, Linda, and Elizabeth Gibb. 2002. "Trauma and Grievance." In *Understanding Trauma: A Psychoanalytical Approach*, edited by Caroline Garland, 81–95. London: Carnac.

Index

Abraham, N. 9
absences 7–8; excavating Tempelhof airfield: objects of memory and the politics of absence 8, 67–82
actor-network theory 111
Adams, Gerry 125, 130, 132
African National Congress (ANC) 53, 59, 60
Agamben, G. 68, 102
Allende, Salvador 24, 33
Aly, G. 70
amnesty 33, 124, 125
Anderson, B. 55
Anderson, D. 8
Andreani, M. 23
anthropology 6
Apel, L. 37, 46, 47
Arab past of Haifa 8–9, 11, 86–97
Arbel, Leo 37, 42, 45, 47–8
archaeology 6; Tempelhof airfield: forced labour camp 8, 67–82
Arendt, H. 3
Argentina 7, 9–10, 100–18; buildings and haunting: 'radioactive zone' 109–11; death flights 109; ghost stories, haunted spaces 104–6; impunity laws 103; living with the specter: the ghosts as *compañeros* 111–15; recovery, memory policies and official narratives 102–4; watchmen, dogs, children: symbolic mediators of haunting 106–9
Aristotle 55
Armenia 3
Arolowitsch, Hasia 47
Ashplant, T.G. 131
Assatzk, M. 70

Assefa, H. 139
Assmann, J. 67–8
Azaryahu, M. 91

Bachelet, Michelle 22, 26, 27
Barkan, E. 3, 6
Barrett, F.S. 54
Barthes, R 12–13
Bartov, O. 11
'Basic Principles and Guidelines': rights of victims 4
Bassiouni, M.C. 4
Basterra, Victor 100–1
Beaudry, M.C. 76
Beier, A. 45
Belarmino Elgueta Pinto, R. 25
Ben-Gurion, David 88, 89, 90, 93
Benjamin, W. 13, 14
Benvenisti, M. 91
Berger, T. 90
Berlovits, Y. 90
Bernbeck, R. 76, 81
Bille, M. 68
blogs 113
Bloomfield, Sir Kenneth 132
Blustein, J. 12
Booth, W.J. 12
Boym, S. 55, 58
Brants, C. 4
Breen, S. 126
Briceño, D'Orival 23
Brin, H. 93–4
Buchli, V. 68
Budraβ, L. 71, 72
Burns, J.F. 125, 126
Buse, P. 112
Butler, J. 67, 69, 80

INDEX

Calveiro, P. 115
Cannadine, David 61
Careaga, Ana Maria 101
Castillo, C. 25
celebrities 47
Chababo, Ruben 105
Chakrabarty, D. 6
Chase, M. 57
children, watchmen, dogs: the symbolic mediators of haunting 106–9, 110
Chile 7, 21–34
cinema 9
clairvoyants 109
Coan, S. 62
Collins, Ed 76
colonialism 8, 54, 59, 95
commemoration: *Stolpersteine* 7, 37–48
compañeros and ghosts: Argentina's former terror sites 100–18
compensation 2, 8, 24, 88
concentration camps 40, 44–5, 46, 71, 72, 74, 77
Constantinople 3
Coppi, H. 40, 70
corruption 60–1
Cossen, F. 9
Crenzel, E. 102
criminal trials 3–4, 6, 10
critical history, role of 6, 61–2; critiquing memory 6–7; engaging with ghosts of the past 9–10; focusing on specific actors 10; rescuing from oblivion 8–9; silences and absences 7–8
Crossland, Z. 68–9, 82
Crusade (1204) 3
cultural studies 6
Cyprus 111

Darkley Church 134
Davidovic, A. 81
Davidovic-Walther, T. 81
Davis, C. 112, 114
Davis, F. 54, 62
Dawson, G. 10, 123, 126–7, 131, 133, 134
de Klerk, F.W. 53
Debus, L. 38
definition of victims 123, 132
Dejnega, M. 74
Demjanjuk, John 42
Demnig, Gunter 37–8, 43, 45
Dening, G. 12, 13
Derrida, J. 9, 111, 112, 113, 114

desire for justice: Northern Ireland 10, 121–41; definition of victims 123, 132; Eames–Bradley Report (2009) 123–4, 125–6, 132–3, 140, 141; fairness 134–7, 138, 141; object-relations psychoanalytic theory 133–7; peace process 123–6, 131, 132, 133, 140; personal memory and 127–30; psychoanalytic insight and writing of history 137–41; reconciliation 123, 124–5, 132–3, 137, 138–9, 140, 141; stuckness 137, 139, 140; West Tyrone Voice (WTV) 126–7; WTV's public discourse and 131–3
detention centres, clandestine (Argentina) 100–18
Deutsche Arbeitsfront (DAF) 70–1
disappeared 2; Argentina 100–18; Chile 21–34
Dlamini, J. 7, 51, 52, 53–5, 56, 57–63
Dockendorff Navarrete, Muriel 31
documentary films 101, 109
dogs, watchmen, children: the symbolic mediators of haunting 106–9, 110
Dohnke, K. 47
Donnelly, R. 126
Drucaroff, E. 116
du Plessis, C. 59
Dymond, T. 12

Eames–Bradley Report (2009) 123–4, 125–6, 132–3, 140, 141
education 24, 26, 27, 34, 54, 58, 61, 107
Efrat, Z. 90–1
Eichmann trial 3
Elkins, C. 8
Eng, D. 82
ethics of nostalgia in post-apartheid South Africa 7, 51–63; distortions of history: ethical implications 59–63; ethics and memory: Margalit and Ricoeur 55–7; ethics, memory and post-apartheid South Africa: Dlamini's *Native Nostalgia* 53–4; memory work 52–3; nostalgia 54–5; post-apartheid South Africa 57–9; validity of experience 59–60
Etkind, A. 112
experience, validity of 59–60
Eyal, G. 90

fairness 134–7, 138, 141
Feierstein, D. 117
Feldman, A. 106

INDEX

Fernández, Cristina 103
Fernándo, R. 34
Fessia, Emiliano 115
film 9
forced labour camp: Tempelhof airfield 8, 67–82
forgetting 39, 80; absence as forgetfulness 77–8, 80; duty to forget 51, 56; pact of 9; and remembering 7, 11, 80
Fowles, S. 69, 77
France 7
Frank, Anne 41
Frei government 33

Gallardo family 30, 32
Garland, C. 133
Gatti, G. 116
Germany 7, 10, 11, 96; excavating Tempelhof airfield: forced labour camp 8, 67–82; *Stolpersteine* 7, 37–48
ghosts and *compañeros*: Argentina's former terror sites 9–10, 100–18
Gibbon, E. 12
Gluck, C. 7
Goebel, A. 39
Goldstein, Y. 96
González García, J.M. 3
González-Ruibal, A. 69, 80, 81, 82
Gordimer, N. 61
Gordon, A. 9, 112–13, 117
Goren, T. 86, 88
gossip or rumour 105–6, 107, 108, 109–10, 114, 116, 117
Greenberg, J. 133, 134
Gross, J.T. 81

Habibi, Emil 92
Hague, William 8
Haifa: Arab past denied 8–9, 11, 86–97
Hajjar, Gregorios 92
Halbwachs, Maurice 10
Hamber, B. 122, 124–5, 133, 138
Hamilakis, Y. 80
Hamlet 113–14
haunting stories and Argentina's former terror sites 9–10, 100–18
Hayner, P. 2
Hazan, P. 5
Heer, H. 40
Heisig, M. 71
Heitmeyer, W. 48
Herman, J.L. 128, 136

Herold, K. 45
Herzl, T. 89
Holocaust 11, 12; Buchenwald 77; concentration camps 40, 44–5, 46, 71, 72, 74, 77; Mauthausen 74; Sachsenhausen 77; *Stolpersteine* 7, 37–48; Tempelhof airfield: forced labour camp 8, 67–82
Horkheimer, M. 117–18
Hungary 38

International Criminal Tribunal for the Former Yugoslavia (ICTY) 4
international law 4
Internet 40, 45, 113, 117
Iraq 94
Israel: Jewish Haifa denies its Arab past 8–9, 11, 86–97
Italy 38
Izaguirre, I. 117

Jaffa 91, 92
James-Allen, P. 2
Janco, Marcel 91
Japan 3, 14
Jerusalem 91, 93
John Paul II 3
Jureit, U. 41

Kadman, N. 90, 92
Karn, A. 6
Karstedt, S. 4
Katz, H. 94
Kawczynski, Rudko 43
Kenya 8
Kersner, D. 114
Kesler, B. 87
Khalfon, A. 88, 95
Kirchner, Nestor 103
Klein, M. 133
Kloth, Hans Michael 45–6
Klüger, R. 46
Knobloch, Charlotte 39
Kohlmann, Elza 45
Kohnstamm, Jackie 42–3, 47
Kordon, D.R. 116
Korean 'comfort women' 3
Koschorke, A. 111, 117
Kubrick, S. 150
Kuttner, Margarete 67, 68
Kuttner, Paul 67
Kwon, H. 112

INDEX

Labanyi, J. 9
Latour, B. 78, 79, 111
Levi, P. 51, 62, 68
Levi, Shabtai 88, 89, 93
Lewin, Bernhard 40
Lewin, Günther 40
Lewin, Horst 40
Liberia 1–3
Lindqvist, S. 40
Llosa, C. 9
local history 40
Londres 38 7, 21–34; 2004 25–6; 2005 26–7; 2006 27; 2007 27–9; 2008 29; 2009 29–30; 2010 30–1; 2011 31–2; 2012 32–4
Lotman, Y. 108
Lüdtke, A. 41
Lufthansa 71–6, 78
Lundy, P. 123, 140
Lydda (Lod) 92
Lynch, Hazlett 126–7, 131

McAdams, D.P. 13
McGonagle, S. 140
McGuinness, Martin 130, 132
McKaiser, E. 53
Magdal 92
Maier, C.S. 10–11, 12
Malamud Goti, J. 102–3
Malema, Julius 59
Mandolessi, S. 116
Mapenzauswa, S. 57
Maqueda, José Luis 110
Margalit, A. 12, 51, 54, 55–6, 58, 61
material culture in archaeological analyses of sites of Nazi crimes 8, 67–82
Matt, S.J. 14
Mayer, A.J. 10–11, 12, 14
memorial project: *Stolpersteine* 7, 37–48
memory 11, 13; Argentina: sites of 100–18; critiquing 6–7; cultural memory 112, 117; ethics of nostalgia in post-apartheid South Africa 7, 51–63; excavating Tempelhof airfield: politics of absence and objects of 8, 67–82; fixed narratives 61, 116; Germany: lives of victims 41; Jewish Haifa denies its Arab past 8–9, 11, 86–97; Northern Ireland: desire for justice 10, 122–3, 127–30, 131, 132, 139; personal 55, 62, 127–30; recovery, memory policies and official narratives 102–4; shared and common/collective 52, 56, 61, 87, 117, 131, 132, 139
Menachem, Z. 89
Meyer, M. 69
Michelet, Jules 12–13
Mieth, F. 10
Milošević, Slobodan 2
Miyeni, E. 53, 55, 58
Montenegro, Leopoldo 32, 34
Monterescu, D. 92
Moore, Gamble 127, 129–30, 138
Morris, B. 86
Morris-Suzuki, T. 14
Moshenska, G. 70, 80
Mourlon, F. 123
Mulka, Robert 46
Muller, A. 61, 62
Muñoz, Ximena 26
Munyaka, M. 58
Murove, M.F. 57
Musih, N. 87, 94
Myers, A.T. 77

Nachama, A. 46
Nakba 8, 94–5, 96
names, street and village 91–2, 95
Nathanson, R. 95
Navaro-Yashin, Y. 111
Neumann, K. 11, 14, 41
non-government organisations (NGOs) 103
Nora, P. 13
Northern Ireland: desire for justice 10, 121–41; definition of victims 123, 132; Eames–Bradley Report (2009) 123–4, 125–6, 132–3, 140, 141; fairness 134–7, 138, 141; object-relations psychoanalytic theory 133–7; peace process 123–6, 131, 132, 133, 140; personal memory and 127–30; psychoanalytic insight and writing of history 137–41; reconciliation 123, 124–5, 132–3, 137, 138–9, 140, 141; stuckness 137, 139, 140; West Tyrone Voice (WTV) 126–7; WTV's public discourse and 131–3
nostalgia in post-apartheid South Africa, ethics of 7, 51–63; restorative and reflective nostalgia 55, 61–2
Nuremberg trial 2

object-relations psychoanalytic theory 122–3, 133–7; desire for justice:

INDEX

psychoanalytic insight and writing of history 137–41
O'Higgins Institute 24, 26–7, 29, 32
Olivier, L. 79
el-Omar, Daher 9, 11, 87, 92, 97
Orentlicher, Diane 124
orientalism 90
Orwell, G. 59

Palestine: Arab past of Haifa 8–9, 11, 86–97
Patterson, H. 131
pavement plaques: Chile 26–7, 28; *Stolpersteine* 7, 37–48
Perez, J.M. 33
Perez, Mariana Eva 110
Phillips, M.S. 14
Piñera, Sebastian 34
Pinochet, A. 21, 24
Poland 71, 72, 93, 96
political taphonomy 76, 77
Pollock, S. 69, 71, 72, 76
Pophanken, H. 71
post-conflict society *see* Northern Ireland: desire for justice
psychoanalytic theory, object-relations 122–3, 133–7; desire for justice: psychoanalytic insight and writing of history 137–41

Quintana, M.M. 113, 116

racial classification 60
Ramla 92
Ratti, C. 108
Rayner, E. 134, 135, 138
Raz-Krakotzkin, A. 89, 90
Read, P. 23, 24, 26, 33
Reati, F. 115–16
reconciliation 6, 56; Chile 29, 33, 34; Germany 41; Israel 95; Northern Ireland 123, 124–5, 132–3, 137, 138–9, 140, 141; truth or truth and reconciliation commissions 2–3, 6, 13, 52, 124–5
reparative justice 2
restorative justice 33, 124, 130, 131
restorative and reflective nostalgia 55, 61–2
retributive justice 2; desire for justice: Northern Ireland 122, 124, 128, 130, 131, 140
Ricoeur, P. 51–2, 55, 56–7, 59, 61, 62

Rieff, D. 11
rights of victims: 'Basic Principles and Guidelines' 4
Riquelme, H. 116
Rivas, P. 25, 30
Robinson, E. 14
Rojas Baeza, P. 116
Roma 38, 41–2, 43
Rosenkovich, Jessica 108
Rosenthal, Edla Charlotte 45
Rotbard, S. 92
rumour or gossip 105–6, 107, 108, 109–10, 114, 116, 117
Russia 112

Sagebiel, Ernst 71
Samuel, R. 61
Sartre, J.-P. 54
Sary, Ieng 2
Schiavi, D. 106–7, 110
Schindel, E. 103
Schrader, Ulrike 42, 47
Schulz, S. 45
Schwab, G. 112
Scilingo, Adolfo 109
Segal, A. 96
Segal, H. 133
Sesay, A. 1
Shakespeare, W. 113–14
Shalev-Gerz, E. 77
Shatner, Mordechai 90
Shaw, R. 10
Siegfried, D. 40
Sierra Leone 1–2, 10
Sikkink, K. 2
Simons, M. 1
Sinti 38, 41–2, 43–4
Sirleaf, Ellen Johnson 3
slavery 3
Slyomovics, S. 91
Smith, D.J. 53
Smooha, S. 87
Smyth, M.B. 122, 125
sociology 6
Soto Roland, F.J. 105
South Africa 124; Constitution 52, 57; ethics of nostalgia in post-apartheid 7, 51–63; *ubuntu* 57–8, 62
Southgate, B. 13
Soviet Union 112
Spain 3, 9, 10
specter, living with the 111–15

INDEX

Srivastava, S. 81
Steinberg, J. 53, 54
Steiner, J. 135–6, 137
Stern, Shimon 94
Stern, Steve J. 24
Stolpersteine 7, 37–48
Stoltz, J. 61
street names 91–2, 95
Suarez, Gabriel 104
supernatural incidents 100–18

taphonomy, political 76, 77
Tarnopolsky, D. 109
Taylor, Charles 1–3, 10
Tel Aviv 94
Tempelhof airfield: forced labour camp 8, 67–82
terror, sites of (Argentina) 100–18
Theune, C. 76, 77
Thompson, J. 12
Thrift, N. 111
Tiberias 92
Todorov, T. 60
Tokyo trial 2
Trollmann, Johann 'Rukeli' 44, 45
Trouillot, M.-R. 70, 77, 80
truth: victims' truth 3–4
truth or truth and reconciliation commissions 6, 13; Liberia 2–3; South Africa 52, 124–5
Tuma, Emil 92
Tumarkin, M. 23
Turner, Ramsey 127–9, 132, 138
Tutu, D. 124

ubuntu 57–8, 62
Ukraine 38
United Kingdom 8, 94, 95–6
United Nations 1, 2; victims: 'Basic Principles and Guidelines' 4
United States 11, 75, 76

Valech, S. 26
Valenzuela, Luisa 112
vampire stories 106
Verbitsky, H. 109
Verwoerd, H. 57
Vezzetti, H. 116
victims, rights of ('Basic Principles and Guidelines') 4
victims' truth 3–4
Videla, Jorge Rafaél 2
Vietnam 112
Viola, L. 114
Vivian, B. 7, 11
von Beust, Ole 38
Vorrath, J. 38

Wadi, R. 32
Walker, M.U. 12
watchmen, dogs, children: the symbolic mediators of haunting 106–9, 110
Wefing, H. 42
Weiss, Tello 106, 115
Weiss, Y. 89
Wenz, F.-H. 71
Weserflug GmbH 71
West Tyrone Voice (WTV) *see* Northern Ireland: desire for justice
White, L. 106, 116
Wiebelhaus-Brahm, E. 2
Wieviorka, A. 14
Wilke, C. 10
Wilson, R.A. 6
Winterstein, Benno 44
Wyndham, Marivic 34

Yahav, Y. 86–7, 94
Yazbak, M. 94
Yiftachel, O. 87
Yoffe, A.B. 91
Young, J. 7
Young, L. 136, 137
Yugoslavia, International Criminal Tribunal for the Former (ICTY) 4

Zanetto, G. 105
Zentek, S. 70
Zionism 87, 89–90, 91–2, 93–4, 95–6
Zochrot 87, 94–6